Understanding the Tea Party Movement

Edited by

NELLA VAN DYKE
University of California, Merced, USA

DAVID S. MEYER
University of California, Irvine, USA

ASHGATE

© Nella Van Dyke, David S. Meyer and the contributors 2014

All rights reserved. No part of this publication may be reproduced, stored in a retrieval system or transmitted in any form or by any means, electronic, mechanical, photocopying, recording or otherwise without the prior permission of the publisher.

Nella Van Dyke and David S. Meyer have asserted their right under the Copyright, Designs and Patents Act, 1988, to be identified as the editors of this work.

Published by
Ashgate Publishing Limited
Wey Court East
Union Road
Farnham
Surrey, GU9 7PT
England

Ashgate Publishing Company
110 Cherry Street
Suite 3-1
Burlington, VT 05401-3818
USA

www.ashgate.com

British Library Cataloguing in Publication Data
A catalogue record for this book is available from the British Library

The Library of Congress has cataloged the printed edition as follows:
Van Dyke, Nella.
  Understanding the Tea Party movement / by Nella Van Dyke and David S. Meyer.
      pages cm.—(The mobilization series on social movements, protest, and culture)
  Includes bibliographical references and index.
   ISBN 978-1-4094-6522-5 (hardback)—ISBN 978-1-4094-6523-2 (pbk.)—
ISBN 978-1-4094-6524-9 (ebook)—ISBN 978-1-4724-0715-3 (epub) 1. Tea Party movement. 2. Political culture—United States. 3. United States—Politics and government. I. Meyer, David S. II. Title.
   JK2391.T43V36 2014
   322.4'40973—dc23

2013041453

ISBN 9781409465225 (hbk)
ISBN 9781409465232 (pbk)
ISBN 9781409465249 (ebk – PDF)
ISBN 9781472407153 (ebk – ePUB)

Printed in the United Kingdom by Henry Ling Limited,
at the Dorset Press, Dorchester, DT1 1HD

UNDERSTANDING THE TEA PARTY MOVEMENT

When the Tea Party movement erupted, it challenged mainstream politics and scholars: where did the Tea Party's resources come from? Who were its supporters? What defined their goals and identities? In this volume, some of the most insightful scholars of social movements today provide convincing answers to these questions. Better than any other, this volume shows why the Tea Party emerged and how it has reshaped the political landscape.

Jack A. Goldstone, George Mason University, USA

The Mobilization Series on Social Movements, Protest, and Culture

Series Editor

Professor Hank Johnston
San Diego State University, USA

Published in conjunction with *Mobilization: An International Quarterly*, the premier research journal in the field, this series disseminates high quality new research and scholarship in the fields of social movements, protest, and contentious politics. The series is interdisciplinary in focus and publishes monographs and collections of essays by new and established scholars.

Other titles in this series

*Dynamics of Political Violence
A Process-Oriented Perspective on Radicalization and the
Escalation of Political Conflict*
Edited by Lorenzo Bosi, Chares Demetriou and Stefan Malthaner

*Beyond NGO-ization
The Development of Social Movements in Central and Eastern Europe*
Edited by Kerstin Jacobsson and Steven Saxonberg

Violent Protest, Contentious Politics, and the Neoliberal State
Edited by Seraphim Seferiades and Hank Johnston

Student Activism and Curricular Change in Higher Education
Mikaila Mariel Lemonik Arthur

Contents

List of Figures and Table   vii
Notes on Contributors   ix
Preface   xi
List of Abbreviations   xiii

Introduction   1
Nella Van Dyke and David S. Meyer

PART I   EXPLAINING THE TIMING AND PACE OF THE MOBILIZATION: POLITICS AND RESOURCES

1   What's New about the Tea Party Movement?   15
Rory McVeigh

2   Three-Layer Movements, Resources, and the Tea Party   35
Tina Fetner and Brayden G. King

3   Social Movement Partyism and the Tea Party's Rapid Mobilization   55
Paul Almeida and Nella Van Dyke

4   The Tea Party and the Dilemmas of Conservative Populism   73
David S. Meyer and Amanda Pullum

PART II   WHO MOBILIZED AND WHY? IDEOLOGY, IDENTITY, AND EMOTIONS IN THE TEA PARTY

5   The Tea Party Moment   99
Abby Scher and Chip Berlet

6   From Fervor to Fear: ICT and Emotions in the Tea Party Movement   125
Deana A. Rohlinger and Jesse Klein

| 7 | Who are "We the People"? Multidimensional Identity Work in the Tea Party | 149 |

Ruth Braunstein

Conclusion 175
Nella Van Dyke and David S. Meyer

Index 185

List of Figures and Table

Figures

1.1	Power devaluation dynamics	20
3.1	College Station, TX, Tea Party rally, October 16, 2009	60
3.2	Tea party membership, June 2010. By permission of the Institute for Research and Education of Human Rights (www.irehr.org)	62

Table

6.1	Overview of respondent demographics	130

Notes on Contributors

Paul Almeida, University of California, Merced

Chip Berlet, Research for Progress

Ruth Braunstein, New York University

Tina Fetner, McMaster University

Brayden G. King, Northwestern University

Jesse Klein, Florida State University

Rory McVeigh, Notre Dame University

David S. Meyer, University of California, Irvine

Amanda Pullum, University of California, Irvine

Deana A. Rohlinger, Florida State University

Abby Scher, Independent Scholar

Nella Van Dyke, University of California, Merced

Preface

When the Tea Party movement exploded onto the American scene in the spring of 2009, we could not help but be fascinated with it, given our area of research. We were struck by its rapid mobilization, by its support from Fox News, as well as by the sight of Republicans engaging in non-institutional protest. As the Chair of the American Sociological Association's Section on Collective Behavior and Social Movements, one of us had the opportunity to schedule a session for the Association's annual meeting focused on the new movement. Because the movement is clearly conservative in orientation, a panel of experts on conservative social movements seemed like an excellent choice, and so I invited Paul Almeida, Tina Fetner, Rory McVeigh and David Meyer to participate. The panel, titled "Social Movement Perspectives on the Town Hall/Tea Party Protests," occurred at the annual meeting of the American Sociological Association in Atlanta in August 2010. The panel proved to be lively and stimulating and very well attended. An audience member suggested that the two of us turn the panel into an edited volume, and so this volume was born.

We wanted the volume to cover different aspects of the movement that are relevant to social movement theory, including political opportunities and threats, resources, framing, ideological roots, and identity. We first invited our distinguished panelists to turn their conference remarks into a chapter, having been impressed by their presentations. We then solicited additional chapters from several scholars who we knew were conducting research on the movement and who we thought would provide coverage of important issues not introduced by the conference panelists. This brought us chapters by Chip Berlet and Abby Scher, Ruth Braunstein, and Deana Rohlinger and Jesse Klein. The resulting volume highlights a range of issues relevant to this movement, illustrating how they are both consistent with social movement theory yet push movement theory ahead.

We want to express our appreciation to our contributors for allowing us to include their fascinating research and theorizing in the book. We also appreciate the support of Hank Johnston, editor of Ashgate's Mobilization Series on Social Movements, Protest, and Culture, and all of the assistance provided by Ashgate's editorial staff.

Nella Van Dyke and David S. Meyer

List of Abbreviations

ALEC	American Legislative Exchange Council
CSI	Center for Social Inclusion
GOP	Republican Party ("Grand Old Party")
ICT	Internet Communication Technology
NAACP	National Association for the Advancement of Colored People
PAC	Political Action Committee
RINO	Republican in Name Only
TARP	Troubled Asset Relief Program
YAL	Young Americans for Liberty

*We dedicate this book to our children,
Elsa and Sadie Van Dyke,
Zena and Jean Meyer*

Introduction

Nella Van Dyke and David S. Meyer

The Tea Party movement emerged on the American political scene in the spring of 2009, shortly after Rick Santelli's now famous rant on CNBC regarding the Obama administration's mortgage relief plans for homeowners, where he encouraged people to mobilize and start a new Tea Party. That April, tax day protests in scores of cities were staged by activists who now defined themselves as supporters of the incipient Tea Party movement. The Tea Party represented a substantial challenge to the Obama administration, and more generally to mainstream politics. It also represented a challenge to analysts of social movements. In this book, we take up the second challenge.

The ostensibly rapid emergence of the Tea Party movement caught political figures and scholars by surprise on a number of counts. First, the Tea Party appellation and mobilization seemed to come from out of the blue. Organizers are always trying to mobilize support for their concerns, and failed efforts leave a trail. A Tea Party, however, was nowhere to be found at the beginning of 2009, but by the summer, Tea Party rhetoric and protests were everywhere. Pre-existing think tanks and lobby groups devoted efforts to promoting the Tea Party. The political action committee "Our Country Deserves Better" even changed its name to Tea Party Express, in an explicit attempt to ride the wave of a movement. New national organizations developed to represent and coordinate action, and hundreds of local chapters emerged across the United States in short order (Skocpol and Williamson 2012, Parker and Baretto 2013).

The extremely rapid mobilization of a very large number of participants reflected the coincidence of more than a decade of investment by well-heeled conservative interests with an unusual opportunity to engage the grassroots, and both the organizations involved and the opportunities and threats that inspired their mobilization merit far more systematic attention from scholars of social movements.

Activists' long-term efforts to build social movements are often overshadowed by sudden mobilization (Reese et al. 2010). Initially, Tea Party protests followed a script that mostly reflected the aspirations of those movement investors, with early Tea Party protests focused heavily on President Obama's health care initiative, but in fairly short order, local Tea Party groups took initiative in defining their own goals and did not always share an agenda with the monied interests supporting the movement, for example in their opposition to raising the debt ceiling. The conflict between the grassroots and the national movement, and within existing national groups, was overshadowed by a fierce and unified opposition to President Obama and health care reform, and opposition to raising taxes. However, over time that unity eroded, especially in the wake of the 2010 election.

As social movement scholars, we want to understand the relationship of the emergent movement to the organizations and interests that tried to promote it, and the conflicts and cooperative efforts among self-described Tea Party groups who didn't always share the same priorities about goals or tactics. Coordinating diversity within social movements is a topic that has only begun to receive the serious attention it merits (e.g., Van Dyke and McCammon 2010).

The notion that the successful mobilization of movements is affected by the world surrounding that movement is well established within the literature, but scholars disagree about just which circumstances promote mobilization for which constituencies (Meyer 2004). Some social movements appear to emerge in response to favorable signals and openings from government, including the civil rights movement and the women's movement (e.g., McAdam 1982, Costain 1992). In contrast, some movements appear to respond to provocation and unfavorable policies (e.g. Meyer 1990, Smith 1996, Van Dyke and Soule 2002).

The Tea Party offers the opportunity to speak to this debate about the relationship between political opportunities and movement emergence. The appearance of the Tea Party followed the adoption of federal policies that organized interests found threatening and offensive, and the proposal of additional provocative policies, including an apparently huge and expensive bailout of large financial firms (TARP), the adoption of a more limited fiscal stimulus bill, and proposals to help troubled homeowners and institute a more extensive system of health care insurance at the national level. The Tea Party emergence also followed a 2008 election that can only be characterized as a massive defeat for libertarians, social conservatives, and establishment Republicans. In the national election, Barack Obama defeated John McCain decisively, and McCain was not even the preferred Republican nominee for social conservatives or libertarians. With Obama at the top of the ticket, Democrats also gained a decisive majority in the House of Representatives and increased the size of their caucus to 60 senators, which represents the number needed to break filibusters. Putative Tea Partiers really saw themselves as facing threats and provocations, and without meaningful effective access to institutional politics.

We have the scholarly opportunity to trace the development of the Tea Party against the backdrop of mainstream politics, and even to view the movement's development over time against changes in mainstream politics. To be sure, protest declined as Republicans, including Tea Partiers, made substantial gains in electoral politics in the 2010 elections. We saw conservatives, often calling themselves Tea Partiers, win elections, but clearly at the expense of grassroots activism.

Scholars have generally viewed social protest movements as a strategy for influence attractive to those who are excluded from other means of influence (Gamson 1990); as a result, the library of studies on social movements in America is heavily weighted toward movements of the left. But the activists animating the Tea Party were not those typically seen as excluded or disadvantaged.

Disproportionately, they were better educated and wealthier than most Americans. Most were not new to politics. And they were also, as a whole, better educated, older, and white. The relative advantages these activists enjoyed surely affected the dynamics of the movement as it developed.

Like many social movements, the Tea Party enjoyed the infusion of outside resources, but the scale and skew of those resources were unprecedented. Students for a Democratic Society, for example, was founded with the help of a very small grant from the Student League for Industrial Democracy (Miller 1994). One Tea Party group, in contrast, the Tea Party Patriots, was funded by a massive million dollar gift given to a group called FreedomWorks for the express purpose of starting the movement, and was the beneficiary of a cultural megaphone via Fox News and conservative commentators elsewhere in the media. Few other modern movements have been able to generate resources on this scale so early on in their existence.

Although the US has a history of conservative mobilizations, the sight of Republican politicians and Republican operatives sponsoring and promoting extra-institutional protest is rare. Indeed, the modern conservative movement had flourished, beginning in the 1960s, by explicitly marginalizing its radical flank, including the John Birch Society and the Ku Klux Klan. Conservative activism has employed protest far less frequently than groups on the left. For example, in Van Dyke's study of 60 years of college student protest (2003), she found that only five percent of protest events were focused on conservative or right-wing issues. Thus, why members of the Republican Party are turning to protest as a form of political action in such large numbers is a question worth examining.

Blessed by outside money and well-established political allies, and filled with activists with extensive resources and experience, the Tea Party could negotiate a far more rapid emergence and effective entry into mainstream politics than most social movements. Tea Partiers made extensive use of both free and paid media as well as newly available online networks. These resources aided rapid growth, but created other dilemmas for the movement. Perhaps the most salient dilemma centered on political identity, as conflicts played out about both ultimate goals and tactics. Political commentators on TV and the web have used a range of adjectives to describe the movement and characterize it in very different ways, ranging from a mobilization of concerned citizens reacting to government overreach, to racist crazies, or an astroturf (non-grassroots) mobilization. However, most of this commentary rests on anecdotal evidence or the rhetoric and actions of a small segment of the movement. Who exactly are the Tea Partiers, and what ideologies motivate their action? How do activists reconcile the multiple group identities constructed by the movement? And how have movement organizers used rhetoric to generate mobilization-inspiring emotions among potential adherents?

The national groups that initially tried to promote grassroots mobilization were mostly business-friendly libertarians. They were opposed to taxation, regulation, and the welfare state, but eager to avoid divisive fights about foreign policy and social issues, including abortion and gay and lesbian rights. For the most part, the business interests funding conservative groups supported immigration reform so that employers could enjoy access to skilled and/or cheap labor. The grassroots support they mobilized, however, included large numbers of social conservatives, prepared to refight old battles about the presence of religion in American life, libertarians who wanted to minimize America's global military presence, and nativists who wanted to restrict immigration. In electoral politics, Tea Partiers disputed the relative merits of supporting strong advocates rather than somewhat more mainstream candidates who might win general elections. Tea Party groups, and the Republican Party they infused, argued vociferously about these issues, with only momentary—and sometimes costly—resolutions.

Division within a large and volatile social movement is hardly unique to the Tea Party, but the extent of the Tea Party movement, and the extensive resources of various factions within it, have provided an ongoing stream of difficulties. The name "Tea Party" as a unifying identity linking diverse conservative interests was likely accidental, but it is not insignificant. When CNBC commentator Rick Santelli called for a "Tea Party" mobilization, activists seized upon the romance and imagined history of America, when the grassroots were powerful, government was small and unintrusive, and things were somehow good. Tea Partiers adapted symbols from the past to unify and infuse their movement, displaying the Gadsden Flag ("Don't Tread on Me") from the American Revolution, and symbolically assuming costumes of revolt that included colonial garb or tea bags. By explicitly linking themselves to an image of pristine patriotism, Tea Partiers asserted an identity steeped in the past. They deployed the tri-corner hat and the Constitution as signs of legitimacy and identity, mostly ignoring the groups that these symbols excluded. Such identity management issues are endemic to social movements.

The contributors to this volume take up all of these issues and others. The Tea Party movement provides an opportunity to consider the dynamics of contemporary reactive or conservative mobilization, in terms of both the factors that facilitated its rapid emergence and growth, as well as the internal dynamics of the movement in terms of participants and their ideologies, identities, and the emotions that have inspired mobilization. The existing social science scholarship on social movements provides useful analytic lenses for understanding the movement, yet the movement challenges these theories in some important ways. Chapters in this volume provide important modifications to movement theory that address these challenges.

Explaining the Timing and Pace of the Mobilization: Politics and Resources

As several of the volume's chapters note, most of the explanations for movement emergence present in the academic literature come from the study of progressive social movements. Conservative populism, represented by the Tea Party, includes an alliance between very well-established business interests and disaffected citizens at the grassroots. In a very clear way, the Tea Party is a less a movement for inclusion than a demand for restoration, all folded into a romanticization of an imagined past. For such a movement, the question of timing presents a challenge to existing theories and requires a different analytic focus. It's not that members of the middle class don't require political opportunities and resources to mobilize, as McVeigh points out in Chapter 1, it's just that they may only be inspired to mobilize these resources and pursue their political opportunities when faced with some sort of grievance or threat. Several of the chapters in the volume explore this important difference and present theoretical contributions to movement theory that incorporate the dynamics present in the Tea Party.

In Chapter 1, McVeigh suggests that the power devaluation theory of movement emergence, which he developed through his study of the 1920s-era Ku Klux Klan, works well for explaining the emergence of the Tea Party. He notes that the Tea Party, much like the twentieth-century Klan, has been a mobilization of predominately middle-class individuals who already enjoyed some level of political access and resources. He argues that a threatened loss of power in three realms, politics, economics, and status, may inspire conservative mobilization. In the 1920s, members of the middle class were motivated to mobilize as they faced national issues including an agricultural recession, immigration, women's suffrage and entrance into the labor force, and the growth of parochial schooling (McVeigh 2009). Those who mobilized were not necessarily those hit hardest by economic problems, but rather those in the middle class who faced some economic challenges, but were motivated to act as the government developed aid policies that they thought would disproportionately benefit members of other groups.

McVeigh suggests that a similar dynamic has occurred with the Tea Party. The movement emerged during an economic recession, which had widespread negative economic impacts. However, while individuals have diverse personal reasons for joining the Tea Party, for the most part the movement does not include those who have been hit hardest by the recession. Rather, it is a mobilization of middle-class individuals who are relatively well off, who are upset about government policies that promise to spend taxpayer money helping members of groups other than their own. In addition, the 2008 Presidential election brought a change in voter demographics, as more minority group members went to the polls. Tea Party members may perceive that their ability to influence politics through institutional channels is declining, as more liberal young people and minorities begin going to the polls. Although not overtly racist like the Klan, the Tea Party is similar to the Klan in that it defines its members as patriotic Americans mobilizing in response to threats from outside (i.e., by questioning Obama's citizenship and calling him socialist).

McVeigh convincingly describes how theories that focus on resources and political opportunities fail to adequately explain the timing of the emergence of the Tea Party. He presents a power devaluation theory as an alternative that focuses on threats to economic, political and social status as the proximate motivations for conservative mobilization. Other volume contributors present other theoretical models for understanding Tea Party movement emergence.

Unlike most progressive movements, which gathered their resources from their own constituents and battled for a voice in the media, the Tea Party has enjoyed an unusual level of support from powerful economic and cultural actors. Fetner and King, in Chapter 2, take an in-depth look at the resources, both financial and cultural, that have been available to the Tea Party and influenced its rapid growth. They propose that the Tea Party suggests important theoretical developments to theories about movement resources, which have typically focused on social movements whose organizational and financial resources developed slowly, and which waxed and waned dramatically at different points in time. They mention the gay and lesbian movement as an example of this type of movement. The Tea Party, in contrast, is one where a massive infusion of resources from elite supporters preceded large-scale grassroots mobilization. Tea Party mobilization benefitted from massive cash support when the non-profit organization FreedomWorks was given a $1,000,000 donation to use to support the Tea Party. FreedomWorks used that money to fund the Tea Party Patriots, one of the largest Tea Party organizations. The Tea Party Patriots provide a great deal of resources to activists, including a web-based search engine where individuals can find local chapters, tools for helping people establish chapters, weekly conference calls, and other forms of support. At the same time, influential cultural resources were provided to the movement by Fox News and other conservative radio and TV programs. Fox News often covered Tea Party protests before they occurred and encouraged watchers to attend, something which has not been seen before in the US.

Clearly the resource dynamics experienced by the Tea Party are different from those experienced by other movements in US history. Fetner and King propose that we think of the Tea Party as a three-layer movement, one that enjoyed a massive infusion of resources from resource-rich supporters, while also benefitting from a robust grassroots mobilization. These two represent the top and bottom layers of a movement, while the middle layer includes the organizations and networks that are so important to mobilization. Movements may be top down or bottom up, depending on where resources are coming from, and the Tea Party represents a top-down movement. Fetner and King suggest that top-down social movements are a trend in the US, as corporations increasingly use their philanthropic resources in a targeted way, intending to promote corporation-friendly policies through their giving, and as policies like the 2010 *Citizens United* Supreme Court decision make it easier for cash to flow anonymously into politics. They suggest that these top-down, three-layer movements face challenges though, in that the source of their resources may shape their trajectory in important ways.

The close ties between the Republican Party and the movement are another unusual feature of the Tea Party. While obviously, in recent years, Republican citizens have been involved in many mobilizations, such as the anti-abortion movement, typically social movements do not enjoy support from the wealthiest Party donors or Party operatives. Movements often have insider allies, but rarely do we see political parties engaging in extra-institutional protest. Movements turn to extra-institutional action often because they do not have sufficient access to the institutional political system to exert meaningful influence. Thus, historically, protest has been an outsider political tactic, not one often used by insiders. The Tea Party offers an interesting contrast, in that it has benefitted from financial, experiential, and organizational support from parts of the Republican Party.

In Chapter 3, Almeida and Van Dyke draw on Almeida's concept of social movement partyism (2006, 2010) to describe this dynamic. Social movement partyism is when oppositional political parties engage in protest action to push their claims. The term comes from social movement unionism, used by labor scholars to describe the use of social movement tactics by labor unions, which typically operate using more bureaucratic means (Johnston 1994, Turner and Hurd 2001). Almeida (2006, 2010) developed the term to describe dynamics in Latin American countries such as El Salvador or Brazil where, after an oppositional social movement came into power politically, the new political party continued engaging in protest. In these cases, the use of extra-institutional protest was a continuation of the tactics the group had been using for years. The Tea Party provides an interesting case in contrast to those in Latin America. The term social movement partyism applies generally to the US case, in that we are seeing a political party, or at least parts of it, sponsoring and encouraging the use of extra-institutional protest in response to perceived political and economic threats. In addition, the Republican Party has been an oppositional party since 2008, when Democrats took over the White House. Tea Party protests, however, are not a continuation of the party's typical political action, as was the case in Latin America. Almeida and Van Dyke describe the resources, including material, social-organizational, cultural, and human, that a political party can provide to a movement, and discuss how these shaped the Tea Party.

Meyer and Pullum, in Chapter 4, offer a contrasting explanation of this conservative mobilization, suggesting that social protest has diffused so widely, both geographically and demographically, that it has now become a standard political tactic for both the left and the right. They situate the Tea Party movement within existing theories on social movements, highlighting how these help explain the movement's emergence and dynamics. As they do so, they draw on Meyer and Tarrow's concept of the "social movement society" (1998), which suggests that protest has become a fairly routine political tactic which has lost its disruptive power as protesters use less confrontational forms of collective action and authorities have learned to manage them. Thus, collective protest is no longer remarkable and has become something used across the spectrum of society, including by political insiders and other segments of society not typically known for their protest activity. The legitimation of protest as an advocacy tactic has paradoxically made it harder for social movements of the excluded to have any political influence. This paradox is especially ironic for the Tea Party, which represents itself as a democratic movement of citizens reclaiming their right to have a political voice and influence.

Who Mobilized and Why? Ideology, Identity, and Emotions in the Tea Party

Virtually all social movements involve diverse participants whose mobilization is driven by a variety of motivations, and the Tea Party is no different. The appeal and ideology of the movement cannot be captured with a single concept. In Chapter 5, Scher and Berlet explore the various ideological strands of the movement, coupled with quotes from individuals they interviewed who were drawn to the Tea Party on the basis of those ideologies. They identify six distinct ideologies promoted by the movement: fiscal conservatism, libertarianism, the Christian Right, white racism, patriot movement ideology, and conspiracy theories. Each of these has a long history in America.

The Tea Party is primarily a middle-class movement, and in many ways includes views consistent with the contemporary Republican Party. Scher and Berlet found that although some members espouse truly populist views, challenging the power of elites, others side with the monied elites and view the Federal government as a threat to the free market, damaging business and threatening America's future with a ballooning deficit. These Tea Partiers represent a traditional Republican fiscal conservatism, with individuals who have turned to the movement in frustration with the Republican Party establishment. Scher and Berlet also talked to Tea Party members who are libertarian, feeling that government has become too big and bloated with regulations. Others adhere to Christian Conservative viewpoints, and are members of what has come to be thought of as the Republican Party base. Most of these individuals support restrictions on abortion and oppose gay and lesbian rights, but are frustrated that Republicans in the government are not upholding conservative principles.

The Tea Party also includes ideological elements that reflect uglier, less mainstream strands of American political thought. Some of these are white racists, who oppose diversity and immigration, and express hostility toward Latinos and blacks. Sometimes this racial antagonism is coupled with a sense of economic threat, the idea that middle-class America is facing economic trouble caused both by a government that squelches business and by poor minorities who take advantage of the system and receive an unfair amount of government assistance. Some Tea Party members adhere to views promulgated by the Patriot movement in the US, whose members feel the need to arm themselves against threats from both outside and within. A related ideological strand of the movement is conspiracy theory. These individuals believe that America and the American way of life are threatened by a host of potential villains, ranging from Muslims to socialists to immigrants. All of these ideological strands have a long history in American political thought, and have come to the fore in the midst of an economic recession and a Republican Party whom many feel has abandoned some of its core principles.

Ideologies alone will not motivate people to join a social movement; rhetoric must invoke mobilizing emotions. In Chapter 6, Rohlinger and Klein present their research on the Tea Party in Florida and how a local group used rhetoric to arouse emotion that inspired mobilization, and how their rhetoric and the emotions it generated changed after the 2010 elections. They highlight the importance of internet communication technology, and how leaders can effectively use the internet and social media to control a movement's message and the emotions it generates, but that this control cannot be taken for granted. They suggest three conditions that affect whether leaders can effectively control movement messaging via the internet. First, the internet forum must serve as a central location for movement communication. If movement members get their information from a variety of sources, a single leader will be less able to control it. Second, area leaders must agree on that messaging. Movements often face conflict when core leaders disagree, and this can result in mixed messaging. Finally, leaders must be willing to use social media and must put time into controlling group content. Leaders often have limited time and therefore do not attempt to control movement messaging.

Rohlinger and Klein illustrate how a Tallahassee, Florida, Tea Party leader established a Facebook page which became a central location for local movement communication. Prior to the 2010 election, one of the area leaders effectively controlled the site and used to it to express an inclusive rhetoric emphasizing pride and patriotism to generate positive emotions which could be shared among a diverse range of potential supporters. Interviews Rohlinger and Klein conducted at local Tea Party rallies revealed that many were motivated to attend based on these positive emotions. However, after the election, the leader became pre-occupied with other pursuits, and no longer controlled the group's Facebook page. Other, more angry individuals began posting messages on the site that emphasized frustration with Republican members of Congress and argued that Obama and other liberals presented a danger to the American way of life. These arguments called upon the emotion of fear to motivate action, and turned off some of the less conservative former supporters of the movement.

The Tea Party movement is complex not only in its ideology, but in the identities that these ideologies call upon. In Chapter 7, Braunstein presents the results of ethnographic research that highlights how a group identity can be complex and sometimes contradictory. A broad, unifying identity which cuts across difference and creates a shared basis for mobilization may have a contradictory meaning when used to advance specific policies. Braunstein documents how the Tea Party claimed a patriotic American identity by defining themselves as "we the people," citizens with a right to participation in the political process, to rally support. This identity, however, is not uncomplicated. When used as a description of movement participants, it is broad and inclusive, and casts a net across partisan divides. However, when used in conjunction with specific policy concerns, the boundaries of the identity shift, casting particular individuals or groups as the enemy depending on the specifics of the issue being discussed. Braunstein describes this type of identity as multidimensional, and one that places the group simultaneously in multiple identity fields, or constellations of allies, antagonists, and other actors. A multidimensional identity can result in contradictory boundaries that groups and individuals have to negotiate.

The "we the people" identity asserted by the Tea Party is sometimes a broad, inclusive identity intended to include all Americans. When members of the Tea Party group Braunstein studied went to train stations to hand out their pamphlets, they attempted to give a pamphlet to anyone who walked by, because all citizens are included in this broad identity group. However, at other times the group would argue that "we the people" are opposed to taxation and the re-distribution of taxpayer money to those who are undeserving. The use of the identity in regards to this specific policy issue casts a narrower net in terms of the citizens that are included. Thus, the same identity casts different boundaries depending on the identity field to which it is applied. Group members negotiate the tension generated by these discrepant boundaries by using an over-arching narrative which is abstract, draws on familiar story lines and characters, and situates the group in time. In this way, when group members disagree about group boundaries in a particular instance, the tension is dispelled through a refocus on the broader identity that originally brought the group together.

Conclusions

Several strong and well-financed Tea Party groups have institutionalized in Washington DC, giving a new name and identity to the advocacy of certain conservative interests. Even without the grassroots, this Tea Party is certain to be a force in American politics for some time to come. Even more significantly, the questions raised by the Tea Party are those that should animate scholarship on social movements for the foreseeable future. The chapters included in this volume illustrate how existing social movement theory provides a partial explanation for the movement's rapid emergence and ongoing dynamics, but they also present important developments for movement theory, advancing it in a way that increases our understanding of the Tea Party movement and others like it.

References

Almeida, P.D. 2006. Social movement unionism, social movement partyism, and policy outcomes: Health care privatization in El Salvador, in *Latin American Social Movements: Globalization, Democratization, and Transnational Networks*, edited by H. Johnston and P. Almeida. Lanham, MD: Rowman & Littlefield, 57–76.
Almeida, P.D. 2010. Social movement partyism: Collective action and political parties, in *Strategic Alliances: New Studies of Social Movement Coalitions*, edited by N. Van Dyke and H.J. McCammon. Minneapolis: University of Minnesota Press, 170–96.
Costain, A.N. 1992. *Inviting Women's Rebellion: A Political Process Interpretation of the Women's Movement*. Baltimore: Johns Hopkins University Press.

Gamson, W.A. 1990 [1975]. *The Strategy of Social Protest*. 2nd ed. Homewood, IL: Dorsey Press.

Johnston, P. 1994. *Success while Others Fail: Social Movement Unionism and the Public Workplace*. Ithaca, NY: Cornell University Press.

McAdam, D. 1982. *Political Process and the Development of Black Insurgency, 1930–1970*. Chicago: University of Chicago Press.

McVeigh, R. 2009. *The Rise of the Ku Klux Klan: Right-Wing Movements and National Politics*. Minneapolis: University of Minnesota Press.

Meyer, D.S. 1990. *A Winter of Discontent: The Nuclear Freeze and American Politics*. New York: Praeger.

Meyer, D.S. 2004. Protest and political opportunity. *Annual Review of Sociology*, 30, 125–45.

Meyer, D.S. and Tarrow, S.R., eds. 1998. *The Social Movement Society: Contentious Politics for a New Century*. Lanham, MD: Rowman & Littlefield.

Miller, J. 1994. *Democracy is in the Streets: From Port Huron to the Siege of Chicago*. Boston: Harvard University Press.

Parker, C.S. and Barreto, M.A. 2013. *Change They Can't Believe In: The Tea Party and Reactionary Politics in America*. Princeton: Princeton University Press.

Reese, E., Petit, C., and Meyer, D.S. 2010. Sudden mobilization: Movement crossovers, threats, and the surprising rise of the US anti-war movement, in *Strategic Alliances*, edited by N. Van Dyke and H. McCammon. Minneapolis: University of Minnesota Press, 266–91.

Skocpol, T. and Williamson, V. 2012. *The Tea Party and the Remaking of Republican Conservatism*. Oxford: Oxford University Press.

Smith, C. 1996. *Resisting Reagan: The U.S. Central America Peace Movement*. Chicago, University of Chicago Press.

Turner, L. and Hurd, R.W. 2001. Building social movement unionism: The transformation of the American Labor Movement, in *Rekindling the Movement: Labor's Quest for Relevance in the Twenty-First Century*, edited by L. Turner, H.C. Katz, and R.W. Hurd. Ithaca, NY: Cornell University Press, 9–26.

Van Dyke, N. 2003. Crossing movement boundaries: Factors that facilitate coalition protest by American college students, 1930–1990. *Social Problems*, 50(2), 226–50.

Van Dyke, N. and McCammon, H., eds. 2010. *Strategic Alliances: Coalition Building and Social Movements*. Minneapolis: University of Minnesota Press.

Van Dyke, N. and Soule, S. 2002. Structural social change and the mobilizing effect of threat: Explaining levels of patriot and militia organizing in the United States. *Social Problems*, 49(4), 497–520.

PART I
Explaining the Timing and Pace of the Mobilization: Politics and Resources

Chapter 1
What's New about the Tea Party Movement?

Rory McVeigh

Beginning in the 1960s, a wave of social movement activism contributed to fundamental change in the United States. African Americans organized to dismantle Jim Crow segregation in the South and to secure voting rights and basic civil rights throughout the nation. Latinos and American Indians, inspired by the example set by the civil rights movement, also took to the streets. Feminists and gay rights activists organized to advocate progressive legislation, but also to change deeply rooted cultural norms that devalue women, gay men, lesbians, bisexuals, and transgendered individuals. Young Americans led a movement against war in Vietnam, and others organized to reverse environmental degradation. While elected officials gave disproportionate representation to the wealthy and powerful, ordinary Americans acted outside institutionalized politics to pressure those officials to respond to calls for progressive change.

Protest of the 1960s also led to a fundamental change in the way that social scientists understood social movement activism. Previously, political protest was viewed as being more similar to crime and deviant behavior than it was to voting, lobbying, or other forms of political action. To a great extent, the fear of the masses reflected in the French social psychologist Gustave LeBon's work remained influential. Writing at the end of the nineteenth century, LeBon described protest participants in the following manner:

> by the mere fact that he forms part of an organized crowd, a man descends several rungs in the ladder of civilization. Isolated, he may be a cultivated individual; in a crowd, he is a barbarian—that is, a creature acting by instinct. He possesses the spontaneity, the violence, the ferocity, and also the enthusiasm and heroism of primitive beings, whom he further tends to resemble by the facility with which he allows himself to be impressed by words and images—which would be entirely without action on each of the isolated individuals composing the crowd—and to be induced to commit acts contrary to his most obvious interests and his best-known habits. An individual in a crowd is a grain of sand amid other grains of sand, which the wind stirs up at will. (1952: 32–3)

While lacking much of the alarmist tendencies of LeBon, dominant theoretical perspectives of the 1950s and 1960s also treated protest as more of a psychological than a political phenomenon. Mass society theory (Kornhauser 1959) and collective behavior theory (Smelser 1962) proposed that changes in the structure of society generate discontent among subsets of the population, freeing those individuals from constraining social bonds. Protest was viewed as a response to anxiety, frustration, and a general sense of anomie.

These scholarly accounts of social protest were turned upside down in the wake of 1960s activism. Many graduates of social science PhD programs in the 1960s and 1970s were schooled in the streets as well as in the classroom. Their own activism on behalf of progressive causes carried over into their emerging scholarship (see Gamson 2011). Not surprisingly, these activist/scholars quickly revealed the extent to which earlier depictions of social movement participants lacked an empirical foundation. Indeed, subsequent research has consistently shown that movement participants tend to be embedded in dense social networks and they participate not to release psychic tension, but to bring about political and cultural change. Rather than focusing on how structural changes can generate anomie and discontent, social movement scholars instead gave attention to how movement activists strategically capitalize on the availability of organizational resources (McCarthy and Zald 1973, Oberschall 1973, Gamson 1975, Morris 1984), exploit favorable shifts in the political environment (Tilly 1978, McAdam 1982, Tarrow 1994), and construct interpretive frames that entice individuals to participate in collective action (Snow et al. 1986).

Progressive social movements have continued to press demands for a more responsive government, and resource mobilization theory, political opportunity theory, and framing theory continue to be useful for analyzing and explaining these movement dynamics. Yet since 2009, one of the social movements that has received the most public attention and has had, arguably, the most influence on American politics, draws support primarily from white middle-class Americans (Zernike 2010). Its members claim to be acting in the spirit of the nation's founding fathers, while they seek to limit the government's role in providing for the welfare of the nation's citizens. Through top-down as well as bottom-up organizing, and with the benefit of free publicity generated by extensive media coverage, the Tea Party movement can boast of millions of members and adherents. A New York Times/CBS News poll conducted in April 2010 showed that 18 percent of respondents identified themselves as Tea Party supporters (see Zernike 2010). Because Tea Party supporters are primarily drawn from Republican voters, Republicans running for public office have come to understand that their political fortunes depend heavily on how they are viewed by Tea Party supporters.

How did the Tea Party gain so many supporters and so much influence? Although a wave of research on the movement is currently underway, as of this writing very little social scientific research has been published on the topic. Much in the same way that research on social movements of the 1960s led to fundamental change in social movement theory, research on the Tea Party could open up new lines of inquiry and generate new insight into social movement dynamics. The emergence of conservative movements such as the Tea Party, as I discuss below, cannot be explained with theories that were developed with progressive movements in mind. The Tea Party, therefore, will require us to develop new tools designed to account for the emergence of conservative collective action. In this chapter, I offer some guidance on how we can most effectively theorize and study Tea Party activism. I begin by discussing the limitations of extant theory. Following that, I compare the Tea Party to another middle-class mass movement in American history—the Ku Klux Klan of the 1920s—and I discuss how the power devaluation model, a theory that I previously developed to account for the rise of the Ku Klux Klan, could be used to study both the emergence and the trajectory of the Tea Party movement.

Grievances Do Matter (for Conservative Movements)

While terms such as "progressive" and "conservative" can be defined in many different ways, here I offer operational definitions that draw attention to a fundamental difference between the two types of movements, with these differences being particularly relevant for explaining their emergence and growth. I see progressive movements as those that are primarily oriented toward winning new rights and privileges for constituents—rights and privileges that are available to other groups in society but have been denied to the movement's constituents. Conservative movements, on the other hand, are oriented primarily toward preserving, restoring, or expanding constituents' pre-existing privileges. This process typically involves protecting traditional economic and social arrangements that offer advantages to constituents—advantages that come at the expense of other groups in society. Conservative collective action is typically instigated by beneficiaries of inequality who are resisting efforts to redistribute wealth and resources or who are resisting other changes that might undermine benefits they receive due to preferential treatment that is given to their own social group.

This fundamental distinction between progressive and conservative movements is critical when it comes to explaining movement origins. As resource mobilization theorists pointed out long ago, many disadvantaged and relatively powerless groups are oppressed and downtrodden for decades, and even centuries, before collective action emerges (McCarthy and Zald 1973, Oberschall 1973, Jenkins and Perrow 1977). Or, in many cases, collective action fails to emerge at all. The presence of grievances and the intensification of grievances are poor predictors of the emergence of collective action among the oppressed (McAdam 1982). Failure to act, in such cases, typically has more to do with the lack of an organizational infrastructure or a political climate that is so oppressive that group members perceive that organizing to bring about change would be futile (Tilly 1978, McAdam 1982, Tarrow 1994). In these cases, social movement researchers have rightly focused on time-variant factors such as the availability of organizational resources and openings in the political opportunity structure that make it possible to act to address longstanding grievances.

This logic, while perfectly sound when applied to progressive movements, does not apply when the goal is to explain the emergence of conservative collective action. Constituents of the Tea Party, for example, are not oppressed and downtrodden. Supporters have ready access to organizational resources, they need not fear political repression when they stage a protest event, and they need not look far to locate influential political allies. Any attempt to explain the emergence of the Tea Party in terms of resources and political opportunities, therefore, begs the question why the movement emerged in 2009 rather than at some other historical moment when resources and political opportunities were just as abundant and accessible. Resources and political opportunities may still be essential for mobilization, but they do not explain the timing of movement emergence. Explanatory power, when studying movements that act on behalf of relatively privileged actors, comes from identifying what has changed over time that provided the impetus to draw upon pre-existing organizational resources and to exploit pre-existing openings in the structure of political opportunity. What new grievances provided the incentive to act?

What about "Threat"?

The Tea Party is just one of many conservative movements that have been active throughout US history, but the vast majority of scholarly attention has been directed toward progressive movements. Conservative movements, however, have not been completely ignored in the academic literature. In some studies, researchers fall back on assumptions about protest participants that were broadly held prior to the 1960s, proposing that conservative movements have more to do with psychological states such as status anxiety and frustration than with political action designed to protect collective privileges (Lipset and Raab 1970, Wood and Hughes 1984, Burris 2001). Yet much recent research suggests that conservative activists, like progressive activists, tend to be embedded in dense social networks (Blee 1991, 2002, MacLean 1994, McVeigh and Sikkink 2001). Little evidence, also, has been provided that indicates that conservative activists are any less rational than progressive activists.

Avoiding irrationalist assumptions about the characteristics of protest participants, some researchers have shown that collective action can result from suddenly imposed grievances (Walsh 1981) or from a disruption in the quotidian (Snow et al. 1998). While reactions to suddenly imposed grievances need not be conservative in nature, these arguments can be applied to conservative movements because members of a particular social group may act in response to sudden changes that are detrimental to their interests. Along these same lines, researchers are increasingly giving attention to how collective action can emerge as a reaction to some form of threat. According to this line of thinking, individuals may act collectively against a real or perceived threat when they conclude that the costs of inaction—or the losses that would result from letting the threat go unanswered— exceed the costs of taking action (Tilly 1978, Goldstone and Tilly 2001, Van Dyke and Soule 2002, Almeida 2003). This general approach is very similar to one that has been applied in studies of racial and ethnic conflict for several decades. In this research, ethnic conflict is shown to be most likely to occur when previously subordinated groups become increasingly capable of competing with majority group members for scarce and valued resources (Blalock 1967, Bonacich 1972, Nielsen 1985, Olzak 1992). Under these circumstances, members of the majority group may initiate collective violence in an effort to drive away or intimidate potential competitors.

Threat is a useful concept in social movement research because it appropriately focuses attention on time-variant grievances that can provide incentives to act collectively for segments of the population that are not held back by a lack of organizational resources or by a closed political opportunity structure. Yet we might think of threat as more of a starting point, rather than a final answer, when it comes to understanding conservative social movements. While conservative action may be understood as a reaction to a threat to collective interests of relatively privileged actors, there remains much to learn about the nature of the threat. We should take care not to neglect the causal complexity of movement emergence, and we should avoid post hoc evaluations that stretch the definition of the "threat" concept so far that it loses explanatory power. Close attention, also, should be given to the context in which collective action emerges. Conditions that pose a threat to constituents of one conservative movement may be irrelevant to other conservative movements. We must also recognize that a threat to collective interests does not always lead to collective action. The link between threat and action, therefore, must be theorized and researched empirically. The power devaluation model, which I describe in the next section, offers precise guidance on where we should look when seeking to explain conservative collective action, but it is also a model that can be easily adapted to different historical and cultural contexts.

The Power Devaluation Model

The power devaluation model is built upon an assumption that individuals are most likely to act in defense of their interests through social movement activism when their power to defend their interests through institutionalized channels is in decline. Individuals may face threats to their interests on a regular basis, but as long as they maintain the capacity to control outcomes and deflect challenges, there will be little incentive to participate in social movement activism. Therefore, a focus on power seems to give us the most purchase when studying conservative movements. Under ordinary circumstances, members of relatively privileged groups seek to protect their interests through institutionalized arrangements that systematically protect their advantaged position, while simultaneously making their advantages appear to be fair, legitimate, and natural (Gaventa 1982, Jackman 1994). Incentives to engage in activism arise when institutionalized power is increasingly ineffective.

As depicted in the simple model in Figure 1.1, the power devaluation model focuses on three key aspects of conservative mobilization: 1) incentives to act, 2) interpretive processes, and 3) movement growth and trajectory. I consider three

Incentives to Engage in Collective Action	Interpretive Processes	Movement Growth and Trajectory
Power Devaluation Economic Political Status	Cognitive shift, predisposing individuals toward collective action Framing opportunity: manipulate supply and demand through cultural attacks and cultural appeals	Utilize pre-existing organizational resources Exploit pre-existing political opportunities

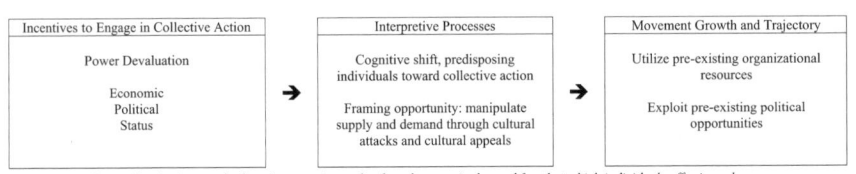

Power devaluation results from increase in supply of, or decrease in demand for, that which individuals offer in exchange

Figure 1.1 Power devaluation dynamics

sources of power devaluation that can potentially generate incentives to engage in conservative activism. These include power rooted in economic exchange, political exchange, and status-based exchange. Conceiving of power as being rooted in exchange (e.g., Simmel 1950, Emerson 1962, Blau 1964) has some distinct advantages when studying conservative movements. As Tilly (1998) notes, durable inequality is reproduced through both "opportunity hoarding" and "exploitation." In some cases, relatively privileged actors secure their advantages by restricting competition (opportunity hoarding). Yet in other instances, privileged actors secure advantages by extracting valued resources from members of other groups (exploitation). It is necessary, then, to consider that for some, conservative collective action may be a response to competitive pressure, but in other instances it may be in response to factors that interfere with processes of exploitation. Tolnay and Beck (1995), for example, call attention to how elite and non-elite white southerners had different motivations for lynching African Americans in the late 1800s and early 1900s. Some white elites saw lynching as useful for maintaining control over labor, while non-elite whites were motivated by a desire to eliminate or drive away competitors. The nature of the threat to white interests, in this case, was very different depending on white southerners' positions within exchange relationships.

I offer a precise way of conceptualizing "power devaluation" so as to avoid post hoc explanations of outcomes of interest that stretch the concept too broadly. We can think of one's "purchasing power" within an exchange market as being determined by supply and demand. Power devaluation results from either increase in supply of those offering the same commodity in exchange or or from a decrease in demand for that which is offered in exchange. Common mediums of exchange within an economic market include labor, wages, goods, services, and money. In a political market, they include votes, money, representation, and patronage. In a status-based market, certain traits and behaviors are exchanged for esteem (Emerson 1962, Blau 1964). We should expect to find that core constituents of a conservative movement are experiencing power devaluation in at least one exchange market (economic, political, or status). Incentives to act would be especially strong if individuals are experiencing devaluation in more than one market. For example, if someone experiences economic devaluation but retains power within political exchange, she might use political power in an effort to restore economic power. Similarly, economic power can be used to restore power devaluation in political or status-based exchange. Simultaneous devaluation in multiple markets, however, provides an incentive to act outside of traditional institutions through social movement activism because institutional action is increasingly ineffective.

Power Devaluation and Interpretive Processes

Decades of research on social movement framing processes has taught us that we should not expect a direct and immediate link between power devaluation and participation in collective action (McAdam 1982, Snow et al. 1986). Individuals act based upon their perceptions of reality, rather than in response to objective conditions. The power devaluation model stipulates that objective power devaluation (as described above) can produce a shift in the way in which those affected understand their own circumstances and also provides framing opportunities for those who wish to organize collective action. When power devaluation disproportionately affects individuals who share a common cultural bond (perhaps based on ethnic or religious identity), it increases the likelihood that those experiencing power devaluation will become aware of devaluation and will view it as a collective rather than an individual problem. Under these conditions, individuals are most likely to be receptive to calls for action as they have become aware of their depreciating power within economic, political, and status-based exchange markets and they are likely to interact on a regular basis with others who share an interest in taking action to restore power.

Recognition of group-based power devaluation provides a strategic framing opportunity for those who wish to organize conservative collective action. Frames that draw upon shared cultural identities (or in some cases seek to construct new cultural identities), while also proposing action to reverse the root causes of power devaluation, should resonate strongly with those targeted for recruitment. Perhaps most importantly, the cultural aspects of the framing may draw support even from those who are not directly experiencing power devaluation but identify with the movement based on its cultural claims. This is especially important because efforts to reverse power devaluation are likely to cause harm to other social groups. Because the movement acts on behalf of relatively privileged actors, frames that appeal to an injustice are likely to lack credibility. Indeed, to avoid a strong backlash and to attract support needed to restore power, there must be some effort to conceal the extent to which the movement is motivated by a desire to protect privileges rather than by a desire to reduce inequality or correct an injustice.

Power Devaluation, Resources, and Political Opportunity

I have argued that conservative movements cannot be explained by resource mobilization theory or political opportunity theories because, unlike movements that represent relatively powerless and disadvantaged groups, conservative movements act on behalf of constituents who typically have ready access to organizational resources and are not denied access to the polity. Yet this is not to say that resources and political opportunities are irrelevant to conservative social movements. Power devaluation generates incentives to utilize pre-existing organizational infrastructure and to exploit pre-existing political opportunities. The skill with which conservative activists are able to do so goes a long way toward determining how strong and influential the movement ultimately becomes.

Klan of the 1920s: Tea Party Precursors?

In seeking to explain the Tea Party phenomenon in the United States, a historical comparison may be instructive. In many respects, the Tea Party movement bears a strong resemblance to the Ku Klux Klan that arose and gained strength in the early 1920s. Before moving forward, it is important to point out that the Klan of the 1920s was different in many respects from the Ku Klux Klan that violently reacted to civil rights gains in the 1960s. Inspired in part by romanticized stories of the original Ku Klux Klan that spread violence and terror throughout the South in the aftermath of the Civil War, the second Ku Klux Klan was resurrected in 1915 by the opportunistic William Joseph Simmons. Simmons, a former preacher with extensive experience organizing fraternal lodges, viewed the Klan as the ultimate fraternity (Jackson 1967).

   Simmons drew heavily upon his own ties to fraternal organizations and to Protestant congregations to attract members and leaders. He had only modest organizing success during the first five years, but in the early 1920s, after putting Edward Young Clarke and Elizabeth Tyler in charge of recruiting, the movement took off (Chalmers 1987). Within a few years, the movement spread into all 48 states and attracted millions of dues-paying members. Unlike the reconstruction era Klan, the Klan of the 1920s grew to be particularly strong in Midwestern states such as Indiana, Ohio, Illinois, and Michigan, and also gained strength in several Western states including Oregon, Colorado, and Oklahoma (Chalmers 1987). Simmons was maneuvered out of his leadership position in 1922, and the organization was taken over by Hiram Wesley Evans (the new Imperial Wizard) and D.C. Stephenson. Stephenson, appointed by Evans as the "Grand Dragon," would be primarily responsible for recruiting and organizing in the Northern states. Both Evans and Simmons sought to capitalize on the Klan's potential to become a force in national politics (McVeigh 2009). Although Klan members of the 1920s did at times commit violent acts, the leadership recognized that containing the violence of its members would be necessary for the Klan to gain broad support and become influential in politics (McVeigh 2009).

   The Klan emerged during a period characterized by racial conflict, as white workers in Northern cities frequently resorted to violence to restrict economic competition and encroachment on neighborhoods and public facilities (Bonacich 1972, Wilson 1980). Someone who is unfamiliar with the 1920s Klan might understandably conclude that the violence and conflict was related to Klan activism and that Klan activism, itself, represented a reaction to increased competition over manufacturing jobs. That conclusion would be wrong. The white working class was under-represented in the Klan's ranks and few Klan members competed directly with African Americans for jobs (MacLean 1994). Klan organizations were often located in communities where African Americans were few in number and posed no local threat to Klan constituents. Indeed, Klan leaders at times condemned the violence that was being directed toward black workers and on several occasions even took credit for a decline in the lynching rate (McVeigh 2009). Klan leaders' rhetoric about their "pure" intentions, of course, should be taken with a grain of salt. Yet it is clear that unlike the Klan of the 1860s and of the 1960s, direct competition with African Americans (or local threats posed by African Americans) had little to do with the movement's phenomenal growth. Klan organizers targeted the white middle class for recruitment, and did not target working-class whites who faced direct competition with African Americans (McVeigh 2009).

During the 1920s, the Klan gave much more negative attention to Catholics and immigrants than they did to African Americans. Leaders of the organization proudly proclaimed that they were establishing a "100 percent American" organization for native-born white Protestants. Klan leaders argued that Catholicism was incompatible with American democracy and was responsible for many of the nation's ills (MacLean 1994). They argued that immigrants, predominantly from Catholic countries, were disproportionately composed of deviants, criminals, and political radicals. Stemming the flow of immigrants, they argued, would go a long way toward preserving America's special status as a nation that was blessed in the eyes of God. As was true in regard to African Americans, however, the Klan thrived in many locations where immigrants and Catholics were few in number and would have posed a minimal threat in terms of localized competition. In my earlier study of the 1920s Klan, I called attention to how many of the issues that Klansmen used to attract members and supporters were national in scope. Increases in the number of Catholic immigrants in New York City and Boston, for example, had significant implications for native-born white Protestants in Indiana in terms of their impact on national politics and on the national economy. Failure to recognize these circumstances leads to a fundamental misunderstanding of the way in which Klan leaders were able to recruit so many supporters in such a short time. In fact, in the Klan's national newspaper, *The Imperial Night-Hawk*, a Klansmen commented on how the Klan was gaining strength in communities where African Americans, Catholics, and immigrants were few in number and posed little threat. He wrote:

> Since every community should be vitally interested in the public welfare of the nation as a whole, and each one has special conditions with which the Klan deals, it cannot be truthfully stated of any place that there is no need of an organization that has to do with national problems and seeks to improve national as well as local conditions. Most of our problems are of national scope and directly concern every community in America. (*Imperial Night-Hawk*, April 2, 1924)

Like today's Tea Party, leaders of the Ku Klux Klan claimed to be calling for a return to principles of governance developed, with divine guidance, by the nation's founding fathers. D.C. Stephenson received his appointment as the Grand Dragon in front of a massive crowd in Kokomo, Indiana on July 4, 1923. His speech, published in the Klan's newspaper *The Fiery Cross*, was titled "Back to the Constitution." Stephenson began his speech by warning of the danger that comes from straying from the standards for governance established by the founding fathers:

> Every subsequent public problem has its origin in some violation of their fundamental attitude, and likewise correction and remedy can be accomplished only through retracting our misguided steps to the standards established by them. Conditions change, but the principles proclaimed on July 4th, 1776, sustained in conflict that was both civil war and revolution, and then embodied in a federal constitution the like of which man has never seen, are as sacred now as they were then, and as more essential to the common welfare today as our modern life is more complex than was the simple life they led. (*The Fiery Cross*, July 6, 1923)

Also foreshadowing Tea Party rhetoric, the Grand Dragon warned his audience about federal budget deficits:

> If in a single year this government were to pay its current unbounded debts, wipe out deficits, liquidate even those pending claims which have been audited and approved, and meet regularly appropriated annual expenses, at least ten billions of revenue would be required. (*The Fiery Cross*, July 6, 1923)

Claiming divine endorsement of a minimalist federal government should have been particularly appealing to Klan members and supporters at the time, much in the same way that it appeals to Tea Party supporters today. To understand the appeal, it is necessary to give attention to the types of people who were drawn to the Klan as well as to the types of changes that were taking place that provided incentives for them to act. Although the decade of the 1920s is often thought of as a time or prosperity preceding the Great Depression, prosperity was unevenly distributed and many were suffering severe economic hardship. In the aftermath of World War I, local economies based on agricultural production, in particular, took a severe hit. Manufacturing industry, concentrated in Northeastern states, was expanding and increasingly relying on unskilled labor, which had negative consequences for artisans and small manufacturers throughout the nation. At a time when capitalists, industrial laborers, and farmers were organizing and pressing demands on the federal government (Clemens 1997, Sanders 1999), many middle-class Americans believed that the unorganized middle class would be left holding the bag. Klan leaders promised to fight on their behalf and asked them to join their cause.

Sources of power devaluation for white middle-class Americans were many during the early 1920s. In my earlier research (McVeigh 2009), I documented the way in which factors such as deskilling of manufacturing production, an agricultural recession, immigration, African American migration, women's entrance into the labor force, women's suffrage, the rise of Parochial education, and Prohibition legislation contributed to economic, political, and status-based power devaluation for many of those who were attracted to the Klan. These conditions created a situation where many middle-class Americans had incentive to take conservative collective action. While many constituents experienced economic hardships, their concern was that government aid would not benefit them but would instead benefit other social groups. Interpretive work was required to transform predisposition to act into collective action. Because the sources of power devaluation were varied, individuals were drawn to the Klan for a wide variety of reasons. Klan leaders sought to unite this diverse middle-class constituency by emphasizing their common cultural heritage as native-born, white Protestant Americans. By linking "power devaluation grievances" to cultural identities, the Klan's leaders were able to develop frames that might have given constituents hope that power devaluation could be reversed.

If power devaluation results from an increase in supply of those offering the same thing as Klan constituents within an exchange market, then cultural attacks could be used to advocate for restricting the supply. Klan framing focused heavily on advocating restriction of immigration and curtailing the rights of Catholics, women, and African Americans. If power devaluation also results from a decrease in demand for that which constituents offer in exchange, then power devaluation could be reversed by appealing to the positive aspects of one's own culture to stimulate demand. Along those lines, Klan leaders organized economic boycotts encouraging people to "trade with a Klansmen" while avoiding commodities produced by Catholic or immigrant labor. They sought to organize a large voting bloc composed of native-born white Protestants that would force candidates for political office to satisfy their political demands. At that time, Klan constituents were split relatively evenly across the Republican and Democratic parties. Klan leaders encouraged constituents to place loyalty to the Klan above loyalty to the party. The Klan promised to deliver votes to candidates who proved to be "100 percent American." The size of the movement, combined with the movement's effectiveness in maneuvering within the political opportunity structure—presenting itself as a patriotic movement concerned solely with protecting American traditions and values—created a dilemma for candidates for public office (including the presidency). To condemn the Klan meant alienating millions of middle-class voters who could determine the outcome of electoral contests. Failure to condemn the Klan, however, could alienate all of those who were excluded by the Klan's racial, ethnic, and (more generally) cultural, boundary construction.

Utilizing a strong organizational infrastructure and taking advantage of an open political opportunity structure, the Ku Klux Klan became a powerful middle-class movement intent on taking action to preserve and restore the advantages of its middle-class constituency during a time of economic and political turmoil.

Power Devaluation and the Tea Party

Political pundits and scholars have noted that Tea Party members are overwhelmingly white and the movement seems energized in opposition to the nation's first African American President. Some survey data also indicates that Tea Party supporters are more likely than other Americans to hold negative views of African Americans (e.g., see Parker and Barreto 2011). It is tempting, therefore, to hypothesize that Tea Party mobilization can be explained in terms of its members and supporters reacting to a perceived threat posed by African Americans. While it is possible that a sense of racial threat or competition plays a role, such an argument, in my view, misses the key forces contributing to Tea Party strength and also misses out on the primary ways in which racial identity is related to Tea Party activism. Even more than was the case for the 1920s Klan, the Tea Party movement is primarily focused on national, rather than local, threats to their interests.

I see many similarities between the rise of the Tea Party and the rise of the Ku Klux Klan in the early 1920s. The Tea Party movement emerged in the midst of the most severe economic recession since the Great Depression of the 1930s. Because of the depth of the recession, economic power devaluation was experienced broadly in the United States. Workers faced declining demand for their labor as unemployment rates soared. Owners of large corporations faced a global decline in demand for their products. As the economic crisis deepened, demand for services and commodities provided by middle-class professionals and small-business owners declined sharply. Notably, however, Tea Party activists vociferously argue against expanded government aid to benefit those who are feeling the brunt of the economic decline. As was the case in the 1920s, many in the middle class sense that any government response to the economic crisis would disproportionately benefit other social groups at their expense. While economic pain resulting from the great recession has been widespread and has undoubtedly affected some members of the Tea Party, supporters of the movement are not drawn from those who are in the greatest need of aid. The movement's central message—cut taxes and cut spending—resonates most strongly with those who are doing fairly well in spite of the great recession and do not want to bear the burden of supporting those who have not fared well.

Political Power Devaluation

While many Americans experienced economic power devaluation during and after the recent recession, the co-occurrence of political power devaluation for core Tea Party constituents, I believe, is key to understanding the movement's rapid growth. As Democrats assumed the leadership of both the House and the Senate, and with Democrat Barack Obama elected as president, all signs indicated that government would enact progressive legislation in response to the crisis that began when Republican George W. Bush was president. It should be noted, however, that the Tea Party anger began brewing before Obama took office, in response to bailouts of endangered financial institutions enacted at the end of the Bush presidency. In the early months of the Obama presidency, conservative fears were realized as the Obama administration pushed through a major economic stimulus bill and launched its effort to enact major health care reform. Good arguments, of course, can be made for increasing government spending during a severe recession and targeting the spending toward poor and middle-class individuals who will be most likely to immediately spend any government funds that come their way. Yet much like the 1920s Klan, many of those who were in the least need of governmental aid—for example those who remained employed and already had quality health care—reacted negatively to the prospects of government funds being directed toward other social groups.

Democratic electoral successes in 2008 reflect political power devaluation for Tea Party constituents. It is useful, though, to use power devaluation concepts to help understand how Democratic ascendency created incentives for Tea Party activism. Under ordinary circumstances, prosperous individuals receive disproportionate attention from elected representatives by virtue of their higher rates of voter turnout and their capacity and willingness to make campaign contributions. The economic crisis, however, temporarily created a situation where candidates running for office had to promise, first and foremost, to take bold action in response to the crisis. The demand for that which relatively prosperous individuals offer in political exchange (votes and contributions) was less of a determining factor than would be the case in a normal election, as politicians had to somehow respond to crisis. Supply-side factors also came into play. Conservative movements often emerge in the wake of significant expansion in the pool of eligible voters (McVeigh 2009). In 2008, Obama benefitted from higher turnout from minority voters and also younger voters. As the nation's population is increasingly composed of racial and ethnic minorities, and as young voters have proven in recent years to be more liberal than older voters on many issues, Tea Party constituents likely sensed a decline in their capacity to protect their privileges through institutionalized politics. Indeed, in the immediate aftermath of the 2008 election, Republican prospects for future growth seemed bleak. Newly emerging constituencies were overwhelmingly Democratic.

Tea Party and Interpretive Processes

Economic power devaluation and, most importantly, political power devaluation, undoubtedly led many potential Tea Party supporters to reevaluate their individual circumstances and their relationship to public policy and political action. As the federal government began to take action to address the economic crisis, many Americans, rightly or wrongly, concluded that proposed government action was detrimental to their interests. Many who, in spite of the economic crisis, retained stable employment and enjoyed access to quality health care were troubled by the way in which the government planned to spend in ways that did not seem to directly benefit them. Because the United States is characterized by high levels of inequality and high levels of residential segregation (by both race and class), these individuals did not need to look far to find others who shared their interests, grievances, and concerns. For many Tea Party supporters, the types of people who stood to benefit from progressive government response to the crisis were both spatially and socially distant.

These circumstances created a framing opportunity for conservative collective action. Many relatively prosperous Americans were likely to be receptive to appeals to organize in opposition to progressive policies which, they perceived, would benefit others at their expense. Simply advocating spending cuts and tax cuts, however, would not be sufficient to turn back the progressive tide. Republicans who offered the same agenda had just suffered a staggering defeat in the 2008 elections. A conservative movement would have to somehow expand its base of support by drawing in individuals who might not readily respond to a straightforward argument about taxing and spending policies.

In the 1920s, Klansmen drew upon racial, ethnic, and religious identities to build a constituency that would be large enough to command attention from elected officials. They strategically constructed interpretive frames that linked economic and political grievances to cultural identities. They used attacks on out-groups to restrict and disable competition, and they touted the cultural superiority of their own group as a justification for taking collective action to preserve their privileges and advantages. Cultural framing obfuscated the extent to which collective action was oriented toward preserving advantages at the expense of others in society. Through this process, the Klan was able to expand its base so that it included those who were not directly affected by power devaluation, but were attracted by the movement's cultural framing.

Norms pertaining to racial, ethnic, and religious bigotry have changed significantly since the 1920s. As a result, the blatant appeals to the supremacy of native-born white Protestants employed by the Klan would have only limited appeal in a contemporary context and would turn away many potential supporters who are offended by such language. Yet due to inequality and segregation in American society, those who are most likely to be receptive to Tea Party appeals are, not unlike Klansmen of the 1920s, disproportionately middle class, white, and native-born. To promote solidarity among potential supporters, and to expand the base of support beyond those who are already up in arms about the government's progressive response to the economic crisis, movement leaders would still need to draw upon cultural solidarity to attract supporters and to justify conservative action. Such a strategy, rather than relying on blatant bigotry, would instead be compatible with practices that Bonilla-Silva has described as "color-blind racism." According to Bonilla-Silva, color-blind racism is an ideology that

> explains contemporary racial inequality as the outcome of nonracial dynamics. Whereas Jim Crow racism explained blacks' social standing as the result of their biological and moral inferiority, color-blind racism avoids such facile arguments. Instead, whites rationalize minorities' contemporary status as the product of

market dynamics, naturally occurring phenomena, and blacks' imputed cultural limitations. (2010: 2)

While some have pointed to expressions of racism and bigotry at Tea Party events, these have been mostly isolated occurrences and Tea Party spokespeople have made a deliberate effort to defend the organization from charges of racism. Certainly, Tea Party representatives recognize that racist tactics similar to those employed by the 1920s Klan would be counterproductive. Yet the Tea Party framing is very similar to Klan framing in another significant way. Like the Klan, Tea Party representatives have sought to characterize progressive policies as foreign, radical, and socialistic. Questions about Obama's place of birth and efforts to create the impression that Obama is a Muslim have helped to reinforce these accusations. Tea Party representatives and supporters, not unlike the Klansmen, have staked a claim to true Americanism while condemning competing agendas as being dangerous and hostile to fundamental principles established by the nation's founding fathers.

Klansmen were more willing than Tea Party representatives to identify specific ethnic or religious groups as the source of dangerous foreign influences. Yet like the Tea Party, Klansmen consistently warned that un-American radical ideas pose a great threat to the nation. As one Klan writer expressed it,

> The enemies of the constitution are within our gates. Communism, I.W.W. ism and anarchy are striking constantly at this fundamental document. The conservation of America and the preservation of the constitution depends upon men and women who love our institution, who are impregnated with the spirit of '76 and who have been baptized under the stars and stripes. (*The Imperial Night-Hawk*, August 1, 1923)

Similarly, by labeling health care reforms as socialistic and by portraying a conservative agenda as being in line with true American principles enacted by the founding fathers through divine inspiration, Tea Party activists provide cover for a political agenda that seeks to preserve privilege by making a minimalist government appear to be patriotic.

Tea Party activists also seek to equate governmental budgets with family budgeting processes. Debt held by the national government is compared to irresponsible individuals who go deep into debt by spending in excess of their means. Individual or family debt, of course, can be addressed by cutting back on expenses or by securing greater income. When it comes to government debt, however, increasing revenue (through taxation) is not an option for Tea Party activists. By solely emphasizing perceived spending excesses, the Tea Party agenda is presented as one that promotes responsibility and traditional values while opponents can be cast as corrupt and irresponsible. This maneuver can activate racial stereotypes in the minds of those targeted for recruitment by the Tea Party much in the way that Ronald Reagan stigmatized progressive policies by promoting the image of the "welfare queen" who lives in luxury while receiving government aid (see Quadagno 1996). The Tea Party has quite successfully concealed the extent to which its agenda aims to preserve privileges of the relatively wealthy during a severe recession. The movement has presented its agenda as being patriotic, while denigrating opponents as un-American and irresponsible. This type of framing is appealing not only to those who have the most to gain from the Tea Party agenda (cut spending and cut taxes) but also to others who may be drawn in by the movement's self-portrayal as one that represents true American values or those who sense that an African American president is seeking to redistribute wealth from white Americans to nonwhite Americans.

Organization and Political Opportunities

Because the Tea Party has relied on broad identity framing rather than direct appeals to specific racial, ethnic, or religious identities, it differs from the 1920s Klan in its capacity to build strong dense networks through regular face-to-face interactions of its members and supporters. Through regular meetings, the Klan was able to promote a strong sense of loyalty to the leadership and toward fellow members. This sense of commitment from so many members helped the Klan to present itself as force to be reckoned with in electoral politics because candidates for office had every reason to believe that the Klan could deliver votes to candidates who promised to do the bidding of the "invisible empire." The Tea Party, therefore, is somewhat vulnerable as it is composed mainly of individuals who are only loosely connected to other members and to a leadership structure. Holding the movement together requires sticking to a simple message about taxes and spending that appeals to all supporters. Branching out by taking on numerous causes, as did the 1920s Klan, could splinter the movement. Because the Tea Party movement has no clear leader, however, it is less vulnerable to scandals that could discredit the movement.

The Klan of the 1920s was rather innovative when it came to staging protest events and using the most recently developed communication technology to promote the organization. The Klan, however, certainly lacked communication tools that are available to the Tea Party. The internet and social media are used effectively to promote the Tea Party agenda. Perhaps most importantly, the movement is aided by the attention that it receives from the media. Mainstream news outlets such as CNN give extensive coverage to Tea Party activities and reporters rarely turn a critical eye to Tea Party claims. Fox News, the clear leader in cable news programming in terms of audience share, is essentially a mouthpiece for the Tea Party agenda, as discussed by Fetner and King in Chapter 2 of this volume. The Tea Party does not represent the views of the majority of Americans, however, and as the 2010 elections showed, Tea Party endorsement can harm candidates in general elections when they must appeal to a diverse constituency. Yet the movement has made effective use of organizational infrastructure and political allies to become a major player in national politics.

Social movements, of course, eventually reach a point where they decline or die. I expect that death for the Tea Party will come from one of two causes. On the one hand, the Tea Party movement will likely die when the economy improves. Widespread economic misery has provided Tea Party activists with a means of discrediting their opposition. By distancing the movement from the Bush administration, Tea Party activists escape blame for the crisis and hammer Obama and the Democrats with accusations of incompetency and socialistic tendencies. Slow progress in terms of job creation makes the framing resonate for many who know little about economics but do know that they are experiencing hard times and they want conditions to change. On the other hand, the Tea Party could die as a result of its own success. If Republicans eventually capture the White House and both houses of Congress with continued Tea Party support, the Tea Party essentially owns the economy and the government. No matter how the economy performs in the aftermath, the incentive for action outside of institutionalized politics will be greatly diminished.

Conclusions

In this chapter I have sought to illuminate the remarkable rise of the Tea Party movement by drawing attention to similarities between the movement and the Ku Klux Klan of the 1920s, and also by discussing the relevance of the power devaluation model for making sense of the movement's emergence and trajectory. Because of the movement's impressive size, elected officials have found it necessary to deal with it on some level. The movement is a useful enemy for politicians representing progressive constituencies, but creates significant problems for Democrats who serve more conservative constituencies and for Republicans who hope to win general elections where Tea Party support is relatively weak. Similarly, the size and political potency of the Tea Party also makes it hard for social movement scholars to ignore. If for no other reason, social movement scholars will need to acquire a better understanding of the Tea Party because the movement has become a significant part of the political field that progressive movements must navigate. Social movements, whether progressive or conservative, do not operate in a vacuum. Understanding movement action involves looking at the way in which a movement interacts not only with the state, but also with other groups in society (Curtis and Zurcher 1973, Klandermans 1997, Armstrong and Bernstein 2008).

A likely consequence of Tea Party research will be a growing interest in examining the sources of collective grievances and intergroup conflict. For several decades, social movement research has taken collective grievances as a starting point and focused on how movements organize to advance collective interests. I believe that a more complete understanding of movement dynamics can be achieved, however, by first analyzing complex social processes that create intergroup conflicts and that distribute power unevenly across groups and individuals.

References

Almeida, P.D. 2003. Opportunity organizations and threat induced contention: Protest waves in authoritarian settings. *American Journal of Sociology*, 109(2), 345–400.
Armstrong, E.A. and Bernstein, M. 2008. Culture, power, and institutions: A multi-institutional politics approach to social movements. *Sociological Theory*, 26(1), 74–99.
Blalock, H.M. 1967. *Toward a Theory of Minority Group Relations*. New York: John Wiley.
Blau, P.M. 1964. *Exchange and Power in Social Life*. New York: Wiley.
Blee, K. 1991. *Women of the Ku Klux Klan: Racism and Gender in the 1920s*. Berkeley: University of California Press.
Blee, K. 2002. *Inside Organized Racism: Women in the Hate Movement*. Berkeley: University of California Press.
Bonacich, E. 1972. A theory of ethnic antagonism: The split labor market. *American Sociological Review*, 37(5), 547–59.
Bonilla-Silva, E. 2010. *Racism without Racists: Color-Blind Racism & Racial Inequality in Contemporary America*. 3rd ed. Lanham, MD: Rowman & Littlefield.
Burris, V. 2001. Small business, status politics, and the social base of new Christian right activism. *Critical Sociology*, 27(1), 29–55.
Chalmers, D. 1987. *Hooded Americanism: The History of the Ku Klux Klan*. 3rd ed. Durham, NC: Duke University Press.
Clemens, E.S. 1997. *The People's Lobby: Organizational Innovation and the Rise of Interest Group Politics, 1890–1925*. Chicago: University of Chicago Press.
Curtis, R. and Zurcher, L. 1973. Stable resources of protest movements: The multi-organizational field. *Social Forces*, 52(1), 53–61.
Emerson, R. 1962. Power-dependence relations. *American Sociological Review*, 27(1), 31–41.
Gamson, W. 1975. *The Strategy of Social Protest*. Homewood, IL: Dorsey Press.
Gamson, W. 2011. From outsiders to insiders: The changing perception of emotional culture and consciousness among social movement scholars. *Mobilization*, 16(3), 251–64.
Gaventa, J. 1982. *Power and Powerlessness: Quiescence and Rebellion in an Appalachian Valley*. Urbana: University of Illinois Press.
Goldstone, J.A. and Tilly, C. 2001. Threat (and opportunity): Popular action and state response in the dynamics of contentious action, in *Silence and Voice in the Study of Contentious Politics*, edited by R.R. Aminzade et al. New York: Cambridge University Press, 179–94.

Jackman, M. 1994. *The Velvet Glove: Paternalism and Conflict in Gender, Class, and Race Relations*. Berkeley: University of California Press.

Jackson, K. 1967. *The Ku Klux Klan in the City, 1915–1930*. New York: Oxford University Press.

Jenkins, J.C. and Perrow, C. 1977. Insurgency of the powerless: Farm workers movements (1946–1972). *American Sociological Review*, 42(2), 249–68.

Klandermans, B. 1997. *The Social Psychology of Protest*. Cambridge, MA: Blackwell.

Kornhauser, W. 1959. *The Politics of Mass Society*. Glencoe, IL: Free Press.

LeBon, G. 1952. *The Crowd: A Study of the Popular Mind*. London: Ernest Benn.

Lipset, S.M. and Raab, E. 1970. *The Politics of Unreason: Right-Wing Extremism in America*. New York: Harper & Row.

McAdam, D. 1982. *Political Process and the Development of Black Insurgency, 1930–1970*. Chicago: University of Chicago Press.

McCarthy, J. and Zald, M. 1973. *The Trend of Social Movements in America: Professionalization and Resource Mobilization*. Morristown, NJ: General Learning Press.

MacLean, N. 1994. *Behind the Mask of Chivalry: The Making of the Second Ku Klux Klan*. New York: Oxford University Press.

McVeigh, R. 2009. *The Rise of the Ku Klux Klan: Right-Wing Movements and National Politics*. Minneapolis: University of Minnesota Press.

McVeigh, R. and Sikkink, D. 2001. God, politics, and protest: Religious beliefs and the legitimation of contentious tactics. *Social Forces*, 79(4), 1425–58.

Morris, A. 1984. *The Origins of the Civil Rights Movement: Black Communities Organizing for Change*. New York: Free Press.

Nielsen, F. 1985. Toward a theory of ethnic solidarity in modern societies. *American Sociological Review*, 50(2), 133–49.

Oberschall, A. 1973. *Social Conflict and Social Movements*. Englewoods Cliffs, NJ: Prentice-Hall.

Olzak, S. 1992. *The Dynamics of Ethnic Competition and Conflict*. Palo Alto: Stanford University Press.

Parker, C.S. and Barreto, M.A. 2011. *Will the Real Americans Please Stand Up? The Tea Party and Contemporary Right-Wing Extremism in the United States*. Princeton: Princeton University Press.

Quadagno, J. 1996. *The Color of Welfare: How Racism Undermined the War on Poverty*. New York: Oxford University Press.

Sanders, E. 1999. *Roots of Reform: Farmers, Workers, and the American State, 1877–1917*. Chicago: University of Chicago Press.

Simmel, G. 1950. *The Sociology of Georg Simmel*. Translated and edited by O.L. Wolff, H. Schiebelhuth, and K. Wolfskehl. New York: Free Press.

Smelser, N. 1962. *Theory of Collective Behavior*. New York: Free Press.

Snow, D.A., Rochford, E.B. Jr., Worden, S., and Benford, R. 1986. Frame alignment processes, micromobilization, and movement participation. *American Sociological Review*, 51(4), 454–81.

Snow, D.A. Cress, D.M., Downey, L., and Jones, A.W. 1998. Disrupting the 'quotidian': Reconceptualizing the relation between breakdown and the emergence of collective action. *Mobilization*, 3(1), 1–22.

Tarrow, S. 1994. *Power in Movement: Social Movements, Collective Action and Politics*. New York: Cambridge University Press.

Tilly, C. 1978. *From Mobilization to Revolution*. Reading, MA: Addison-Wesley.

Tilly, C. 1998. *Durable Inequality*. Berkeley: University of California Press.

Tolnay, S. and Beck, E.M. 1995. *A Festival of Violence: An Analysis of Southern Lynching, 1882–1930*. Urbana: University of Illinois Press.

Van Dyke, N. and Soule, S.A. 2002. Structural social change and the mobilizing effect of threat: Explaining levels of patriot and militia mobilizing in the United States. *Social Problems*, 49(4), 497–520.

Walsh, E.J. 1981. Resource mobilization and citizen protest in communities around Three Mile Island. *Social Problems*, 29(1): 1–21.

Wilson, W.J. 1980. *The Declining Significance of Race: Blacks and Changing American Institutions*. 2nd ed. Chicago: University of Chicago Press.

Wood, M. and Hughes, M. 1984. The moral basis of moral reform: Status discontent vs. culture and socialization as explanations of Anti-Pornography Social Movement adherence. *American Sociological Review*, 49(1), 86–99.

Zernike, K. 2010. *Boiling Mad: Inside Tea Party America*. New York: Times Books.

Chapter 2

Three-Layer Movements, Resources, and the Tea Party

Tina Fetner and Brayden G. King

When Anna Kroyman, who runs a telephone sales business out of her home in Monticello, Indiana heard about the government bailout of big business, she was fed up. She was inspired by Rick Santelli's rant from the floor of the Chicago Board of Trade opposing federal assistance to homeowners facing foreclosure. She went online to learn about the Tea Party and found TeaPartyPatriots.org, a professionally developed and maintained website of the social movement organization of the same name. The site was a source of information about local and national Tea Party organizations, and it also contained a feature that allowed Anna to enter her zip code to find a local Tea Party group. When she found that the closest group was two hours away, Tea Party Patriots taught her how to start her own group and register it with them, in case other Monticello residents wanted to join. She also made connections with other Tea Party leaders around the country and found support in their communications:

> TeaPartyPatriots.org—they are the beating heart of the movement. They started it and their website was a connection for groups all over the country to find each other ... I looked at Tea Party Patriots and I saw nothing in my area, but I did see that groups had popped up in the very beginning, in Texas, California, other parts of the country, Florida. So, I emailed those group leaders that were on Tea Party Patriots to say "How did you do it? How did you get your group? How did you get people to know you were there?" And all I got was support, "Don't give up; don't give up." I said "When we get twelve members, I'm going to hold a meeting," and they said "Don't wait. If you get five people, hold a meeting. If you get three people, hold a meeting." (Anna Kroyman, telephone interview, May 13, 2011)

Anna did exactly that and became the founder of the White County Tea Party Patriots group. Anna's transition from bystander to activist was surprisingly rapid. Feeling that something needed to change, she was able to easily get information, make connections with others, start an organization, and connect with a national network of similar groups. Studies of social movement emergence to date have not revealed such a smooth incorporation of individuals into activism, such a seamless transition from the emotional state of dissatisfaction to a fully mobilized state of participation in a functioning and active social movement.

What facilitated this rapid movement emergence? Three important factors were 1) an infrastructure that allowed people to quickly identify local Tea Party organizations or to start a new group if none was available, 2) a set of powerful media allies in Fox News and conservative talk radio, which not only broadcast news about the emergent movement, but actively promoted its events and valorized its participants, and 3) wealthy entrepreneurs and corporate sponsors who provided valuable resources to the movement. Although the movement would never have gained the national prominence that it did without the support of volunteer activists, the resources and infrastructure provided by established actors, like entrepreneurs and the media, magnified the influence of these local activists, enabling them to quickly build a powerful, national movement.

The Tea Party is unique in a number of ways, but one of the most distinctive features of the Tea Party was its rapid emergence and rise to national political power. The large amounts of resources available to the movement from its outset—indeed even before its beginning—put the Tea Party on a fast track relative to other movements scholars have observed. The Tea Party mobilized quickly, facilitated mass protest almost immediately, identified and supported candidates for local elections, and became an instantly recognized cultural and political phenomenon.

Certainly one of the factors that made this rapid emergence and rise to influence possible was the abundance of resources made available to would-be organizers like Anna. Compared to most new social movements, the Tea Party, from the very beginning, was resource-rich. As several investigative journalists have revealed, the movement had the support of wealthy individuals and corporations who have donated money to the cause, built movement infrastructure, and promoted movement events and protests. In this chapter we consider the challenges that corporate resources, which so few social movements have access to, might pose to a body of social movement theory that has culled its insights largely from social movements in which resources are scarce—often profoundly so. We ask: Are resources just resources? Does the source or the timing of resources influence a movement's political focus? Are the political interests of a movement endogenous to the resources' source? These questions, perhaps not as obvious to us when studying progressive movements, are made clear in the current era of corporate-supported "grassroots" movements. The Tea Party is certainly the most prominent of these movements, giving us a window into the dynamics that link corporate interests and grassroots activism.

Resources in Social Movement Theory

Social movement scholars have known for decades that resources are important to social movement mobilization. McCarthy and Zald's seminal work on resource mobilization theory (1977) posits that activism is akin to other tasks that involve complex coordination. Organizational strength, resources in the form of both money and personnel, and network ties are crucial to establishing and maintaining a social movement. These are also important influences, resource mobilization theory holds, for movement outcomes such as policy success. Claims of the value of resources to social movements have withstood substantial empirical analysis (for an extensive review, see McCarthy and Zald 2001).

In particular, social movement scholarship on resources has focused on the organizational infrastructure that supports and facilitates activism. Social movement organizations both emerge from and are embedded within networks that support their growth (e.g., Diani 2003). Coalitions between movements facilitate movement growth and goal attainment (Van Dyke and McCammon 2010). Andrews (2001) argued that these organizations and networks constitute a movement's infrastructure, which supports activism by providing leadership and other needed resources. His analysis of the Mississippi civil rights movement demonstrates that movements in areas with strong movement infrastructure had a larger impact than movements in areas with weaker infrastructures (see also Andrews 2004). Soule and King (2008) found that the kind of organizational infrastructure matters to movement survival, especially in times of economic turbulence when resources are low. Large, generalist organizations that have complex organizational abilities have a higher rate of survival during economic downturns than small, specialist movement organizations. For all of our idealistic hopes for the prosperity of mom-and-pop grassroots movements, past research clearly shows that the movements that prosper tend to have the support of complex and resource-plentiful organizations.

However, this body of work primarily focuses on social movements that emerge under conditions of scarce resources, and for good reason. Most social movements address issues of oppression, injustice, or inequality on behalf of a socially and/or economically marginalized group or social sector. In these cases, movement participants must roll up their sleeves and work to raise funds and recruit volunteers to sustain their activism. Resources from wealthy donors are not immediately available. Movement organizers usually start small and become more resource-rich after initial, incremental successes. Plentiful resources usually only come after a long period of movement gestation during which a small cadre of leaders and activists create infrastructure, allowing them to develop a core group of supporters and movement ideas (Morris and Staggenborg 2004). Resource injections are often episodic, sparked by the success of a movement event or a sudden shift in the political environment, but the majority of movements are characterized by high uncertainty and extreme fluctuation in resource availability (see Summers-Effler 2010 for vivid examples). Movement leaders continually deal with the question, where will resources come from next?

The Tea Party, however, did not emerge under conditions of scarce resources. Although clearly not all local Tea Party organizations enjoy the benefits of resource munificence, the emergence of the Tea Party movement occurred at a time when corporations and other elites infused the right-wing movement sector with resources, looking for voices to carry an agenda consistent with their private interests. As we discuss below, the Tea Party's emergence was initially sustained by large-scale donations by corporations and wealthy individuals and by free cultural support from Fox News and other conservative media venues (Skocpol and Williamson 2012). The Tea Party was, compared to other new movements, a resource-rich movement, perhaps even one in which resources ran ahead of the grassroots participants. This phenomenon poses an important theoretical challenge to social movement scholars: does the timing and source of resources matter to the development of a movement? Putting political ideology aside, does it matter when and how a movement is funded?

Three-Layer Movements

To conceptualize the role of resources and movement infrastructure in resource-rich social movements, and to connect them to other movements as well as to existing scholarship, we posit the three-layer movement, in which movement infrastructures are supported from above by donations from resource-rich donors, as well as from below by grassroots supporters and protest participants. Although the three-layer movement is by no means exclusive to the Tea Party, this movement typifies this structure and thus provides an ideal setting to examine how resources and their timing of availability may shape movement dynamics.

We conceptualize resource-rich social movements as being composed of three layers. The bottom layer consists of grassroots activists and their participation, energy, and contributions. Above them, as social movement theory already knows, is an infrastructure of organizations and networks that coordinate activism and mobilize participants. The top layer, where it exists, is a set of well-funded supporters of the movement who contribute resources to building and maintaining the movement infrastructure and sponsoring mobilization of the grassroots. In addition to corporate and elite sponsors, the top layer also consists of the various foundations, think tanks and media organizations that provide leadership and cultural resources for a movement.

Bottom-up movements are what we think of when we imagine a truly grassroots movement: activists build networks and institutions, form a collective identity, create collective action frames, mobilize participants, and utilize elite ties when available. Poor people's movements, as described by Piven and Cloward (1977), or early labor movements typify bottom-up movements (Cornfield 1991). Bottom-up movements initially have few elite allies with deep pockets and are often engaged in political conflict with wealthy interests, and therefore rely on indigenous resources to shape the early development of their movements (Morris 1981). Other movements are primarily grassroots, but are also sustained by contributions from corporate partners or sympathetic wealthy individuals. Usually these movements initially begin through grassroots organizing and then develop business ties after they have achieved some success and recognition. One example is the lesbian and gay movement, which developed alongside lesbian and gay business ventures, primarily in urban enclaves (Armstrong 2002). These movements often draw extensively from a middle and professional class of supporters and have more social ties to sources of wealth.

The Tea Party, as far as we can tell, is a top-down movement, in which a top layer of business corporations and wealthy donors used their resources to construct the necessary movement infrastructure used to mobilize grassroots participants. The Tea Party's access to resources is substantial and was present from the first moments of movement emergence. Few movements have such a resource-rich top layer during their formation period, probably because the interests of corporations and the very wealthy are mostly addressed outside the realm of social movements. These resource-rich movements may emerge when there are blockages to direct influence of polity insiders or, such as in the Tea Party, when the movement's goals are election-based and therefore require the mobilization of a large number of people to engage in activism (e.g., vote for a particular candidate). In addition, as can be seen in the case of corporate-sponsored grassroots organizing (Walker 2008, 2010), businesses may inject resources into a movement in order to promote their private interests in a less transparent form than direct lobbying. When wealthy actors seek to influence the political process directly, through lobbying or traditional public relations, they risk destroying the credibility of their argument as the general public may see their attempts as blatantly self-interested. By using social movements as vehicles, business corporations and wealthy individuals can influence public opinion, electoral victories, and legislative action without losing credibility.

So, to what extent can resource mobilization theory simply be applied to top-down movements like the Tea Party? To what extent does resource abundance matter to social movements? How does the relationship between rich donors and grassroots activists affect movement goals? How does the abundance of resources affect collective action frames, collective identity, and movement strategy? Is resource abundance sufficient to produce desired outcomes? Below, we examine the Tea Party as one example of how an infusion of top-down resources influences mobilization and movement outcomes and compare it to other movements that have benefitted from top-down resources during their emergence. Just as important, we consider the extent to which the existence of three-layer movements challenges existing theory on movements and resources.

Tea Party Resources

As Skocpol and Williamson (2012) carefully document, several resource-rich organizations had a hand in the emergence and mobilization of the Tea Party movement. They demonstrate that even before the emergence of the Tea Party, several "highly ideological right-wing billionaires" (Skocpol and Williamson 2012: 102) who want the Republican Party to shift to the libertarian extreme and have a long record of lobbying, supporting think tanks and funding institutions, saw an opportunity for mass mobilization on the right when the Tea Party began to emerge. Skocpol and Williamson's account is consistent with the writing of a number of investigative journalists. For example, Jane Mayer's exposé of corporate funding in the *New Yorker* (2010) follows the Koch brothers' development of right-wing think tanks and lobbying organizations through the establishment of FreedomWorks, which sponsored the creation of the Tea Party Patriots. Chris Good's work in *The Atlantic* (2010) and Andrew Goldman's piece in the *New York Magazine* (2010) provide additional information about the complexity of the political influence of the apparatus created by the Koch brothers and key Republican insiders such as Dick Armey. While we may not have a comprehensive understanding of all the resources available to the Tea Party, we are confident that these accounts are sufficient to establish our premise that this was a well-funded movement even before activists began protesting. Given that, we wish to consider the mechanisms through which these various "top-layer" providers of movement resources provided support to the Tea Party movement.

Facilitating Grassroots Mobilization

Although some have accused the Tea Party of being an "astroturf" movement, there is a sector of this movement that is genuinely grassroots. The biggest organization to mobilize mass participation is the Tea Party Patriots, a network of local, grassroots social movement organizations. The group is organized around a website that contains a search engine through which individuals can enter their zip code to learn about local social movement organizations in their area. This web-based search engine has been an important mechanism for mobilization, encouraging participants to join local groups or to start new ones when no one else had. Tea Party Patriots also hosts a weekly internet conference call to set the organization's agenda, plan events, and provide support across local social movement organizations. Journalists have claimed that the group's emergence was sponsored by FreedomWorks, the 501(c)(4) organization funded by the Koch brothers and run by Republican strategist Dick Armey (Beutler 2009, Fang 2009). FreedomWorks has at times denied this connection, but the group did admit that it had received a $1,000,000 donation from an anonymous source to distribute among local Tea Party organizations in advance of the 2010 midterm elections (Khan 2010). Other news accounts have disclosed emails between Tea Party Patriots and FreedomWorks (Good 2009, Roth 2009a).

Although Tea Party chapters are indeed founded by local activists who run their organizations independently, their activism has been greatly facilitated by the technical mechanisms established by FreedomWorks. The social network built through the TeaPartyPatriots.org website is populated with grassroots members, but the capacity to build this social network was created with resources provided from above. By avoiding the appearance of being funded directly by corporate sponsors, Tea Party organizations are able to maintain grassroots involvement while still benefitting from a well-established infrastructure supported by corporate sponsors.

Astroturf Organizations

Some Tea Party organizations benefit from more direct connections to wealthy supporters. Members of organizations affiliated with the Tea Party Patriots, in fact, have publicly criticized other organizations for being GOP-controlled "astroturf" organizations. For example, the Tea Party Express was founded by a political action committee (PAC), the Our Country Deserves Better PAC, in 2009. Its primary activism has been a series of bus tours of the United States, holding rallies in cities along the stops and supporting Tea Party candidates. The group has purchased advertising to support the election efforts of candidates: over $200,000 for Delaware's Christine O'Donnell and over $500,000 for Alaska's Joe Miller, who was elected to the US Senate (Beckel 2010). However, most of the money raised by the Tea Party Express appears to go back to the coffers of its PAC's founders, a Republican consulting firm, Russo, Marsh, and Rogers, which received over $850,000 over the period from July through November 2009 (Roth 2009b).

Unlike the Tea Party Patriots, a network of groups locally organized by independent activists, the Tea Party Express has close ties to the Republican Party, is organized hierarchically and makes its strategic decisions from a small group of powerful leaders with deep pockets. When it holds rallies to appeal to mass audiences, it is not so much about mobilizing mass participants as raising funds to direct either to candidates or to the founders of the group. The Tea Party Express, inasmuch as it represents the masses at all, has the qualities of synthetic grassroots organizing characteristic of astroturf organizations (Lyon and Maxwell 2004).

Other organizations claim to be activist, but seem to be more oriented to generating revenue. For example, the Tea Party Nation, founded in 2009 by Judson Phillips of Tennessee, hosts a social networking site for conservative activists and sponsored the 2010 National Tea Party Convention, at which Sarah Palin was the keynote speaker (Vogel 2009). The convention supported the Tea Party movement by hosting workshops for training leaders of local organizations. The group was criticized by other Tea Party activists for charging over $500 attendance fees and for paying $100,000 to Ms. Palin. In the controversy, the fact that this organization was not a nonprofit group emerged (Zernike 2010). These actions led many supporters of the Tea Party to distance themselves from this group.

Cultural Support

Perhaps the most important top-layer resource made available to Tea Party activists has been the conservative media's support for the Tea Party's cultural efforts: identity-building, issue-framing, mobilization of participants and communication to mass audiences. For example, Fox News took a leadership role in publicizing Tea Party events. This role extended beyond mere reporting of the news as it organized tax day Tea Party events branded with its logo and hosted by its on-air personalities. They made direct pleas to their viewers to attend Tea Party events and to join the movement (Hananoki 2009). Fox News covered the Tea Party on its news programs, as well as giving the movement extensive attention on its opinion shows such as *Fox & Friends*, *The O'Reilly Factor*, *Hannity*, *America Live with Megyn Kelly* and before its cancellation, *Glenn Beck*. As Fox News has an audience share that dwarfs other television news sources in the United States, the work it did to publicize and support the Tea Party reached a mass audience that other fledgling (or even established) social movements could never dream of (see, for example, Amenta et al. 2009, Andrews and Caren 2010, Sobieraj 2011 on news coverage of protests).

Fox News is not the only cultural outlet actively supporting the Tea Party movement, however. Conservative talk radio personalities like Rush Limbaugh, Michael Savage, Glenn Beck and Sean Hannity, the most widely listened to radio hosts in the country, have spent countless hours discussing their support of the Tea Party to their listeners (Skocpol and Williamson 2012). Writers on conservative blogs, newspaper columns, and political monographs including Michelle Malkin and Anne Coulter have argued in support of the Tea Party online and in print, as well as by appearing as pundits on television and the radio. Other print media such as the *Wall Street Journal* have provided space for opinion pieces supporting the social movement (e.g., Noonan 2010, Williams 2010). While some of this media support may stem from the movement winning the support of allies, much as Lipsky (1968) argued most powerless movements do, the Tea Party movement from the beginning (from the moment Rick Santelli mobilized people to take action during his rant on CNBC) has had a powerful advocacy partner in conservative media.

There are primarily three types of support that large amounts of resources provided to the early activism of the Tea Party: 1) the building of organizational apparatus/structure (including the organization of Tea Party events to mobilize supporters—e.g., tax day protests), 2) the election of Tea Party candidates in the midterm elections, and 3) the cultural promotion of Tea Party events and protestors in large-scale media outlets. These sources of funds not only provided start-up money but also created channels through which efficient fundraising could occur. According to Skocpol and Williamson (2012), these resources also serve a number of additional functions to support the Tea Party movement. For example, big funders offer training to grassroots organizers, they sponsor speakers who will provide programming at local Tea Party meetings, they host social networks for grassroots activists, and they sponsor the large national gatherings that Tea Party activists can attend.

Movements with Top-down Resources

Rather than being entirely unique, the Tea Party movement's links to wealthy funders seems to be following a historical trend in neoconservative politics. Looking at other movements that have benefitted from ties to business interests or wealthy elites may give us a greater understanding of the challenges and opportunities facing top-down movements and, in particular, the Tea Party movement.

Businesses have a recent history of funding movements that promote ideologies or policies that align with their private interests. Typically, corporations promote nonprofit organizations indirectly by funding foundations and charities through their philanthropic endeavors (Galaskiewicz 1997, Guthrie 2010), with some of these funds finding their way to activist organizations (McQuarrie 2010). While some corporate funding falls under the label of "corporate social responsibility," there is also a link between corporate outreach and their promotion of specific political agendas. This link became more pronounced in the 1970s and 1980s. Prior to this time, corporate giving was largely seen as charitable and intended to produce social goods. However, in the 1970s and 1980s, a sea change in corporate funding of foundations and charities took place, spurred in part by the rise of the neoconservative movement and the redirecting of resources to foundations and nonprofit organizations that were aligned with this movement.

Irving Kristol, one of the leading early voices of neoconservatism, argued forcefully in the editorial pages of the *Wall Street Journal* that businesses ought to be selective in which forms of philanthropy they pursue:

> When you give away your own money, you can be as foolish, as arbitrary, as whimsical as you like. But when you give away your stockholders' money, your philanthropy must serve the longer-term interests of the corporation. *Corporate philanthropy should not be, cannot be, disinterested.* (1977: 18; emphasis added)

Kristol echoed Milton Friedman's earlier admonition (1970) that businesses did not have "social responsibilities" except to create a profit. Other forms of philanthropy or corporate giving went against the shareholder mandate to create wealth. This mantra was repeatedly voiced by neoconservative critics who believed the business community was indirectly supporting the liberal agenda when they donated funds to social causes merely to improve the public good. They envisioned a new agenda of corporate giving that would direct resources—and thereby qualify them for corporate tax credits—to foundations possessing "an ethos of antiregulatory, anti-bureaucratic entrepreneurship as the basis of a reconfigured, decidedly more market friendly and antistatist" agenda (O'Connor 2010: 125).

Although corporations at that time were still prevented from funding direct forms of political advocacy, this shift in attitude led to the proliferation of corporate givers funding nonprofits with conservative leanings that could be persuaded to promote policies and ideas aligned with their own private interests. Two of the most visible foundations, the John M. Olin Foundation and the Federalist Society, began to actively promote the law and economics movement—the organized push to change the tenor of academic debate and to promote market (and conservative) friendly scholarship in law schools (Teles 2009). Of course, funders of this movement, which notably included the Coors family, intended to change more than just how law was theorized by scholars; ultimately, conservative donors and activists hoped to create a cadre of legal professionals that would replace the liberal elite they perceived had a hold over the judicial system. The result of this movement was to create a school of thought, gradually adopted by prestigious law reviews and law school sponsors, that would become the home of the most conservative lawyers and judges in the generation to come (e.g., Antonin Scalia was the first faculty adviser for the University of Chicago's chapter of the Federalist Society). The movement not only helped conservative activists to form a more-or-less pro-market ideology, in part because of the increasing concentration of law and economics scholars in elite law schools (Manne 2005), but it also created the organizational and social infrastructure that would form the spine of the market-facing legal community. Future Securities and Exchange Commission regulators, federal judges, and Justice Department administrators would come from that community.

The legal sphere was not the only part of society to be affected by the shifting of corporate funds to conservative-leaning nonprofits. The Bradley Foundation, the Capital Research Center, the Heritage Foundation, and other nonprofit think tanks and watchdog groups benefitted (O'Connor 2010). However, perhaps a more lasting legacy of shift in funding was to move even traditionally liberal foundations, like the Brookings Institution, more to the right. Although many of these foundations were ideologically predisposed to favor free market policies, corporate resources also made them easily susceptible to seeing things the way their corporate sponsors saw them. Foundations' promotion of particular policy solutions was suddenly more vulnerable to corporate influence.

More deceptive and insidious than funding foundations has been the corporate practice of directly funding grassroots campaigns. Since the early 1970s, corporations have become increasingly involved in funding grassroots lobbying campaigns, groups made to look like grassroots movement activists but that are primarily or solely funded by corporations. Walker (2009) argues that this trend has had a major impact on civil society in the US and not in entirely positive ways. Although corporate funding of grassroots activity has almost certainly increased participation, more generally, it has increased the civic sector's dependence on corporate resources, thereby weakening social capital and the development of civic skills. Moreover, Walker (2012) argues that the main purpose of these corporate efforts is to gain some control over their stakeholders and to align public opinion with their corporate interests. Thus, these campaigns are specifically engineered to shape public opinion to support corporate-friendly policies (e.g., lower corporate taxes). Thus, firms that use more direct lobbying, that have in-house public affairs offices, and that have already donated significant funds to Republican PACs —that is, the most politically engaged firms—are the most likely to engage in grassroots lobbying.

Foundation funding and corporate sponsored grassroots activism are both indirect means to influence policy and electoral outcomes; however, in the past businesses have been prevented from direct sponsorship of or campaigning for a candidate by strict campaign laws. However, the 2010 Supreme Court decision in *Citizens United v. Federal Elections Commission* further changed the nature of corporate-sponsored political activity. The case ruled that Citizens United, a nonprofit political advocacy organization, could legally show a political advertisement criticizing then presidential candidate Hillary Clinton 30 days before the election. While the ruling might have been implemented as a mere rebuttal of campaign reform, the Court instead interpreted the law generally to apply to First Amendment rights held by all citizens, including those of the corporate variety. Thus, business corporations were given new leeway in exercising their free speech by engaging in direct political advocacy. The timing, of course, perfectly coincided with the rise of the Tea Party. Under this new liberalization of corporate free speech, businesses now have unfettered freedom to fund activism.

Although there is no guarantee that movement activists, including the Tea Party, will unilaterally side with their corporate sponsors on every issue (and, in fact, the crisis over Congress's raising of the debt ceiling indicates that sometimes they do not), the examples cited above suggest that corporations intend to co-opt movement activists to serve their interests. While corporate leaders may share a similar political ideology with these activists, this ideological resonance is secondary to the political interests of the firm in determining why and how they seek to fund movements. Businesses and wealthy individuals have followed the advice of Irving Kristol in using their nonprofit funding to assist organizations and movements that they believe will push candidates and policies that serve their own private interests. The Tea Party movement, in this light, is an ideal candidate for corporate funding. The Tea Party, emerging shortly after the election of President Obama and a significant weakening of traditional Republican PACs and interest groups, was perfectly suited as a vessel for the promotion of corporate interests.

The availability of top-down resources facilitated the emergence of the Tea Party by helping activists to quickly build an organizational infrastructure that made it easy to recruit participants to the movement, find organizations near them, and coordinate, organize, and participate in protest activities. It is clear that a large pool of material and cultural resources was directed to supporting Tea Party movement emergence, though it is not known exactly how large that pool was. Unlike most fledgling movements, the Tea Party had a very robust set of start-up funds instantly available upon movement emergence. The infrastructure built by corporate and individual donations quickly and nimbly connected like-minded individuals, brought them together with others in their geographic area, directed them to existing organizations, and informed them about upcoming protest activities. This organizational infrastructure also trained future Tea Party leaders and gave interested individuals information on how to start a local organization if one did not yet exist. It provided abundant, free advertising of Tea Party-sponsored protests and events. To use the language of rational choice theory, this quickly constructed infrastructure removed the usual barriers to mobilization by substantially reducing the cost of participation for interested individuals. An important question for social movement scholars is what impact the availability of top-down resources has had on the movement's ideology and goals. Does the injection of top-down resources during the movement's origin affect its long-term viability?

Theorizing the Consequences of Top-down Resource Mobilization

Our conceptualization of a three-layer movement offers a twist to our understanding of movements' relationships with and dependence on resources. Extending resource mobilization theory's basic idea that much movement activity can be explained by their access to resources, this conceptualization pushes us to consider the source of resources as an important determinant of a movement's trajectory and outcomes. Movements that build their resources from the bottom-up face different challenges and opportunities than those that are injected with resources from the top-down. In this section we consider how movements that originate with a dependence on top-down resources may differ from other social movements. We discuss these implications for the Tea Party movement specifically and for social movement theory more generally.

Sequencing of Movement Emergence

Big-money movements call for social movement theorists to reconsider our understandings of the sequence of movement emergence. Social movement theory's current assumptions about the work of building a movement, framing issues, developing collective identities, and charting out strategic action may be out of sync with a top-down movement's ability to quickly mobilize grassroots bases, even before movement participants have settled on a coherent set of issue frames or strategic goals. Does the presence of large-scale resources obviate the need to carefully prepare for mobilization? As discussed above, it may be possible to form and mobilize a relatively large movement before a cadre of leadership develops.

Similarly, top-down movements may experience different rates of decline than bottom-up movements. Having grown to depend on resources from wealthy donors early on, these movements may be especially susceptible to failure when the political environment changes and their agenda no longer becomes central to the advancement of their wealthy sponsors' interests. Dependence on corporate resources or other sources of wealth may inhibit their ability to develop strong social capital and ties to the community that would sustain the movement through setbacks (Walker 2009). The lack of a well-developed grassroots base may increase the vulnerability of these movements to an early demise. One of the intriguing puzzles of the Tea Party phenomenon is whether a movement that was so heavily influenced by top-down resources during its formation can maintain coherence and unity as the movement grows and whether it will ever be able to completely wean itself from those resources to form a truly grassroots movement.

Although it is too early to forecast the fate of the Tea Party movement, one journalist's qualitative sampling of Tea Party protests suggests that attendance has declined significantly since their peak in 2010, and some cities that once had a strong Tea Party presence no longer exhibit much party activity (Seitz-Wald 2011). Sociologist Theda Skocpol suggests that by the spring of 2012, the number of Tea Party groups had fallen by 40 percent from its peak (Arrillaga

2012). Evidence of the movement's decline is consistent with the hypothesis that top-down movements fluctuate more in strength and participation, and are more susceptible to failure, than other movements.

Infrastructure Development

Despite our concerns about the long-term viability of top-down movements, the emergence of the Tea Party provides no doubt that these movements can proliferate rapidly and efficiently develop widespread support and participation. While social movement theory understands clearly that organizations and movement infrastructures support collective action, for the most part little attention is paid to how this infrastructure is built. Rather, most scholarship takes for granted that organizational infrastructure is pre-existing and indigenous to the communities in which they form (Morris 1981). Reliance on local, indigenous resources may not be as necessary as was once true.

With new technologies, like the internet and social media, social movements can build infrastructures very quickly, establish networks, organize communication, and facilitate protest events at a much lower cost than was true in the past (Earl and Kimport 2011). If we were to consider only the Tea Party's online infrastructure as a resource, we might jump to the conclusion that this was the most important transformation that allowed them to quickly mobilize tens of thousands of participants in a national reform movement. But in reality, social movements vary in their effectiveness in using web technology to mobilize participation and spread their perspectives. In the case of the Tea Party movement, it seems to be the combination of the availability of technology and a strong supportive infrastructure developed through top-down resources that made local organizers so effective in creating a community of activists. Without top-down resources an effective online social network might not have emerged when and how it did, but perhaps more important than this, without the extremely active support of conservative media outlets who blasted the Tea Party's message into millions of American homes, it is unlikely that most participants would have ever found their way to the websites. In this sense, the conservative media opened the opportunity for online activism to become an effective outlet for the Tea Party.

Cultural Processes

One of the central tenets of social movement theory is that the process of constructing a collective identity that defines activists and connects them to their social change goals is a necessary step in movement emergence. However, the Tea Party has offered an interesting counter-example in which collective identities that have long been used to signal connection with national interests—labels such as American, patriot, and of course the term Tea Party itself—have been marshaled to bring identity coherence to a heterogeneous group of activists. Moreover, the labels have been used to draw a sharp boundary between Tea Party insiders and the outsiders who support government programs and policies. That the protestors have adopted the claim to the identity "real Americans" and named the government itself as an outsider to American identity is a puzzle worth social movement theory's attention.

Rather than point to the corporate donations that built movement infrastructure in this case, however, the likely source of this collective identity coup is the cultural support provided by television news and talk radio. Fox News in particular has been explicitly supportive of the Tea Party protests (Hananoki 2009). The 24-hour news cycle has provided cultural support in unprecedented amounts. Whereas most social movements must hold "endless meetings" to hash out collective identities and manage problems of boundary maintenance (Polletta 2002), the Tea Party has held its meetings virtually through celebrity opinion-makers such as Glenn Beck and Sean Hannity, as well as a stream of pundits, politicians, and Tea Party activists, 24 hours a day, 7 days a week.

The financial value of this cultural support is astronomical, and we argue that it should be included in the calculation of top-down resources supporting this activism. But the question for social movement theory is whether this cultural support created a process for collective identity-building that is unlike that of resource-scarce social movements, or whether the process was the same, but just accelerated by these cultural resources.

Agenda and Outcomes

By imagining a social movement as having three layers—grassroots resources, infrastructure and organizational resources, and resources from corporate and wealthy donors—we can consider how the scale of resources might affect the pattern of movement emergence. For example, it raises questions about the relationship between wealthy or corporate donors and grassroots participants. Do grassroots supporters of big-money movements, to a greater extent than traditional movements with scarce resources, play a substantively different role in establishing the political goals of the movement, or in determining the strategic plan for social change?

This dynamic is especially important and impactful when a movement gets funding from a wealthy source early in its existence before movement leaders have had a chance to formulate a coherent set of objectives. In short, corporate sponsors may be able to co-opt a movement before it ever has a chance to decide what it is or what it seeks to accomplish. A movement's dependence on resources undoubtedly makes it more likely to succumb to the will and influence of the powerful actors that fund its activities (Jenkins and Perrow 1977, Piven and Cloward 1977, Pfeffer and Salancik 1978). Typically movements are co-opted following a successful tactic, which tends to lead to de-radicalization, but movements that originate with a dependence on top-down resources may already be sufficiently captured by these interests that they are never able to develop goals outside of the specific agenda set by their wealthy donors. Although movement activists may be ideologically motivated to pursue a radical agenda of government reform, their ability to push for reforms that go against the interests of their corporate funders may be limited.

We can take the example of another top-down movement, the religious right, as a lesson in the efficacy of this form of movement. Over its 30-year history, the religious right in the United States has built a tremendous infrastructure for activism, connecting churches with activist organizations, reshaping the policy agenda of the Republican Party, and influencing electoral outcomes at federal, state, and local levels (see, e.g., Fetner 2008). It has also influenced policy outcomes to some extent, such as in placing limits on access to abortion and preventing the implementation of federal anti-discrimination protections for lesbians and gay men (Werum and Winders 2001). In this movement, large pools of resources were amassed from the grassroots, as mail-in donations to movement organizations through direct-mail solicitations, as donations to local churches, or as donations and profits of the media empires created by televangelists and evangelical radio broadcasters (Diamond 1995). To the extent that mega-churches, media empires, and wealthy donors contributed to this movement, this would certainly be considered a substantial top-layer of big-money resources, akin to the Tea Party. However, with the exception of elite allies like Republican insider Paul Weyrich, who nurtured the emergence of the movement, the movement's emergence was, as far as we can tell, a product of grassroots support for socially conservative political activism. In the Tea Party, the top-down resources fostered the emergence of the movement itself.

In the Tea Party, we already can see some early measures of the impact that this new movement has had on the political landscape. For example, the 2010 midterm elections were certainly influenced by Tea Party activism, with several Tea Party candidates elected to office. Tea Party activism has also held sway in the Republican Party, as party leaders such as Ohio Senator John Boehner make clear that the Republican agenda includes the small-government preferences of the Tea Party. In the House, Wisconsin Representative Paul Ryan's rise to Republican stardom and the 2012 vice-presidential nomination was on the wings of his budget proposal that included severe cuts to cherished social programs such as Medicare and Medicaid.

Many of the issues around which the Tea Party is most mobilized are also those important to particular corporate sponsors. By channeling the movement's attention to particular policy issues and providing the means to organize around certain policy issues, wealthy funders may be influencing the goals and tactics of the movement. For example, in the fall of 2010, the coal industry's lobbying group, the Federation for American Coal, Energy, and Security, paid for buses, hotels, and other accommodations to bring 1,500 West Virginians to Washington DC to participate in a Tea Party rally to protest federal regulation of mountaintop removal mining.[1] The coal industry is not the only group to organize Tea Party

---

[1] The details of the protest and its relationship to the coal industry lobbying group can be found at http://www.commondreams.org/view/2010/09/15-4 (accessed July 22, 2011). A press release from the lobbying group can be found at http://kycoalblog.org/2010/09/14/appalachian-coal-communities-to-rally-at-capitol/ (accessed July 22, 2011).

rallies to support its specific policy goals. The Center for Responsive Politics reported that the health insurance industry became the biggest donor to the Tea Party in 2010, using the party to organize protests against the Democrat-sponsored health reform act. During their campaign against health reform, health professional groups donated $2.7 million to the Tea Party Caucus alone. One consequence of this injection of resources was to create a tighter coupling of the insurance industry's efforts to defeat health reform and the Tea Party's policy focus.[2]

Of course, there has been some backlash among Tea Party grassroots organizers who resent corporate intrusion. A *Washington Post* article from September 2010 reported that an effort to hold a national Tea Party convention in Nevada that summer fell apart because local activists would not support what they saw to be an overly commercialized event (Gardner 2010). The founder of the Nevada Patriots said about the failed convention, "They were trying to come in not so much to gather with the local people but to really just put on an event that maybe didn't have a good intention to begin with. It looked like a commercial event, and it just never really gained traction because the local tea party leaders here didn't get behind it."

Policy depends on how you define an agenda, and in terms of the Tea Party, the agenda is not clear or altogether explicit. In particular, the agendas of grassroots supporters and wealthy donors do not necessarily match, making for a muddy, confusing agenda that is not clearly articulated and contains self-contradictions. For example, it is reasonable to assume that the policies of wealthy, corporate donors include reduced taxes on the wealthy and deregulation of the industries of these various corporations, especially the energy industry. However, grassroots supporters looking for smaller government and debt reduction may push their elected representatives to pursue fiscal policies that endanger the health of the business sector, as we saw happen when Tea Party legislators in the House of Representatives nearly sabotaged Congressional efforts to raise the debt ceiling. It remains to be seen whether the policy "wins" for the wealthy will undermine the Tea Party's grassroots support or whether some ideological "wins" among grassroots supporters will cause their corporate sponsors to become less enthusiastic about supporting the Tea Party in the future.

Taken together, these questions show that social movement scholarship should pay greater attention to resource-rich social movements like the Tea Party. The Tea Party shows us that top-down resources from corporations or wealthy donors can potentially affect the sequencing of movement emergence (and possibly decline), the development of movement infrastructure, the cultural processes of collective identity formation and issue-framing, as well as the agenda-setting and outcomes of the social movements they support. The Tea Party can be seen as one of several movements that represent elite interests, and as such it poses some new questions

---

2 Details about the Center for Responsive Politics' analysis can be found at the following websites: http://dyn.politico.com/printstory.cfm?uuid=7396EF48-9D3E-D830-C4BA8BF98C47C321 and http://www.opensecrets.org/news/2010/07/members-of-tea-party-caucus-major-r.html (accessed July 22, 2011).

that social movement scholarship, which has focused on bottom-up movement emergence, has not yet had to address.

References

Amenta, E. et al. 2009. All the movements fit to print: Who, what, when, where, and why SMO families appeared in the *New York Times* in the twentieth century. *American Sociological Review*, 74, 636–56.

Andrews, K.T. 2001. Social movements and policy implementation: The Mississippi Civil Rights Movement and the War on Poverty, 1965 to 1971. *American Sociological Review*, 66(1), 71–95.

Andrews, K.T. 2004. *Freedom is a Constant Struggle*. Chicago: University of Chicago Press.Andrews, K.T. and Caren, N. 2010. Making the news: Movement organizations, media attention, and the public agenda. *American Sociological Review*, 75(6), 841–66.

Armstrong, E.A. 2002. *Forging Gay Identities: Organizing Sexuality in San Francisco, 1950–1994*. Chicago: University of Chicago Press.

Arrillaga, P. 2012. Tea Party 2012: A look at the conservative movement's last three years. *Huffington Post* [Online]. Available at: http://www.huffingtonpost.com/2012/04/14/tea-party-2012_n_1425957.html [accessed 04/14/12].

Beckel, M. 2010. Independent expenditures by Tea Party Express help activists earn another Senate primary victory. *OpenSecrets blog* [Online]. Available at: http://www.opensecrets.org/news/2010/09/independent-expenditures-by-tea-par.html [accessed July 11, 2011].

Beutler, B. 2009. FreedomWorks' long history of teabagging. *Talking Points Memo* [Online]. Available at: http://tpmdc.talkingpointsmemo.com/2009/04/freedomworks-long-history-of-teabagging.php [accessed June 16, 2011].

Cornfield, D.B. 1991. The US Labour Movement: Its development and impact on social inequality and politics. *Annual Review of Sociology*, 17, 27–49.

Diamond, S. 1995. *Roads to Dominion: Right-Wing Movements and Political Power in the United States*. New York and London: Guilford Press.

Diani, M. 2003. *Networks and Social Movements: A Research Programme*. Oxford: Oxford University Press.

Earl, J. and Kimport, K. 2011. *Digitally Enabled Social Change: Activism in the Internet Age*. Cambridge, MA: MIT Press.

Fang, L. 2009. Spontaneous uprising? Corporate lobbyists helping to orchestrate radical anti-Obama Tea Party protests. *Thinkprogress.org* [Online]. Available at: http://thinkprogress.org/2009/04/09/lobbyists-planning-teaparties/ [accessed April 20, 2011].

Fetner, T. 2008. *How the Religious Right Shaped Lesbian and Gay Activism*. Minneapolis: University of Minnesota Press.

Friedman, M. 1970. The social responsibility of business is to increase its profits. *New York Times*, SM17.

Galaskiewicz, J. 1997. An urban grants economy revisited: Corporate charitable contributions in the Twin Cities, 1979–81, 1987–89. *Administrative Science Quarterly*, 42(3), 445–71.

Gardner, A. 2010. "Tea party" movement faces challenge of having no single leader, goal. *washingtonpost.com* [Online]. Available at: http://www.washingtonpost.com/wp-dyn/content/article/2010/09/21/AR2010092105411.html [accessed August 3, 2011].

Goldman, A. 2010. How oil heir and New York arts patron David Koch became the Tea Party's wallet. *New York Magazine* [Online]. Available at: http://nymag.com/news/features/67285/ [accessed May 27, 2011].

Good, C. 2009. The Tea Party Movement: Who's in charge? *The Atlantic* [Online]. Available at: http://www.theatlantic.com/politics/archive/2009/04/the-tea-party-movement-whos-in-charge/13041/ [accessed May 27, 2011].

Good, C. 2010. Peeling back the layers of the Kochtopus. *The Atlantic* [Online]. Available at: http://www.theatlantic.com/politics/archive/2010/09/peeling-back-the-layers-of-the-kochtopus/62372/ [accessed May 27, 2011].

Guthrie, D. 2010. Corporate philanthropy in the United States: What causes do corporations back?, in *Politics and Partnerships: The Role of Voluntary Associations in America's Political Past and Present*, edited by E.S. Clemens and D. Guthrie. Chicago: University of Chicago Press, 183–204.

Hananoki, E. 2009. REPORT: "Fair and balanced" Fox News aggressively promotes "tea party" protests. *MediaMatters.org* [Online]. Available at: http://mediamatters.org/reports/200904080025 [accessed August 3, 2011].

Jenkins, J.C. and Perrow, C. 1977. Insurgency of the powerless: Farm worker movements. *American Sociological Review*, 42(2), 249–68.

Khan, H. 2010. Tea Party Patriots gets $1 million to fund local groups—The Note. *ABC News "The Note"* [Online]. Available at: http://blogs.abcnews.com/thenote/2010/09/tea-party-patriots-gets-1-million-to-fund-local-groups.html#tp [accessed June 1, 2011].

Kristol, I. 1977. On corporate philanthropy. *Wall Street Journal*, March 21, p. 18.

Lipsky, M. 1968. Protest as a political resource. *American Political Science Review*, 62(4), 1144–58.

Lyon, T.P. and Maxwell, J.W. 2004. *Corporate Environmentalism and Public Policy*. Cambridge: Cambridge University Press.

McCarthy, J.D. and Zald, M.N. 1977. Resource mobilization and social movements: A partial theory. *American Journal of Sociology*, 82(6), 1212–41.

McCarthy, J.D. and Zald, M.N. 2001. The enduring vitality of the resource mobilization theory of social movements, in *Handbook of Sociological Theory*, edited by J.H. Turner. New York: Kluwer Academic/Plenum, 533–65.

McQuarrie, M. 2010. Nonprofits and the reconstruction of urban governance: Housing production and community development in Cleveland, 1975–2005, in *Politics and Partnerships: The Role of Voluntary Associations in America's Political Past and Present*, edited by E.S. Clemens and D. Guthrie. Chicago: University of Chicago Press, 237–68.

Manne, H.G. 2005. How law and economics was marketed in a hostile world: A very personal history, in *The Origins of Law and Economics: Essays by the Founding Fathers*, edited by F. Parisi and C.K. Rowley. Cheltenham, UK and Northampton, MA: Edward Elgar, 309–27.

Mayer, J. 2010. Covert operations: The billionaire brothers who are waging a war against Obama. *The New Yorker* [Online: August 30]. Available at: http://www.newyorker.com/reporting/2010/08/30/100830fa_fact_mayer?currentPage=all.

Morris, A. 1981. Black Southern sit-in movements: An analysis of internal organization. *American Sociological Review*, 45, 744–67.

Morris, A. and Staggenborg, S. 2004. Leadership in social movements, in *The Blackwell Companion to Social Movements*, edited by D.A. Snow, S.A. Soule, and H. Kriesi. Malden, MA: Blackwell, 171–96.

Noonan, P. 2010. Why it's time for the Tea Party: The populist movement is more a critique of the GOP than a wing of it. *Wall Street Journal*, 17 September, Declarations section.

O'Connor, A. 2010. Bringing the market back in: Philanthropic activism and conservative reform, in *Politics and Partnerships: The Role of Voluntary Associations in America's Political Past and Present*, edited by E.S. Clemens and D. Guthrie. Chicago: University of Chicago Press, 121–50.

Pfeffer, J. and Salancik, G.R. 1978. *The External Control of Organizations: A Resource Dependence Perspective*. New York: Harper & Row.

Piven, F.F. and Cloward, R.A. 1977. *Poor People's Movements: Why They Succeed, How They Fail*. New York: Vintage Books.

Polletta, F. 2002. *Freedom is an Endless Meeting: Democracy in American Social Movements*. Chicago: University of Chicago Press.

Roth, Z. 2009a. FreedomWorks says jump, Tea Partiers ask how high. *Talking Points Memo* [Online]. Available at: http://tpmmuckraker.talkingpointsmemo.com/2009/08/freedomworks_says_jump_tea_partiers_ask_how_high.php [accessed June 16, 2011].

Roth, Z. 2009b. Majority of Tea Party group's spending went to GOP firm that created it. *Talking Points Memo* [Online]. Available at: http://tpmmuckraker.talkingpointsmemo.com/2009/12/majority_of_tea_party_groups_spending_went_to_gop.php [accessed July 11, 2011].

Seitz-Wald, A. 2011. Tea Party at its Dregs? Major Convention Attracts Few. *thinkprogress.org*. [Online]. Available at: http://thinkprogress.org/politics/2011/03/21/152046/at-the-dregs-major-florida-tea-party-convention-attracts-few [accessed April 23, 2013].

Skocpol, T. and Williamson, V. 2012. *The Tea Party and the Remaking of Republican Conservatism*. Oxford and New York: Oxford University Press.

Sobieraj, S. 2011. *Soundbitten: The Perils of Media-Centered Political Activism*. New York: NYU Press.

Soule, S.A. and King, B.G. 2008. Competition and resource partitioning in three social movement industries. *American Journal of Sociology*, 113(6), 1568–610.

Summers-Effler, E. 2010. *Laughing Saints and Righteous Heroes: A Theory of Persistence and Transformation in Social Movement Groups*. Chicago: University of Chicago Press.

Teles, S.M. 2009. Transformative bureaucracy: Reagan's lawyers and the dynamics of political investment. *Studies in American Political Development*, 23(1), 61–83.

Van Dyke, N. and McCammon, H.J., eds. 2010. *Strategic Alliances: New Studies of Social Movement Coalitions*. Minneapolis: University of Minnesota Press.

Vogel, K.P. 2009. Tea parties emerge as revenue stream. *Politico* [Online]. Available at: http://www.politico.com/news/stories/1109/29943.html [accessed August 3, 2011].

Walker, E.T. 2008. Contingent pathways from joiner to activist: The indirect effect of participation in voluntary associations on civic engagement. *Sociological Forum*, 23, 116–43.

Walker, E.T. 2009. Privatizing participation: Civic change and the organizational dynamics of grassroots lobbying firms. *American Sociological Review*, 74(1), 83–105.

Walker, E.T. 2010. Industry-driven activism. *Contexts*, 9(2), 44–9.

Walker, E.T. 2012. Putting a face on the issue: Corporate stakeholder mobilization in professional grassroots lobbying campaigns. *Business & Society*, 51(4), 561–601.

Werum, R. and Winders, B. 2001. Who's "in" and who's "out": State fragmentation and the struggle over gay rights, 1974–1999. *Social Problems*, 48, 386–410.

Williams, J. 2010. Tea Party anger reflects mainstream concerns. *Wall Street Journal*, 2 April, Declarations section.

Zernike, K. 2010. Tea Party disputes take toll on convention. *New York Times* [Online]. Available at: http://www.nytimes.com/2010/01/26/us/politics/26teaparty.html [accessed July 11, 2011].

Chapter 3
Social Movement Partyism and the Tea Party's Rapid Mobilization

Paul Almeida and Nella Van Dyke[1]

The Tea Party movement in the United States emerged as a potent force on the political landscape within a brief 18-month period. The conservative movement surfaced nationally convening rallies and demonstrations in dozens of American cities by Tax Day (April 15) in 2009 (Rafail et al. 2011). The movement continued to gain momentum through the summer of 2009 as it mobilized against the Democratic Party's health care reform program. In the movement's early days, many in the mass media and the Democratic Party leadership labeled the Tea Party protests "astroturf," as opposed to grassroots, due to the heavy involvement of the Republican Party and associated think tanks in their mobilization. Journalists like Rachel Maddow exposed how Tea Party protests have been promoted and sponsored by Republican Party operatives. The involvement of the Republican Party in public protest actions is a fairly unique phenomenon. In fact, official Republican Party participation in protest actions has been virtually absent from the social movement landscape in the United States for almost 40 years, with the exception of anti-abortion protests in some parts of the country such as annual rallies in Washington DC. In this chapter, we use the tools of social movement scholarship to explore Republican Party involvement in the movement and its contribution to the movement's mobilization. In particular, we draw from studies that examine the multiple contributing roles political parties play in facilitating large-scale collective action.

We argue here that this mobilization reflects an instance of *social movement partyism*, a situation in which an oppositional political party manifests behavior similar to what we characterize as social movement action (Almeida 2006, 2010)—that is, organizing collective action outside of more institutionalized political settings, such as rallies, marches, and street protests (Snow et al. 2004). The term is akin to "social movement unionism" whereby labor unions alter their more conservative collective bargaining approach to resolving labor issues to organize social movement-type campaigns (Johnston 1994, Turner and Hurd 2001, Van Dyke et al. 2007). In the case of social movement partyism, the political party instead of the labor union behaves as a social movement. We would like to

---

[1] The authors contributed equally to this chapter, names are listed in alphabetical order.

point to two dimensions where the social movement partyism framework may be useful in understanding the rapid emergence of the Tea Party on a national scale:

1. Interests and motivations for an oppositional party to use social movement-type strategies.
2. Rapid and extensive mobilization using oppositional party resources—or why we should be especially interested when a political party behaves like a social movement.

While political parties would not advocate protest mobilization unless they see a benefit to extra-institutional grassroots mobilization, their reasons for doing so may vary. No matter what their motivation, however, parties possess a variety of resources that may be beneficial to a social movement. In the following pages, we explore how the theory of social movement partyism helps explain the rapid emergence of the Tea Party movement and Republican involvement in it, as well as the implications the movement has for social movement theory.

Social Movement Partyism: Interests and Motivations

Much has been written about the external allies of social movements and why actors inside the state may be especially beneficial, including McCarthy and Wolfson's study of the channeling of social movements by the state (1992), Santoro and McGuire's work on "Institutional Activists" (1997), Banaszak's recent work on the women's movement and "state-movement intersections" (2005, 2010), research on state actor–social movement coalitions (Stearns and Almeida 2004), Jack Goldstone's writing on the blurring of state and nonstate actors (2003), as well as Ron Aminzade's studies of nineteenth-century French political parties (1995). However, we know much less about why institutionalized entities such as political parties would seek out a social movement form of political participation. We believe this is a very different question to address in the literature on social movements and elite allies—why the elite ally—in this case a national political party—would itself take on the characteristics of a social movement.[2] Much more research exists on how a social movement develops into or becomes incorporated within a political party (Snow et al. 2004, Van Cott 2005) than on why an institutionalized party begins engaging in social movement-type tactics.

We should note from the outset that we are not suggesting that involvement in Tea Party protest has been an official tactic of the national Republican Party. As Bailey and colleagues note, "The Tea Party is an organized interest or movement associated with the Republican Party, but not the same as the Republican Party.

---

2 A cautionary note is acknowledged here in that we want to recognize that the Tea Party movement is composed not only of GOP sympathizers, but also of independents, libertarians, disaffected Democrats, and a variety of other conservative forces.

This is consistent with the conception of political parties as coalitions of interests" (2012: 771). As we will show here, Republican Party members, donors, and operatives have been highly involved in the Tea Party, but we are not suggesting that the Republican Party establishment has embraced the Tea Party, nor that the Tea Party embraced the Republican establishment. On the contrary, some Tea Party activists "have expressed disdain for most existing GOP organizations and 'establishment Republicans,'" (Skocpol and Williamson 2012). That said, the evidence suggests that elements of the Republican Party immediately embraced the Tea Party movement and become involved as members, donors, or supporters, in what Skocpol and Williamson call "a scramble for the head and heart of the Republican Party" (2012: 100). Thus the question remains, why would a political party, or at least elements of it, become involved in social protest?

One possibility is that social movement tactics have become so widespread that any group, whether they be political insiders or outsiders, will now use them. Meyer and Tarrow (1998) advance this idea of a social movement society in their work, including a piece by Meyer in this volume. They suggest that protest has become more widespread in contemporary society and that wide-ranging and diverse constituencies now engage in protest activity. Further, they argue that the professionalization and institutionalization of social movements has made social movements a part of the standard, institutionalized political system. The social movement society thesis suggests that Republican Party insiders are using movement tactics because these actions are so standard and usual now that any group might use them. Protest activity is now largely inseparable from more standard tactics within the institutional political world. While it is hard to argue with these hypotheses, we think that the Tea Party case requires explanation beyond movement society theory. Why did Republican Party operatives decide that 2009 was the time to turn to protest tactics, rather than at some other time in the last 20 years? The answer to this query requires considering the political climate of the time.

In earlier work, one of this chapter's authors documented the rise of social movement partyism in Latin America (Almeida 2006, 2010). In the Latin American cases of Bolivia, Brazil, Ecuador, El Salvador, Nicaragua, and Uruguay, social movement partyism occurred after oppositional social movements had mobilized for many years, won electoral victories, and become officially recognized political parties. These former social movement political parties, while engaging in institutional political action, also continued to participate in social protest mobilization and action in the 1990s and 2000s. For these groups, participation in non-institutional social activism reflected a continuation of political action strategies they had been engaging in for years. As Tilly (1978) notes, past action and habits of action often shape a group's repertoires of action. After becoming recognized political parties, these groups turned to protest mobilization in response to economic austerity programs being threatened by the party in power, policies that would privatize water rights, medical care, and other social service programs and infrastructure.

The threats were perceived as an erosion of economic rights to state-subsidized protections for the middle and working classes of Latin America. In many of the countries where social movement partyism surfaced there was a network overlap of double affiliation (Diani 1995) whereby key activists simultaneously belonged to social movement-type organizations such as a labor union or an agricultural cooperative and to a political party. This double affiliation provided the skeletal structure to build the broader alliance between social movements and opposition political parties. For example, labor militants in Nicaragua's public sector unions also served as parliamentary representatives in the national legislature for the Sandinista political party. In Ecuador, leaders of indigenous peoples' organizations also served as representatives in the Patchukutik political party while major representatives of coca farmer associations in Bolivia ran for local and national office under the banner of the MAS political party. This particular pathway of organizing like (and with) social movements partially explains the electoral success of left-of-center political parties in Latin America or the so called "pink tide" (Almeida 2010).

The US Tea Party case bears some similarities and deviations from the Latin American cases, and provides us with the opportunity to further develop the theory of social movement partyism. Unlike the left-of-center political parties, which continued participating in movement protest after they became political parties, the Republican Party in the US has existed for over 150 years as a political party. Thus, it is not engaging in its usual and traditional form of political action when it turns to social protest. On the contrary, mobilizing people for social protest is something we would not expect to see from an established political party. Social movement theory tells us that informal organizations are more likely to mobilize people for disruptive collective action and that professional organizations with a paid staff typically confine their action to more conventional "insider" tactics (Staggenborg 1988). Although scholars such as Minkoff (1999) remind us that the organizational types that engage in social protest are varied, ranging from advocacy organizations to more radical movement organizations, little research examines political party involvement in protest mobilization. Thus, this case presents us with the opportunity to contribute to social movement theory by considering the conditions under which an institutional political actor turns to non-institutional action.

Republicans at the Tea Party

Journalists have documented widespread Republican involvement in the Tea Party movement. The Tea Party Express and Tea Party Patriots, the most well-known national Tea Party organizations, both have ties to the Republican Party. The Tea Party Express was formed by a Republican political action committee "Our Country Deserves Better." The Tea Party Patriots was formed by an organization called FreedomWorks, founded by ex-Republican Congressman Dick Armey, the former House majority leader. Dick Armey's other recent employment involved working as a lobbyist for DLA Piper, a lobbying firm whose current and former clients include a number of pharmaceutical and health care industry businesses (Maddow 2009). Thus, it is not surprising that FreedomWorks might sponsor mobilization against the Democrats' health care initiative. FreedomWorks' President is Matt Kibbe, the former senior economist for the Republican National Committee. Before that, he was chief of staff for Republican Congressman Dan Miller of Florida. The fact that the two national Tea Party organizations have direct ties and received their funding from Republican-connected organizations illustrates the influential connections between the party and movement.

Although individual Tea Party activists and local Tea Party groups are not necessarily directly affiliated with the two large national organizations, many local organizations have received support, both financial and otherwise, from the Republican-funded national organizations. In their case study of a Boston area Tea Party group, Williamson and her colleagues (2011) describe multiple connections between the group and the big national organizations. In April 2010, the Tea Party Express came to a Tax Day protest organized by the Boston group, providing a great deal of publicity to the action. Group members receive training in grassroots organizing from the Koch-funded group American Majority. The Boston group is registered as an affiliate on the Tea Party Patriots website. Thus, this local organization receives several forms of support from the national groups of the Tea Party-Republican nexus.

In another local example, one of the authors of this chapter observed a Tea Party rally in College Station, Texas in October 2009. Local Texas Tea Party chapters organized the event in protest of President Barack Obama's keynote address at ex-President George H.W. Bush's "Points of Light" Conference on volunteering in America (see Patel 2009). Four out of five of the tables set up at the event represented a chapter of the Republican Party. They included Texas A&M College Republicans, Brazos County Young Republicans, Republican Party of Brazos County, and Hands Off Texas (a state-wide Republican organization). The fifth table at the event was a very small stand set up by the Lyndon Larouche PAC (LaRouchePAC) and manned by a single person.

The Brazos County Young Republicans hung a large "register to vote" banner in front of their table. Hands Off Texas was created in September 2009 with the explicit goals of capturing Republican majorities in national and Texan congressional elections in 2010 as well as reclaiming the White House in 2012 (http://www.handsofftexas.com/). Between 500 and 1,000 people attended this Tea Party rally (see Figure 3.1). Local Republican organizations sponsored the event and appear to have focused their efforts during this activity on mobilizing votes for the midterm elections. The Tea Party protest of a summit exalting civic engagement and volunteerism provides another instance of social movement partyism—local Republican chapters organizing a protest rally to attract votes for the upcoming electoral cycle.

The Press has uncovered the presence of Republican operatives as protesters at town hall meetings held in 2009 by many members of Congress to discuss

Figure 3.1   College Station, TX, Tea Party rally, October 16, 2009

the proposed health care legislation and other topics. For example, a woman who claimed to be politically unaffiliated challenged Wisconsin Representative Steve Kagen, a Democrat, on health care at a town hall meeting in early August. However, a local TV station discovered later that she was a former Republican staffer who had worked for Mr. Kagen's opponent in his Congressional race (Stolberg 2009). Republican Party members and affiliated media commentators have all encouraged these mobilizations, including Fox News and its promotion of the Tea Party events on tax day 2009. Republican politicians have spoken at many Tea Party events, and many have claimed an affiliation with the movement.

Inside the State

In July 2010, as politicians prepared for November's Congressional elections, Michele Bachmann, Republican Representative from Minnesota, started a Tea Party Political Caucus in Congress. The Caucus immediately included 28 members. One hundred thirty-eight candidates ran as Tea Party candidates in the election, all of them registered as Republicans (44 enjoyed a victory) (*New York Times* 2010). Just prior to the November 2012 election, the Tea Party Caucus boasted 60 members (Tea Party Caucus 2012). Although not all Tea Party activists supported the formation of the Caucus, on the grounds that it presented the threat of cooptation by the Republican Party and was not consistent with the anti-institutional ethos of the Tea Party (Vogel 2010), the Caucus and Tea Party activists have nonetheless maintained close ties. For example, in May of 2012, the Caucus held a symposium on the economy and American Dream featuring former Republican Presidential candidate Herman Cain. Attendees included members from TeaParty.net, the Tea Party Patriots and Tea Party Express (teapartycaucus-bachmann.house.gov 2012). Tea Party activists are frequent guests at events held by the Caucus.

Thus, there is significant evidence of close ties between the Republican Party and the Tea Party. While Republicans have been involved in other mobilizations in recent history, including mobilization against abortion and against the civil rights movement, Republican Party participation is rarely as direct or explicit as it has been with the Tea Party. As noted earlier, the Republican establishment has not necessarily backed the Tea Party, but instead support has come from more extremist or fringe Republicans who had long sought to have more influence within the Party (Skocpol and Williamson 2012). Why then has at least some faction of the Republican Party involved itself in a grassroots social movement at this point in time? The Tea Party movement in the US and Republican sponsorship and involvement occurred only after the Republican Party had *lost* a significant amount of institutional political power. In the 2008 election, the Republican Party lost control of both the White House and the House of Representatives, and conservatives faced a political system dominated by the Democratic Party to an extent not seen since 1993. Thus, following the 2006 and 2008 Congressional and Presidential elections, the Republican Party became more of an oppositional party. Public opinion polls showed declining support of the Afghan and Iraq occupations pushed aggressively by the Bush administration. At the same time, by late 2008 the economic crisis had arrived in full force with hundreds of thousands of Americans losing their source of employment and/or their homes via the foreclosure crisis. The Republican Party found itself in dire need of rejuvenating its base of support and overall credibility. In addition, Theda Skocpol and her colleagues argue that longtime Republican funders had been looking for a way to connect to the grassroots and mobilize the grassroots around their agenda (Williamson et al. 2011, Skocpol and Williamson 2012).

Opposition parties need to develop mechanisms to increase their electoral strength in future elections and weaken the dominant party in power (Stearns and Almeida 2004). By creating media events with social movement-type rallies, the opposition party can raise issues and attempt to bring public opinion on its side. Polling data suggests that a majority of Americans were aware of the Tea Party's existence by mid-2010 (about three-fourths of Americans had heard about the Tea Party movement and formed a positive or negative attitude)—that is, the Tea Party made itself known within US public opinion in a little over one year through the use of large protest events and the disruption of political meetings such as the town hall meetings held by Democratic members of Congress (Pew Research Center 2010).

The movement has effectively mobilized people by socially constructing the "threat" of rights erosion, big government, and tax increases. In Charles Tilly's

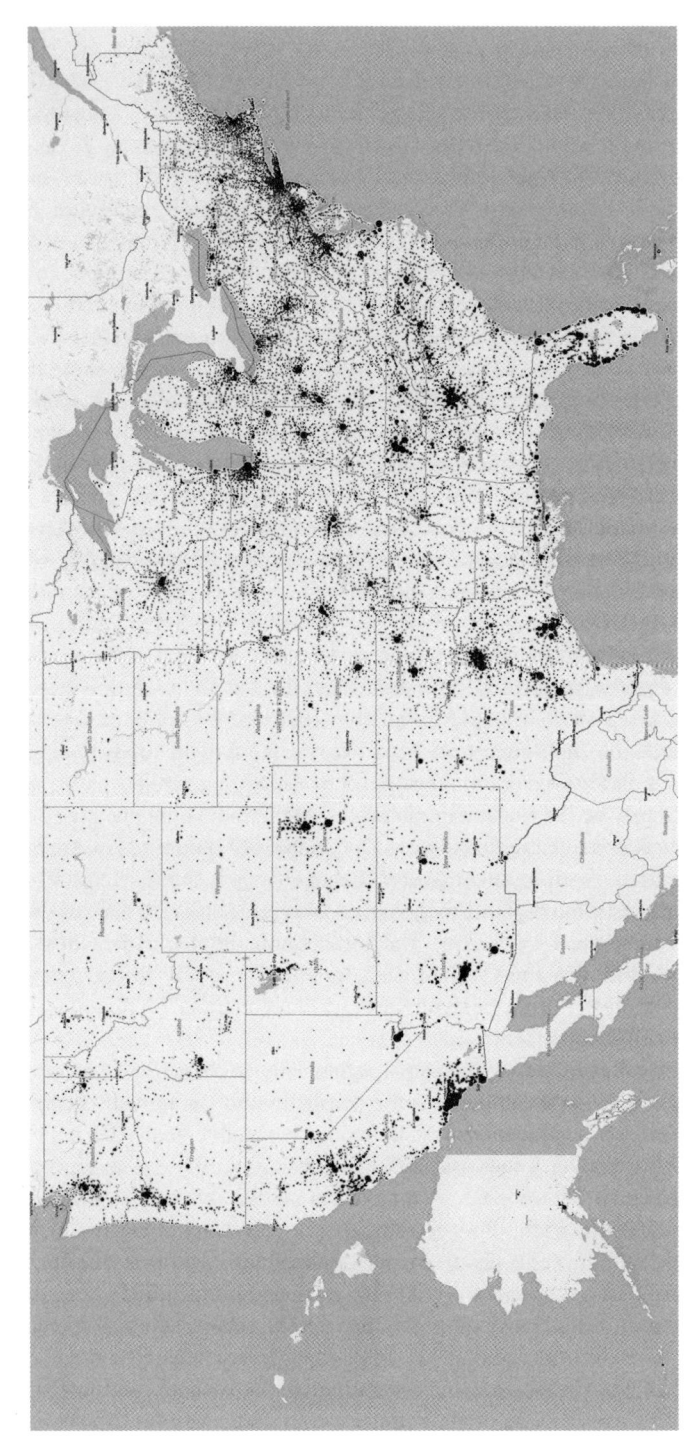

Figure 3.2 Tea party membership, June 2010. By permission of the Institute for Research and Education of Human Rights (www.irehr.org)

original formulation of opportunity and threats as incentives to collective action (1978), he predicted that action motivated by collective threats would lead to more rapid mobilization than that motivated by opportunities because people respond to loss more dramatically than they do to new advantages. The Tea Party appears to socially construct and emphasize threats purportedly presented by the Obama administration (e.g., government takeover of private firms, deficit spending, socialized medicine, etc.) more than it does opportunities for action and influence (e.g., now we have the opportunity for change, allies are ready to help, etc.). However, structural opportunities such as town hall meeting venues do provide institutional access and proximity to political elites to express grievances (Tarrow 1994). And, as Skocpol and Williamson (2012) point out, the movement and more extremist Republicans faced opportunities in the wake of the failed Bush Presidency, when the Republican establishment was in no position to determine what happened next. So concepts of both threat and opportunity serve scholars well in research on Tea Party emergence and sustained mobilization. An especially interesting avenue for research is to analyze how such a movement actively constructs its own cognitive scheme around threats—in terms of stories and narrative (Polletta 2006).

Rapid and Extensive Mobilization

The most impressive part of the Tea Party in our view is its rapid growth in the political landscape beginning on Tax Day, April 15, 2009 (as well as its ability to take up several political issues such as tax reform, government spending, health care, and immigration). By June 2010, just over one year after the movement's emergence, it enjoyed widespread membership across the United States (Figure 3.2).

In this dimension, rapid and sustained mobilization, we believe there is room to make further contributions to resource mobilization theory. A specific focus on the unique and rich assets of a national political party is critical. Social movement scholars have documented the crucial role that resources can play in mobilization (McCarthy and Zald 1977, Morris 1981, Cress and Snow 1996, 2000). As Cress and Snow (1996) suggest, these resources range from leadership and office space to moral support. However, little research considers the resources that political parties may bring to a movement.

Polity members, such as national political parties, enjoy an enormous amount of structural power and resources. Not just in the United States, but in many parts of the world, traditional mobilizing structures, such as labor unions, religious institutions, and so on, may be weakening (of course we want to be cautious here in terms of world regions when making such claims). Political parties, especially in democratic nations, remain one of the most important unified national organizations in existence (Almeida 2010) and possess a vast array of resources. In fact, they possess all of the resources that have been suggested as important to social movement success, including cultural, social-organizational, human and material resources (Edwards and McCarthy 2004). National political parties have the potential to provide all of these forms of resources to mobilization:

1. **Material**. Political parties have access to stockpiles of liquid capital which are extremely fungible and mobile. This financing is provided by corporations, wealthy individuals, and PACs.
2. **Social-organizational**. Political party voting records present a vast potential membership database and a bureaucratic structure that is organized in every county and perhaps zip code in the United States.
3. **Cultural**. Political parties have media contacts, media allies, and media access (including print media, electronic Listservs, websites, blogs, but probably more important, talk radio and television).
4. **Human**. Political party activists are already accustomed to mobilizing massive numbers of people for electoral campaigns; these skills can easily be transferred to social movement-type rallies and easily "spillover" (Meyer and Whittier 1994, Whittier 2004).

Let us consider each of these resources in turn and how they have facilitated this rapid mobilization.

Material

FreedomWorks, the Republican-affiliated organization described previously, received a $1 million donation from an anonymous source, which some have linked to Republican financiers the Koch brothers (Mayer 2010, Fenn 2011). The donation was given for the express purpose of aiding in the mobilization of the Tea Party. Funds from this source were used to found the Tea Party Patriots and set up its website, which acts as a resource for local activists. A number of other Republican-affiliated organizations, including Americans for Prosperity, a Republican-affiliated think tank, and the Republican PAC, Our Country Deserves Better, have used their financial resources to support the Tea Party. It is extremely unusual for a social movement to have available funds of this magnitude even as it is just beginning to mobilize (or at any time, for that matter). For further discussion of the resources provided by Republican-affiliated individuals or organizations, see Chapter 2 in this volume by Fetner and King.

Social Organizational

Political parties possess a social organization whose geographic reach and thoroughness is, arguably, unmatched by any social organization in the country. Every voting precinct in the country has a named Party Chairman (unless the position is vacant), and voter registration records are publicly available. The explicit support of the Tea Party provided by the Republicans made the use of Republican voter registration lists a logical mobilizing tool for Tea Party activists.

Surveys of Tea Party members find that the vast majority are Republicans, and those who identify as Independents are Republican-leaning (Greenberg et al. 2010, Quinnipiac 2010, Zernike and Thee-Brenan 2010, Abramowitz 2011). There is some evidence that the Tea Party made use of the Republican Party's social reach in its mobilization. For example, Williamson and her colleagues (2011) describe how Tea Party activists in Brockton, MA, created a contact list of Republican Party members from voter registration records. Another example, described earlier, is the Tea Party protest on a college campus that included official representation from four different Republican organizations. While these are only examples, there is little question, given the movement's membership base, that the Republican organizational structure has aided the Tea Party movement.

Cultural

The emergence of Fox News on the Cable News scene represents a dramatic departure from conventional news outlets. Fox News, many have argued, serves largely as a mouthpiece for the Republican Party. Journalist Rachel Maddow documents how many of the commentators offering their analysis of the Presidential race on Fox News were actually paid consultants for the Republican Mitt Romney campaign (Maddow 2012). Thus, it may come as no surprise that Fox News has been heavily involved in promoting Tea Party events and the movement's agenda. The Tea Party has received a tremendous boost from the national media, specifically Fox News. Williamson and her colleagues (2011) document the extensive news coverage received by Tea Party protests *prior* to their occurrence. Fox show hosts, including Glenn Beck, Sean Hannity, Greta Van Susteren, and Neil Cavuto, all staged shows at Tea Party events, including the inaugural Tea Party rallies on tax day in 2009. The largest Tea Party event, held September 12, 2009 in Washington DC, was co-sponsored by Glenn Beck, at that time a Fox News host. Williamson et al. suggest that Fox News should be thought of as a social movement organization which provides both infrastructure and a sense of shared collective identity to Tea Party activists. They say, "Overall, it is hard to avoid the conclusion that Fox News provides much of what the loosely interconnected Tea Party organizations otherwise lack in terms of a unified membership and communications infrastructure" (Williamson et al. 2011: 30).

Human

Political parties mobilize voters on a regular and routine basis. Party operatives have skills in framing issues to appeal to voters, preparing messages and talking points for the media, and mobilizing voters, all of which are useful and can be adapted for use in extra-institutional mobilization. At the national level, the two major Tea Party organizations are run by individuals with extensive experience in institutional, party politics. Thus, they come to the organizations with a great deal of political human capital. At the local level, Republican-affiliated organizations offer workshops and educational materials to anyone interested in using them, and there is anecdotal evidence that Tea Party organizations have made use of them. The Boston area Tea Party group studied by Williamson and colleagues encouraged members to attend training sponsored by Americans for Prosperity, a Republican-oriented think tank. In July 2010, Americans for Prosperity held a summit called Texas Defending the American Dream. Attended by 500 people, the forum served as a training session for the Tea Party movement (Mayer 2010). A longtime political operative in the employ of Americans for Prosperity spoke at the rally, saying "We love what the Tea Parties are doing, because that's how we're going to take back America!" In an interview with the *New Yorker*, she described how the Americans for Prosperity "help 'educate' Tea Party activists on policy details, and give them 'next-step training' after their rallies, so that their political energy could be channelled 'more effectively'" (Mayer 2010: 2). She also told the magazine that Americans for Prosperity had given Tea Party activists lists of elected officials to target. The organization also provides talking points to Tea Party activists, directions to protests, and "Tea Party finder" websites.

The Tea Party Patriots has a professionally run website (teapartypatriots.org) where individuals can enter their zip code and be informed about local chapters in their area. The website also provides information on forming new chapters, and offers users the opportunity to connect with other activists in order to share information and support. The group sponsors a weekly conference call where it plans future events and provides support to local chapters. Thus, there are multiple Republican-affiliated or -funded organizations providing human capital resources to the Tea Party.

Conclusions

The Tea Party movement is remarkable in its rapid, national mobilization. It is also unique in the direct links between it and parts of the Republican Party. Social movement theory has much to offer our understanding of the Tea Party movement, while the Tea Party's unique features can assist scholarship by pushing existing research in new directions. These new arenas of research include the motivations that lead a political party to abandon solely institutionalized actions in legislatures and mobilize in the streets and the particular properties of political parties that can lead to rapid and widespread mobilization.

We have described how Republican involvement in the Tea Party was likely motivated by a number of factors, including a combination of political opportunities and threats. While the Republican Party enjoys a great deal of access to political power as well as financial resources, and thus opportunity, at the same time the Party had just experienced a massive electoral defeat, losing the White House as well as control over Congress. Public consternation over the federal economic bailout and the health reform bill, and a general dislike of President

Obama among some segments of the population, provided elements of the Party with the ability to participate in a massive grassroots mobilization, and it did so. We suspect that social movement partyism typically occurs when a political party enjoys a combination of opportunities and threats. However, we would not suggest that all episodes of social movement partyism are exactly the same.

In Latin America, social movement parties also faced a combination of both opportunities and threats. The political system had opened up allowing oppositional movements to become a recognized part of the formal political system in the 1990s with the advent of the third wave of global democratization (Markoff 2006). Yet at the same time, domestic austerity and structural adjustment programs proposed by the party in power presented threats that inspired their turn to social movement action to resist. Thus, the US and Latin American cases both represent social movement partyism in an environment that presents opportunities, but where mobilization occurs in response to the threat of political and economic policies that are counter to the mobilizing group's goals. In both regions political parties engaged in social movement action in response to political and economic threats. A key difference between the two cases, however, is the extent to which the social movement tactics represented a new form of action on the part of the party—a disjuncture with their previous political repertoire. In the US case, social movement partyism reflects a profound shift in party tactics, whereas in the Latin American case it does not. Indeed, disruptive protest is an internal resource for poorly financed oppositional parties in Latin America, whereas the Tea Party relies heavily on elite external funding to sustain protest campaigns.

Another fundamental difference between Latin American anti-austerity mobilization and Tea Party protests resides in the social construction of threat. Austerity measures generally do punish the working class and marginalized populations in the city and countryside (Vreeland 2003). Hence, labor and community activists as well as oppositional political parties can anchor their mobilizing frames on the economic threats of austerity measures with experiential credibility (Snow and Benford 1988). The Tea Party activists and the Republican Party have largely postponed their threats as imminent and in the future in a more artificial fashion, whereby attempts at protecting the welfare state through taxation, government investment, and expanding public health care are portrayed as creeping socialism. The social construction of the threat by Tea Party mobilization is based less on experiential credibility and more on putative future threats. This may partially explain the weaker results of Tea Party candidates in the 2012 House and Senate elections. The alleged future threats may not be able to be sustained as a mobilizing mechanism unless they are eventually reinforced by actual events and outcomes suggested by the constructed ideological maps.

No matter what the social context, political parties provide an array of resources to social movements, including material, social organizational, cultural, and human resources. Whether the Tea Party movement could have mobilized as rapidly or with its large geographical reach without the array of resources provided by the Republican Party is questionable. A massive infusion of liquid capital right at the beginning of the movement facilitated its rapid and widespread mobilization. Activists used Republican Party registration lists and webpages to recruit participants. The Fox News network provided an accessible cultural mouthpiece and explicitly recruited people for participation in Tea Party protests. An array of Republican-affiliated organizations provided training to local activists, as well as educational materials, talking points, and strategy suggestions for the movement. The availability of this array of resources is extremely unusual for social movements, and in part illustrates why social movement scholars need to pay attention to and theorize about the movement.

The long-term effect of Republican involvement in the Tea Party remains to be seen. Sociologist Theda Skocpol (Arrillaga 2012) argues that the movement has been largely co-opted by the Republican Party. And as this has happened the number of Tea Party organizations has dropped by 40 percent. Whether the movement will be completely incorporated into mainstream Republican Party politics or will remain an extra-institutional political force remains to be seen.

References

Abramowitz, A. 2011. Partisan polarization and the rise of the Tea Party movement. Paper presented at Annual Meeting of American Political Science Association, Seattle, WA. Retrieved from http://ssrn.com/abstract=1903153.

Almeida, P.D. 2006. Social movement unionism, social movement partyism, and policy outcomes: Health care privatization in El Salvador, in *Latin American Social Movements: Globalization, Democratization, and Transnational Networks*, edited by H. Johnston and P. Almeida. Lanham, MD: Rowman & Littlefield, 57–76.

Almeida, P.D. 2010. Social movement partyism: Collective action and political parties, in *Strategic Alliances: New Studies of Social Movement Coalitions*, edited by N. Van Dyke and H.J. McCammon. Minneapolis: University of Minnesota Press, 170–96.

Aminzade, R. 1995. Between movement and party: The transformation of mid-nineteenth-century French republicanism, in *The Politics of Social Protest: Comparative Perspectives on States and Social Movements*, edited by J.C. Jenkins and B. Klandermans. Minneapolis: University of Minnesota Press, 39–62.

Arrillaga, P. 2012. Tea Party 2012: A look at the conservative movement's last three years, *Huffington Post* [Online]. Available at: http://www.huffingtonpost.com/2012/04/14/tea-party-2012_n_1425957.html [accessed April 14, 2012].

Bailey, M.A., Mummolo, J., and Noel, H. 2012. Tea Party influence: A story of activists and elites. *American Politics Research*, 40(5), 769–804.

Banaszak, L.A. 2005. Inside and outside the state: Movement insider status, tactics, and public policy achievements, in *Routing the Opposition: Social*

Movements, Public Policy, and Democracy, edited by D. Meyer, V. Jenness, and H. Ingram. Minneapolis: University of Minnesota Press, 149–76.
Banaszak, L.A. 2010. *The Women's Movement Inside and Outside the State*. Cambridge: Cambridge University Press.
Cress, D.M. and Snow, D.A. 1996. Resources, benefactors, and the viability of homeless social movement organizations. *American Sociological Review*, 61, 1089–109.
Cress, D.M. and Snow, D.A. 2000. The outcomes of homeless mobilization: The influence of organization, disruption, political mediation, and framing. *American Journal of Sociology*, 105, 1063–104.
Diani, M. 1995. *Green Networks: A Structural Analysis of the Italian Environmental Movement*. Edinburgh: Edinburgh University Press.
Edwards, B. and McCarthy, J.D. 2004. Resources and social movement mobilization, in *The Blackwell Companion to Social Movements*, edited by D.A. Snow, S.A. Soule, and H. Kriesi, Oxford: Blackwell, 116–52.
Fenn, P. 2011. Tea Party funding Koch brothers emerge from anonymity. *US News and World Report*, February 2.
Goldstone, J. 2003. Bridging institutionalized and noninstitutionalized politics, in *States, Parties, and Social Movements*, edited by J. Goldstone. Cambridge: Cambridge University Press, 1–24.
Greenberg, S.B., Carville, J., Gerstein, J., Craighill, P.M., and Monninger, K. 2010. Special report on the Tea Party Movement. *Democracy Corps* [Online]. Available at: http://www.democracycorps.com/attachments/article/821/Tea-Party-Report-FINAL.pdf [accessed April 28, 2013].
Hands Off Texas! 2013. [Online]. Available at http://www.handsofftexas.com [accessed December 9, 2012].
Johnston, P. 1994. *Success while Others Fail: Social Movement Unionism and the Public Workplace*. Ithaca, NY: Cornell University Press.
McCarthy, J.D. and Wolfson, M. 1992. Consensus movements, conflict movements, and the cooptation of civic and state infrastructures, in *Frontiers in Social Movement Theory*, edited by A.D. Morris and C.M. Mueller. New Haven, CT: Yale University Press, 273–97.
McCarthy, J.D. and Zald, M.N. 1977. Resource mobilization and social movements: A partial theory. *American Journal of Sociology*, 82(6), 1212–41.
Maddow, R. 2009. *The Rachel Maddow Show*, August 11 [Online]. Available at: http://www.msnbc.msn.com/id/32386235/ns/msnbc_tv-rachel_maddow_show/ [accessed September 7, 2009].
Maddow, R. 2012. *The Rachel Maddow Show*, September 17 [Online]. Available at: http://www.msnbc.msn.com/id/49074791/ns/msnbc-rachel_maddow_show/t/rachel-maddow-show-monday-september-th/ [accessed October 15, 2012].
Markoff, J. 2006. Globalization and the future of democracy, in *Global Social Change: Historical and Comparative Perspectives*, edited by C. Chase-Dunn and S. Babones. Baltimore: Johns Hopkins University Press, 336–61.
Mayer, J. 2010. Covert operations. *New Yorker*, August 30.

Meyer, D.S. and Tarrow, S.R., eds. 1998. *The Social Movement Society: Contentious Politics for a New Century*. Lanham, MD: Rowman & Littlefield.

Meyer, D.S. and Whittier, N. 1994. Social movement spillover. *Social Problems*, 41(2), 277–98.

Minkoff, D.C. 1999. Bending with the wind: Organizational change in American women's and minority organizations. *American Journal of Sociology*, 104(6), 1666–703.

Morris, A. 1981. Black Southern Sit-In Movement: An analysis of internal organization. *American Sociological Review*, 46, 744–67.

New York Times. 2010. How the Tea Party fared. *New York Times* [Online]. Available at http://www.nytimes.com/interactive/2010/11/04/us/politics/tea-party-results.html [accessed August 31, 2012].

Patel, V. 2009. 1,000 protesters include few from A&M, *The Eagle* (Bryan-College Station Newspaper). October 17.

Pew Research Center. 2010. Distrust, discontent, anger and partisan rancor. [Online]. Available at http://www.people-press.org/2010/04/18/section-6-tea-party-and-views-of-government-overreach [accessed October 15, 2012].

Poletta, F. 2006. *It Was Like a Fever: Storytelling in Protest and Politics*. Chicago: University of Chicago Press.

Quinnipiac poll. 2010. March 16–21 [Online]. Available at http://www.quinnipiac.edu/x1295.xml?ReleaseID_1436 [accessed December 9, 2012].

Rafail, P., Walker, E.T., McCarthy, J.D., and Gromis, A. 2011. Explaining the spatial distribution of the 2009 tax day Tea Party protests. Paper presented at the American Sociological Association Meetings, Las Vegas, NV (August 2011).

Santoro, W.A. and McGuire, G.M. 1997. Social movement insiders: The impact of institutional activists on affirmative action and comparable worth policies. *Social Problems* 44(4), 503–19.

Skocpol, T. and Williamson, V. 2012. *The Tea Party and the Remaking of Republican Conservatism*. Oxford: Oxford University Press.

Snow, D.A. and Benford, R.D. 1988. Ideology, frame resonance, and participant mobilization. *International Social Movement Research*, 1, 197–217.

Snow, David A., Soule, Sarah A., and Kriesi, Hanspeter 2004. Mapping the terrain, in *The Blackwell Companion to Social Movements*, edited by D.A. Snow, S.A. Soule, and H. Kriesi. Oxford: Blackwell, 3–16.

Staggenborg, S. 1988. The consequences of professionalization and formalization in the Pro-Choice Movement. *American Sociological Review*, 53(4), 585–606.

Stearns, L.B. and Almeida, P.D. 2004. The formation of state actor-social movement coalitions and favorable policy outcomes. *Social Problems*, 51(4), 478–504.

Stolberg, S.G. 2009. "Public Option" in health plan may be dropped, *New York Times*, August 16.

Tarrow, S. 1994. *Power in Movement: Social Movements, Collective Action and Politics*. New York: Cambridge University Press.

Tarrow, S.G. 2011. *Power in Movement: Social Movements and Contentious Politics*. 3rd ed. Cambridge: Cambridge University Press.

Tea Party Caucus. 2012. Tea Party Caucus hosts Herman Cain and Tea Party groups for discussion on economy. [Online]. Available at http://teapartycaucus-bachmann.house.gov/membership [accessed August 31, 2012].

Tilly, C. 1978. *From Mobilization to Revolution*. New York: Addison Wesley.

Turner, L. and Hurd, R.W. 2001. Building social movement unionism: The transformation of the American Labor Movement, in *Rekindling the Movement: Labor's Quest for Relevance in the Twenty-First Century*, edited by L. Turner, H.C. Katz, and R.W. Hurd. Ithaca, NY: Cornell University Press, 9–26.

Van Cott, D.L. 2005. *From Movements to Parties in Latin America: The Evolution of Ethnic Politics*. Cambridge: Cambridge University Press.

Van Dyke, N., Dixon, M., and Carlon, H. 2007. Manufacturing dissent: Labor revitalization, Union Summer and student protest. *Social Forces*, 86(1), 193–214.

Vogel, K.P. 2010. Tea party vs. Tea Party caucus, *Politico*. Available at http://www.politico.com/news/stories/0810/40528.html [accessed August 31, 2012].

Vreeland, J.R. 2003. *The IMF and Economic Development*. Cambridge: Cambridge University Press.

Whittier, Nancy. 2004. The consequences of social movements for each other, in *The Blackwell Companion to Social Movements*, edited by D.A. Snow, S.A. Soule, and H. Kriesi. Oxford: Blackwell, 531–52.

Williamson, V., Skocpol, T., and Coggin, J. 2011. The Tea Party and the remaking of Republican conservatism. *Perspectives on Politics*, 9(1), 25–43.

Zernike, K. and Thee-Brenan, M. 2010. Poll finds Tea Party backers wealthier and more educated. *New York Times*, April 14.

Chapter 4
The Tea Party and the Dilemmas of Conservative Populism

David S. Meyer and Amanda Pullum

Keli Carender started blogging in January 2009, just after Barack Obama took the oath of office. An underemployed math teacher and improv comic, she adopted the pen name "Liberty Belle" and called for conservatives to come out and oppose the Obama administration and take back America. She described herself as

> a girl who has come to realize that the people of the USA are in dire need of a basic Economics lesson as well as a review on individual rights and freedom. I am a girl who is dedicated to filling that educational void. I will not sit idly by and watch as social democrats, socialists, or communists attempt to dominate this country. I am ready to do my part and fight for liberty. Join me? (Carender 2009a)

She expressed distrust of government, arguing that Republicans could offer better answers to the nation's pressing problems, and that their success in doing so was predicated upon pressure from the grassroots. In her first post, she described her goals, and her strategy for achieving them:

> I believe we should have a "Solution Revolution." No more flowery language, no more rhetoric. GOP Solutions are straight-forward, real, alternative solutions to the problems we face. We need to sit down and actually create SOLUTIONS that are based in OUR principles like the free market, fiscal conservatism, individual freedom and liberty, self-responsibility, and the importance of family. From there we put it on every website, talk show, hold press conferences, send email alerts, pamphlets, calls, door to door, send out groups of "educators" into communities to have meetings where we describe and discuss our SOLUTIONS to their problems, etc. ... BOLD and DIFFERENT and REAL ... Once we have solutions for all of the hot button issues (energy, healthcare, education, etc.) we put it together in a simple, user-friendly format which states the problem, our solution, the Democrats' solution, and why ours is better, all side by side. Let's rush the field in every medium—like comedy, viral videos, and merchandise (i.e. "agitprop"). (Carender 2009c)

Articulate and dramatic, yet a novice to politics, Liberty Belle served as an icon for the emerging Tea Party movement (Ward 2010, Zernike 2010). In addition to her blog, she organized demonstrations in Seattle, and theatrically confronted Congressman Norman Dicks in a town meeting about health care. Waving a $20 bill at Dicks, she demanded that he take her money—if he thought it was legitimate for government to take money from American citizens for health care. Dicks refused the offer, and the video of Carender confronting him went viral, generating more than 70,000 hits on YouTube, and more on conservative websites (Carender 2009b).

The image Carender projected is a familiar one in American politics and American social movements: she is the average citizen, not particularly engaged in politics, who is provoked by threats from government into political action. She has expressed no interest in a long-term career in politics, electoral or otherwise, but sees herself as a participant in a growing movement that can restore a vision of limited Constitutional government that respects the rights of individuals. Carender is also not alone.

Over the last two years, activists have organized demonstrations to "Take Back America" across the United States. Sometimes donning faux colonial costumes, self-described Tea Party activists appropriated a version of American history that cast themselves as patriots fighting against a tyrannical government: a government that bailed out large banks, that mandated and regulated health care, that might regulate greenhouse gases, and, most vehemently, that taxed. (Placards used TEA as an acronym for "Taxed Enough Already.") Vigorously embracing a populist democratic rhetoric, Tea Party activists were insistent about restoring an America that was responsive to the needs of THE PEOPLE.

The vigor and volatility of the Tea Party movement has been understandably enticing to journalists. We expect that scholars are already following the news, and that in the coming years we will see analytical treatment of the mobilization, tactics, and impact of the Tea Party. Right away, we've seen interesting developments on all of these issues. The Tea Party has been a forceful presence in the Republican Party, producing victories for dissident candidates in Republican primaries, affecting the rhetoric of the Party's leaders, and establishing a caucus in Congress. It has also generated a large number of dramatic events, including nationally oriented demonstrations in Washington DC, and many smaller demonstrations at the grassroots.

At once, the rhetoric and activities of the broad Tea Party movement promise a campaign to *redemocratize* the United States, although the definitions of democracy are generally vague, implicit, or contradictory. Activists like Carender promise a different approach to government and politics than the two large parties. The notion that a social movement can be a source of democratic renewal, even in America, is hardly new. The question is whether the resources necessary to promote a campaign like the Tea Party make the promotion of any classical vision of democracy unlikely. While the social movement is historically a form sometimes used by constituencies to redress democratic deficiencies, the form has also been used by constituencies with very different aims. We mean to explore the tension between grassroots mobilizations animated by democratic rhetoric and the potentially less democratic claims on policy.

We situate our study of the Tea Party in the larger world of social movement theory, established in both Sociology and Political Science. The Tea Party represents an analytical challenge for such theories, which generally view social movements as the province of groups that are otherwise disadvantaged, who cannot get what they want without employing protest. Such approaches focus on the relationship between a challenging movement and the world around it. And, the balance of writing on social movements is heavily slanted to movements of the left. We begin by sketching out some of the concepts helpful in making sense of the Tea Party established in theory. We then look at the mobilization of the Tea Party movement and its relationship to the political context. We note the linkage between grassroots activism and well-heeled funders supporting activism as their best political strategy—for the moment, noting the peculiar and evolving relationship of the Tea Party movement and the Republican Party. We observe potential rifts within the Tea Party, and between the grassroots activists and their organized and well-funded sponsors. We conclude by returning to the social movement society hypothesis, noting that an ostensibly populist democratic movement, like the Tea Party, is dependent upon elite sponsorship that may have no long-term interest in democratization.

Social Movements and the Social Movement Society

Broadly speaking, the history of social movements in the United States is one animated by fights for political inclusion lodged by (and on behalf of) groups without the political access or resources to exercise influence without protest. For the most part, the largest movements of the first two centuries of American life represented people who were visibly excluded, most notably, workers, African Americans, and women. (To be sure, populist conservatism and nativism have also episodically mobilized in opposition to the threats from those rising constituencies.)

After World War II, however, there were large and often sustained mobilizations by groups composed of people who ostensibly enjoyed access to mainstream American life and politics. Antinuclear weapons, environmental, and antiwar campaigns, to name a few, were animated by the middle class, who claimed that they lacked meaningful access to decisions that affected their lives. In effect, their efforts argued that the availability of conventional democratic remedies for redress—party activism, election campaigns, lobbying and more routine civic engagement—were insufficient means for making claims. On the left and the right, activists identified similar categories of culprits: self-interested politicians who ignored them, well-established interest groups who looked after narrow concerns, non-responsive government, and mobilized opponents.

Over the last 50 years, in the United States, and indeed in other wealthy countries, it seems that the routine means of access to political influence have been inadequate and unsatisfying for virtually everyone. Thus, we have seen the permanent establishment of groups that represent interests that are only occasionally visible to the larger public (e.g., various corporate and trade associations, such as the American Legislative Exchange Council (ALEC) or Citizens United, peace concerns, abortion rights (for and against), gun rights (for and against)). We have also seen groups that would seem to have ready access to routine channels of influence augment their efforts with protest campaigns.

Nearly 15 years ago, Meyer and Tarrow (1998) proposed the concept of a "social movement society" to unify a series of such observations about social protest in the contemporary era. They claimed that social movement tactics had widely diffused across causes and constituencies, and had become a routinized part of modern politics, more accepted, and less disruptive. They argued that increased frequency of protests was accompanied by other changes in politics and life that made the social movement less disruptive:

- the general public became more tolerant to protest as a political tactic;
- police and other state authorities developed negotiating strategies to manage protests to increase predictability for all concerned and minimize disruption;
- social movement organizations formalized, bureaucratized, and established themselves as more or less constant presences in political life;
- this formalization created a professional identity for organizers;
- as protest was increasingly accepted as a tactic of political influence, it was no longer confined to those holding intense passions or lacking institutional means of redress; and
- activists employed a narrower range of social movement tactics, emphasizing less disruptive, threatening, or costly approaches to invite broader participation—for example, staging a large and colorful demonstration on a weekend in a public location negotiated with authorities rather than staging ongoing civil disobedience campaigns.

They noted that the implications of such changes were largely unexplored, and posed fundamental questions about contemporary democracy. They asked whether the social movement society represented an increased democratization of political life in advanced industrialized societies or the effective neutering of a tactic that had sometimes been useful to those without other access to political influence. They suggested that the more crowded social movement landscape made it harder for any new cause or constituency to break through the clutter of movements. When social movements become routinized, they asked, do they also become routinized so as to be less consequential?

Previous understandings of social movements have viewed social protest as an effort to even the odds by those who are poorly positioned to make claims effectively through conventional politics. The disadvantaged could use disruption to bring attention to their cause, to engage latent support, and to mobilize countervailing resources. In relatively closed or repressive polities, this meant that anyone outside the ruling group might try to launch protest movements. In advanced industrialized democracies, however, people who were disadvantaged politically, economically, or socially were the ones who would use protest to try to make gains. Either way, movements were a tool for enhancing democratic participation in politics.

The social movement society theory focused on those advanced industrialized democracies. The signal social movements of the 1960s, particularly in the United States, supported the notion that people who could get what they wanted in other ways would avoid protest. The large movements of the time were animated by ethnic minorities seeking civil rights and inclusion and young people seeking to end the war and enhance their opportunities to participate in decisions about both political life and higher education, and women seeking meaningful inclusion in politics and economic opportunities.

But by the 1970s, social movements emerged representing constituencies that had more tenuous claims to being disadvantaged, often organizing and mobilizing on issues that might have little direct effect on their lives. These conservative movements eschewed the violent actions employed by earlier organizations, such as the Ku Klux Klan or White Citizens Councils; instead, they adopted and adapted the tactics and rhetoric of the civil rights movement to battle government action intended to promote egalitarianism. As an example, white, mostly working class, people in Boston neighborhoods used protest to stop the integration of their schools—in the name of democratic control. By the 1980s, the repertoire of social movement actions, including demonstrations and even civil disobedience, had extended to people and causes that were not dramatically disadvantaged, and they were often making claims on behalf of others. The peace and environmental movements, for example, were led by educated and middle-class people who could engage in more conventional politics, including participating in electoral politics; indeed, they often did—in addition to movement tactics. True to the expectations of the social movement society, it had become common for a wide variety of movements to protest, using a relatively narrow and increasingly non-disruptive tactical repertoire to do so.

Most recently, Tea Party activists have attacked the policies of the Obama administration, claiming a democratic lineage that started with the founders of the American republic. Employing what has become the usual social movement repertoire, including demonstrations, lobbying, and electoral activism, they charged that the Obama administration's efforts, particularly on health care, violated both the Constitution and basic notions of democracy. Since the passage of a first round of health care reform, a variety of Tea Party organizations have sought to maintain their efforts and focus attention on new issues.

Here, we examine the democratic rhetoric of the Tea Party movement, including the constructed narratives about its origin. We compare the language and stories with what we know about the actual infrastructure of the movement, including its organizational base and its demographic support.

Social Movement Theory and the Tea Party

The Tea Party's sudden emergence and generally unexpected mobilization led to a flush of attention. When directed to the midterm elections, mainstream media coverage was extensive and often hyperbolic, as reporters and analysts tried to make sense of an ostensibly new force in American life. We're not convinced, however, that "a movement that few people took seriously has become the most obsessed-over and overanalyzed political backlash since the 1960s" (Weigel 2010).

Of course, contemporary political figures with all kinds of axes to grind have seized upon the Tea Party to find authentic American democracy, horrific American nativism, regular citizens newly engaged in politics, marginalized crazies newly legitimized, an astroturf lobby for wealthy interests (e.g., Garcia Bedolla 2010),[1] or a backlash against government intrusions on health care, bank bailouts, gun regulation, taxation, or antipathy to the election of the first black President. Given the standards of evidence on the web and in contemporary political dialogue, we can claim all of these things and find an anecdote to support the claim. More significantly, given the sloppy and diverse nature of social movements in America—and elsewhere—it really isn't surprising that we can use any volatile social movement as a kind of Rorschach on which to project our preferred political interpretation. This, of course, *isn't* new. Like most American movements, the Tea Party is diverse and divided, composed of multiple organizations and more or less loosely associated individuals who agree on some things and disagree on others, but clearly situate themselves on the right side of the political spectrum. The success of the Tea Party in sustaining itself and exercising influence on politics and policy will surely reflect the extent to which activists and organizations are able to agree to cooperate on proximate goals and strategies (Meyer and Corrigall-Brown 2005).

Tea party activists, journalists, and public opinion pollsters have claimed that the Tea Party represents people who do not normally depend upon social protest to try to get what they want from the political process. The few polls we have show Tea Party supporters to be better educated, more affluent, and whiter than the American population at large—not unusual for some kinds of social movements (*New York Times*/CBS 2010). The social movement society claim (Meyer and Tarrow 1998) is that more diverse causes have adopted the more moderate spectrum of protest movement forms and tactics. We see these tactics in the form of rallies,

---

1 "I can think of no other social 'movement' that can claim political patrons of this magnitude," Garcia Bedolla (2010) writes. We can. The civil rights movement, for example, enjoyed the support of elected officials in the North and top-level officials in all presidential administrations from Truman to Johnson. More recently, advocates for gays and lesbians being allowed to serve openly in the military have been able to call on the support of the Secretary of Defense and the chair of the Joint Chiefs of Staff, and supporters of government funding for stem cell research have drawn upon the almost unanimous support of both academic science and drug and biotechnology companies.

lobbying, electoral politics, or calls for boycotts (and sometimes "buycotts," in which Tea Partiers pledge to support particular businesses). We need to figure out what it means to protest in American politics, when virtually everyone else is doing the same thing.

In its initial flourishes, the Tea Party clearly responded to policy initiatives, reacting strongly against the financial bailout of 2008–2009, and mounting vigorous opposition to the proposed health care reform. The mobilizations against the Obama administration's efforts have been strong and focused. Forwarding an affirmative agenda, however, beyond advocacy of limited or "Constitutional" government, has been slow and contested, and the Tea Party has struggled to negotiate a relationship with mainstream institutional politics. We see this struggle in the electoral realm, as Republicans argue about the wisdom of primary electorates choosing purer Tea Party candidates who may be weaker in general elections than their less pure opponents. Both monied interests and voters at the grassroots have repeatedly confronted the dilemma of supporting the purer advocate or the stronger candidate.

Meyer and Staggenborg (1996) speculated that virtually every consequential movement in American politics would spur a substantial countermovement. The Tea Party has provoked specific responses, both from new groups—or ideas of groups, like the Coffee Party—and from long-established movement organizations, including the NAACP and its efforts with organized labor in a One Nation campaign. However, in addition to counter-mobilization, movements must also address dissent within their ranks. A campaign that employs the inflammatory rhetoric that has appeared in some Tea Party events attracts a range of people, including those particularly attracted by that rhetoric. Although such people don't necessarily commit to ongoing organizational participation, they may well be attracted to dramatic—and violent—action. Like other movements, the Tea Party will sweep up a broad range of people in its wake and it is quite possible that somewhere down the line, someone proclaiming affiliation with the Tea Party will do something destructive or violent (Wright 2007). Of course, this has happened before within movements on the left and the right. While the community that studies social movements and protest was right to reject the mass society approaches of the 1950s that argued activism was the result of social anomie or psychological disaffection, there may nevertheless be anomic or sociopathic people participating in movements. This is one version of the negative radical flank dilemma (Haines 1984, 1995) that confronts many movements; violent action can end up discrediting and marginalizing a movement. These few violent activists can also spur a positive radical flank effect, making the larger non-violent Tea Party appear more reasonable by comparison.

More than most recent American movements, the Tea Party offers a story about the founding of America and the long-term meaning of America. Tea Partiers tell stories about the founding and the Constitution, and portray their efforts as fulfilling and restoring its vision. Of course, this isn't completely new. Activists often claim discrete elements of American history, interpreting them in ways that serve their present ends (Lepore 2010). What's more, like most political campaigns, the tales Tea Partiers tell about the founding, the Constitution, or even contemporary tax policy, don't necessarily line up well with the opinions of people who are more expert on those matters. The stories that we tell about the past that win acceptance aren't necessarily those that are most accurate (Meyer 2006).

We will now make some more general observations about the emergence of the Tea Party and the predications of social movement theory.

Political Opportunities

Political opportunity theory is supposed to help us understand how the claims, tactics, and trajectory of a movement are affected by the world outside that movement, with a particular focus on formal politics (Meyer 2004). Research focuses on both formal institutional characteristics as well as political alignments. In its short life, the Tea Party has spoken back to an ongoing debate in the field.

In one of the most influential statements of the political opportunity approach, McAdam (1982) argued that African American activists responded to positive signals and the presence of powerful allies in institutional politics, or, more generally, political openings. Costain (1991) found the same story in reference to women's movements. But in reports on other movements, we can see mobilization in response to policy setbacks and the exclusion of allies from institutional power (e.g., Meyer 1990).

We can generalize from these observations to suggest a broader theory based on the notion that different groups turn to protest from different structural conditions, specifically: movements of people generally excluded from political influence would depend upon openings, whereas movements composed of people used to institutional access would respond to policy provocations and political exclusion. This means that groups of the excluded will mobilize when they are poised to influence policy. Paradoxically, however, some kinds of movements are likely to mobilize when they are least likely to get what they want—but perhaps they can stop or slow initiatives they find abhorrent. (This approach looks more like the curvilinear relationship between opportunities and mobilization that Tilly (1978) offered than like subsequent iterations of political opportunity theory emphasizing openings.)

The Tea Party movement provides a clear case of a constituency mobilizing in response to bad news, that is, perceived exclusion, and the threat of unwanted policy initiatives. The Tea Party represents the mobilization of conservatives in the face of defeats and threats, and the absence of viable institutional alternatives for influence.

Note that even with such a short life, there are different narratives for the emergence of the Tea Party, all starting with defeat. Some trace the beginning to 2007, with the mobilization of Ron Paul supporters who were disaffected with their candidate's prospects for winning the Republican presidential nomination. Others mark the Tea Party's emergence with Carender's blog, or with CNBC correspondent Rick Santelli's February 2009 rant against the government bailout of the financial industry and mortgage holders. Alternative narratives focus on Glenn Beck's 9/12, Tax Day protests, or the health care town meeting shout downs. In all of these stories, the Tea Party is a response to a government (and in Beck's case, a culture) *that is not listening* to at least one large segment of the citizenry.

At the most obvious level, there is a reasonable case to be made here. Barack Obama, running on a progressive platform that emphasized health care reform and tax increases for the wealthiest Americans, was elected with a decisive margin in 2008, and his candidacy demonstrated coattails that far exceeded those of his predecessor, George W. Bush. Democrats picked up nine seats in the United States Senate, going from a bare majority dependent upon the support of two independents to a filibuster-proof 60 votes (after Pennsylvania Republican Arlen Specter changed parties). Democrats also picked up 21 seats in the House of Representatives, and a margin of 69 votes. This meant that the liberal wing of the Democratic Party enjoyed firm control of the House, and that the center of gravity in the Senate had shifted substantially to the left as well.

Most people take to the streets only when they believe that protest is the best strategy for them to get what they want from politics. People opposed to the financial bailout (an approach supported by the Bush administration and many visible Republicans) had few institutional routes to influence. Conservatives faced a national Executive and Legislature that were both unusually insulated from their direct influence. Republicans in the House, many of whom had promised not to compromise with Democratic colleagues, found few prospects for influencing the legislative agenda and responded by taking their case *outside* the House. Booing or heckling a presidential speech was about as much as any House Republican *could* do. If the archaic rules of the Senate afforded the minority relatively more political leverage, it was still leverage only to block or stall the Obama administration's initiatives. Meanwhile, even if the judiciary were more explicitly conservative, it is not an institution obviously responsive to citizen advocacy. In short, there were no conservative allies in a position to deliver very much to dissatisfied citizens.

Untethered by the responsibility of governance, conservative rhetoric was untempered. The shift of gravity understandably moved from the minority leaders in the House or Senate—who really couldn't do much more than talk—to advocates better positioned to speak more clearly and more provocatively. Radio and television personalities, particularly Rush Limbaugh and Glenn Beck, became the most colorful, prolific, and provocative opponents of the Obama administration. The hundreds of Republican legislators were a less promising target for influence than the more diffuse politics of the streets and social movements.

This is a clear case in which interests and advocates who would normally work through lobbying and electoral politics were essentially forced into the light, politics outdoors, and the more polemical rhetoric that flourishes in such settings.

Can we imagine a Tea Party movement emerging in response to a John McCain presidency? It is far more likely that conservative activists would see more direct and promising routes to influence than protest in the streets, and would therefore temper their rhetoric and tactics. They would be more wary of alliances with unreliable allies and employing disruptive tactics when they saw they might have something to lose. Grassroots democratic populist politics would take a backseat to the exigencies of power and a reluctance to complicate the lives of allies facing more threatening opposition. Again, this isn't surprising. Conservatives were tempered in their criticisms of President George W. Bush on matters of fiscal responsibility, preferring him to the Democratic opposition. And, more recently, left and liberal activist groups have had a hard time mobilizing strong opposition to President Obama's efforts, even as they have been profoundly disappointed by the president's vigor and follow-through on promises about the wars, the economy, civil liberties, health care, science, and gay and lesbian rights.

White People's Politics

Social movements are always about more than their expressed concerns, and surely part of the Tea Party's politics confront race. To be sure, we see a few visible African American or Latino supporters within the Tea Party, and it is a gross oversimplification to suggest, as opponents sometimes do, that the Tea Party is primarily a white backlash against the first African American elected to the Presidency. Nevertheless, research suggests that some Tea Party sympathizers' discontents are based, at least in part, on racist sentiments and the fear that white control of American political institutions may be threatened (Garcia Bedolla 2010, Parker and Barreto 2013).

The activists appearing in Tea Party events, and the people who register their support in public opinion polls, are overwhelmingly—if not exclusively—white. It is worthwhile to think about what this means. We might start by noting that movements of the middle class in American history have almost always been overwhelmingly white, and that left-liberal movements, including antinuclear and environmental campaigns, have wrestled with finding ways both to increase their racial/ethnic diversity and to increase the appearance of such diversity.

The veracity of the adjective "white" as a descriptive is not really at issue. More problematic, and more interesting, is whether that description affects the way a political movement develops. Specifically, is white a mobilizing identity that affects who gets engaged in the movement and how? Do white movements operate with different constraints and opportunities than those filled with other populations? Do American political institutions, ranging from elected officials to the police, respond differently?

Scholars who have written on race and social movements (see, particularly, recent work by Okamoto 2003 and Martinez 2008) focus on ethnic minorities, in which phenotypic appearance is a factor in grievances and political claims, and is therefore a mobilizing identity. Mobilization in such cases is likely to follow a different model than movements that construct identities explicitly based around beliefs about collective goods that are ostensibly available to everyone.

Here, Tilly's curvilinear framework of opportunity helps. For African Americans in the 1950s and 1960s or for women in the 1960s and 1970s, openings and some institutional allies were essential for extra-institutional mobilization to seem safe and/or promising enough to engage sufficient numbers of people. This relationship, however, where openings are necessary for social protest mobilization, is historically contingent. When a group is sufficiently incorporated into mainstream American politics (or for that matter, any politics) that its representatives can employ routine measures (voting, campaign contributions, lobbying, and so forth) to represent their concerns, new mobilization will only occur around new grievances and/or visibly reduced access for that constituency. Mobilizing on the basis of gender or race after these groups have gained some institutional access becomes more difficult and more complicated.

White people's politics responds to grievances and exclusions, and activists will talk about new threats, insults, and the lack of meaningful mainstream political alternatives. They will also point to a past, distant or proximate, in which those things were not the case: when allies were in government, when policies were less problematic or threatening, and when government's ambitions better matched their own. We want to stress that this works for the left and the right. Antinuclear weapons activists in the 1980s lauded government initiatives to control arms. Second amendment activists praise an institutional design that protects individuals' access to firearms.

We think that this affects tactics as well as other elements of the presentation of claims. The Tea Party rally that included spitting and shouting at African American members of Congress brings to mind a comparison with the early years of the civil rights movement.

In the 1950s and 1960s, civil rights activists used non-violent tactics for many reasons. To be sure, the movement grew out of, partly, well-established pacifist organizations, so there was an institutional set of practices and ideology. Beyond that, leaders, particularly clerics like Martin Luther King, were theologically and ideologically committed to non-violence as a way of life. They saw a connection between ends and means, and also saw non-violent action for social justice as inherently good—regardless of its efficacy.

But there were tactical concerns as well. Civil rights leaders were well aware of the threat they represented to local white political figures and, more broadly, to images of an America that some people cherished. They were self-conscious about training activists to wear their best clothes and look mainstream—and safe. They were also committed to training activists entering potentially confrontational situations *not* to react to verbal provocations or physical violence. They were keenly aware that they were fatally disadvantaged in any battle involving physical force. They presented themselves as non-violent for both ideological and tactical reasons.

In contrast, the threats of recourse to violence at large Tea Party events have been explicit. Even candidates for political office have discussed "second amendment" remedies to tyrannical government, and demonstrators have carried posters depicting weapons. We think that this results from a feeling of entitlement among some of the Tea Partiers; they believe that their rights (to assemble, to resist government, to bear arms) are well established and legitimately incontestable. Like other conservative groups, they fear structural or political shifts that might jeopardize these rights (Van Dyke and Soule 2002). Much of the rhetoric about their opponents is polemical and/or condescending. They seek a government response, but not discussion or conciliation with their opponents. (Surely, we can find that campaigns on the left side of the spectrum have shared *some* of these characteristics. Tea Party activists have been quick to point out dismissive comments about the intelligence or ethics of Ronald Reagan or George W. Bush offered by liberal activists.) The point, however, is that white people's movements are based in constituencies who already feel a sense of connection and entitlement in mainstream politics (McVeigh 1999). White peoples' movements that discuss democracy suggest that it is a condition that they previously enjoyed, and a process that might not be defined by access to the polls or citizenship rights so much as a protected or advantaged status.

When several members of Congress walked through an assembly of Tea Party protesters on their way to the Capitol building, they received a hostile response. Members of the Black Congressional Caucus, including civil rights hero Rep. John Lewis, reported hearing racial epithets, and videos available on YouTube show Rep. Emmanuel Cleaver responding to being spit upon. Inside the corridors of the Capitol, Rep. Barney Frank heard anti-gay slurs. These elected officials all supported some version of comprehensive health care reform, but it is impossible to view such attacks as being primarily about health care. In a *Politico* report reprinted on Republican Congressman John Campbell's website, the authors noted:

> Several Republicans said their party acted no worse than Democrats did during the Bush years. "When the CodePinkers and [Michael] Moore et al. were up here, you should've heard some of the things they were saying," said Rep. Greg Walden (R-Ore.). "At any time there is a heated public debate, people say things they shouldn't say. We don't condone it ... It wasn't appropriate then, and it wasn't appropriate now." Walden told POLITICO that the GOP leadership was upset about members inciting people in the gallery. "They shouldn't clap," said Walden. "And the leadership said that doesn't belong." (Thrush and Cogan 2010)

But Rep. John Campbell (R-Calif.) said that the outbursts were "a reflection of widespread passion and anger that exists throughout the country." And while he said that such behavior "is never helpful," he also suggested that much of the anger stems from the feeling—amplified exponentially by the passage of health care reform—that the country is slipping out of his party's hands.

The notion of entitlement is further underscored by comments from Tea Party supporters that the members of Congress had intentionally provoked the Tea Partiers by walking through the front door of the Capitol, rather than taking available underground tunnels. As one blogger notes:

> The question I have is, why did these Congresspeople, including Emmanuel Cleaver (the alleged "spitee", who actually walked too close to a protester shouting "kill the bill" and got sprayed), Barney Frank, and Nancy Pelosi deliberately march into the demonstration and confront the Tea Partiers? After all, wasn't it Nancy herself who said she was "frightened" by these supposedly violent people? Is it possible that they wanted to provoke a reaction from the crowd to be used by the media to demonize the Tea Party movement (i.e., "Pick the target, freeze it, personalize it, and polarize it")? Is it also possible that when there was nothing sufficiently provoked by the lawmakers' confrontation, they decided to fabricate it? I believe their previous record of untruthfulness supports this hypothesis. (Thomas 2010).

Such comments did not come only from bloggers. Minnesota Republican Rep. Michele Bachmann said that Speaker Nancy Pelosi was trying to provoke an overreaction by walking out of the Capitol. "In three years I have never seen Nancy Pelosi cross the street, the way that you saw in that picture," Bachmann told Sean Hannity. "They deliberately went through that crowd perhaps to try and incite something." Bachmann said the Democrats were "slandering" Tea Partiers by calling them racist. Bachmann said:

> It is a smear technique, but now it is beyond smearing people this is actually out and out slandering people. Again, 30,000 freedom loving people, they were picking up their own litter afterwards. These were the nicest people you would ever want to meet, happy people. I think there's been a prearranged caricature that is being written, whether it is from the White House, whether it is from the—I don't know where coming from. (Zimmerman 2010)

The point is that some Tea Partiers, and some of their institutional sponsors, could excuse (or deny) an extremely hostile reaction to elected officials as a response to unwarranted provocation, a provocation that was provided by their support for a comprehensive health care reform, and the physical presence of black, female, and gay legislators near the Capitol.

The democratic rhetoric of the Tea Party has, in many instances, explicitly rejected the notion that a government elected by majorities should enjoy the capacity to govern, or that those officials deserved any special deference or respect by virtue of being elected. *It is, then, a democracy that is based on assertion of privilege, described as rights, and more forcefully predicated on substantive claims rather than process.*

Resource Mobilization

Although the preceding narratives emphasize a provocation or disappointment spurring the Tea Party, it is important to stress that the Tea Party advocates were not starting from scratch, even though the appellation of "tea party" was new. Large business interests were organized against some of the Obama administration's initiatives years before Obama came to power. Most notably, FreedomWorks (fronted by former House Republican leader Dick Armey), the libertarian Club for Growth, pro-business Americans for Prosperity, and American Majority were all established before Obama's election and funded by very wealthy sponsors who sought both to promote an ideological vision and to protect a financial interest. As Jane Mayer's profile of the billionaire Koch brothers (2010) notes, the promotion of a conservative ideology with hundreds of millions of dollars serves business concerns worth many times that. Moreover, she notes, the Koch brothers had accepted the input of big government initiatives when they were helpful to the business.

This is not to say that the people who assembled in town meetings across the United States to shout at members of Congress who might support health care reform were insincere. Rather, we want to emphasize that coordinated campaigns and social movements more generally are not spontaneous affairs, but are organized. Well-heeled financiers and professional organizers dedicated themselves to stoking activism in the town halls, on the Washington mall, and in the streets more generally. Conservatives were also adept in using internet networks, conservative radio shows, and Fox News to promote their analyses and their activities. The point is that frustrated citizens with grievances about taxes or health care found support, material, organizational, and ideological, for their opinions.

The key issue here is that large and established interests found common cause with populist anger, and lacked alternative approaches to influence. It's important to note that these business interests, in addition to lobbying or donating to campaigns, chose to put money toward mobilizing groups of discontented citizens and encouraging their participation in traditional protest tactics. Groups like FreedomWorks invested in grassroots mobilization because it was their best opportunity to express their claims publicly and effectively. The alliances between the grassroots and their business sponsors, however, are something that cannot be taken for granted, but must be renegotiated from issue to issue.

Tea Party Coalitions

At the national level, the Tea Party has been represented by several different organizations, which, upon even cursory inspection, turn out to share some short-term concerns, but seem to have very different visions of the future. This is not uncommon for American social movements, which are composed of coalitions of groups and affiliated individuals united, for a time, on a program of common concern. For reactive movements that respond to bad news, such movements generally focus on a set of pressing issues, such as nuclear power, access to abortion, or opposition to a war. Within such a coalition, groups will share a common short-term agenda, but often differ in their analyses and in affiliated issues that matter to them. As an example, the Nuclear Freeze movement represented a coalition that spanned absolute pacifists, far left groups, and advocates of an older tradition of nuclear arms control (Meyer 1990). Such a coalition functions only in opposition and fragments when political authorities start to respond in any way.

The demands of the Tea Party movement are somewhat less defined, with the appellation glossing over a broad range of concerns and substantial differences on matters of policy and politics. The Tea Party label has become an all purpose designation for mobilized opposition to President Obama's political agenda.

Of all the national groups, the Tea Party Patriots seems best to embody the conservative democratic ethos the movement claims. Organized by a small number of experienced activists, it has styled itself as something of a clearinghouse for conservative grassroots politics. Claiming more than 2,500 local allies, the group's initial goal was to support grassroots activism. Articulated in terms of limited federal government, free markets, and fiscal responsibility, it also prizes personal liberty and the rule of law. The Tea Party Patriots has self-consciously tried to develop a model of organization based in the grassroots, immune to cooptation or decapitation (Rauch 2010). The activist leaders read and recommend Alinksy as a model for grassroots organizing, and explicitly reject the notion of building a stable Washington-based institutional structure. They have also suffered from fundraising difficulties.

After the 2010 election, however, at a press conference at the National Press Club, the Tea Party Patriots announced the receipt of a $1 million donation from an anonymous donor. Criticizing the legitimacy of other groups using the Tea Party appellation, they announced that they would support Tea Party electoral efforts without giving donations to candidates or consultants, or endorsing specific candidates. They also announced that former Congressman Ernie Istook would join the group as an adviser, as part of their effort to establish a permanent presence in American politics.

In contrast, the Tea Party Express is a renamed organization established by a long-time Republican political consultant, Sal Russo. Originally called "Our Country Deserves Better," Russo renamed the group when grassroots Tea Party activism took off. It is far more focused on candidates than any particular policy position, save for safe positions against taxes and against the "nationalization of industry." The group funneled money and expertise into several campaigns, notably those of Joe Miller (Alaska) and Sharron Angle (Nevada). It is the largest independent group supporting Republican candidates, spending more than $5 million on primary campaigns of candidates it endorsed. More than half of this money has gone to consulting firms controlled by Russo or his wife. The group has been effectively functioning as a conduit for grassroots money given to conservative Republicans and translated into a consulting service by Russo and his allies.

Tea Party Nation is a for-profit organization that has been visible only in organizing national conferences for delegates who pay relatively high registration fees. These delegates can participate in workshops on politics and issues, and hear well-compensated speakers. It operates as a business more than as a movement group, offering services or entertainment to the Tea Party movement. The first national conference, in Nashville, featured Sarah Palin, speaking for a reported $100,000 fee. One observer emphasized the ideological diversity and demographic similarities (affluent, old, and white) of the participants (Raban 2010). Several conservative members of Congress canceled commitments to attend. Subsequent conferences have been canceled, presumably because of the failure to attract large paying audiences.

The most visible group was probably Glenn Beck's 9/12 Project, designed to build national unity around "9 principles and 12 values." Beck himself renounces the identity of a Tea Party supporter, explaining that he will work with Tea Partiers when they have common purposes (Leibovich 2010). The 9/12 Project has worked with conservative politicians, but endorses spiritual/religious values that resemble self-help rhetoric. Principle 2, for example, announces: "I believe in God and He is the Center of My Universe." Principle 4 expresses personal goals with a bit of a political edge: "The family is sacred. My spouse and I are the ultimate authority, not the government." Beck clearly has concerns beyond political mobilization.

Other groups appear to be little more than websites. The National Tea Party Federation is styled as a clearinghouse for Tea Party groups, and is committed to communication among allies, response to criticism, and "to continue to build the brand equity of the Tea Party movement." It explicitly renounces "9/11 truthers" and "birthers." The Tea Party and Revolution offers little specific information, although it reprints the Bill of Rights on its website. The surely desirable URL, teaparty.org, was obtained by Dale Robinson, an anti-immigration activist, and has been disparaged by other Tea Party activists. The website emphasizes an anti-immigration stance.

Underneath these Tea Party sites are longer-established interest groups and think tanks, which are often more specific in their claims, more tightly organized, and less directed to the grassroots mobilization of the moment.

The two most visible organizations, FreedomWorks and Americans for Prosperity, are groups that spun off from Citizens for a Sound Economy, an organization founded by the Koch brothers, who own several large business interests and are particularly concerned with preventing environmental regulation that may stifle their coal and oil business. Citizens for a Sound Economy was founded in 1984; Americans for Prosperity grew out of it in 2004. It is focused on "fiscal responsibility," and emphasizes cutting taxes, reducing regulation of business, and limiting the reach of the judiciary. It does not stress a social agenda at all.

Similarly, FreedomWorks "fights for lower taxes, less government and more economic freedom for all Americans ... it drives policy change by training and mobilizing grassroots Americans to engage their fellow citizens and encourage their political representatives to act in defense of individual freedom and economic opportunity." Initially led by former Congressman Dick Armey, who served as Republican Majority leader in the House of Representatives, it has worked with Tea Party Express to support conservative Republicans. Armey urged grassroots groups to focus on the electoral payoff, and to avoid divisive social issues. Tea

Party activists criticized Armey and FreedomWorks for being more interested in Republican fortunes than American values (Vogel 2010).

The Tea Party has become a catchall label for conservative activists who disagree among themselves about both substantive and strategic matters. The 2010 election provided a focus for these activists, but also a source of both unity and division. Specific candidates must articulate policy preferences on the whole range of issues that often separate Tea Partiers into libertarian and social conservative camps.

Policy Issues and Political Alliances

Within the social movement society, there exist formalized and bureaucratized social movement organizations on both the left and the right. Like any new movement, as the Tea Party has developed, it has created relationships—both cooperative and adversarial—with existing conservative groups. In addition, although established business interests may exert a large degree of influence over the organizations they fund, local grassroots organizations and individual Tea Partiers don't necessarily agree with these agendas.

The initial battles for the Tea Party were rather simple ones in terms of political coalitions. Tea Party citizen groups and well-established conservative groups agreed on opposing the financial bailout—after it had been passed. Opposition to taxation (in general, on principle) was also an easy area of agreement, as was opposition to President Obama's health care reform effort. The tactic of shouting down efforts to explain the proposed reform at town meetings was a vision of democracy based on assertion rather than dialogue. No doubt, some elements of the populist critique of government health care in general, most notably support for eliminating Medicare, would have a hard time surviving in an open and informed dialogue.

And finding subsequent areas of agreement between the populist right and big business interests will be more complicated. To be sure, these groups might forge alliances to support gun rights (not particularly salient for big business) or oppose legislation on climate change (not immediately salient for right-wing populists), but these issues have not been at the top of the Democratic Party's agenda.

Other issues are more difficult and complicated. As it has been since the 1970s, conservative populism is split between libertarians and social conservatives. If some issues, like taxation generally, can paper over differences in the populist ranks, other issues can exacerbate them. To date, the Tea Party groups have, for the most part, avoided taking strong positions on divisive issues, including drug law reform, same-sex marriage, or US foreign and military policies. As we will show below, there is a split between the grassroots and the sponsors on such issues.

As the Tea Party's electoral efforts to date have been in support of selected Republican candidates for office, activists have had to deal with the range of forces in the Republican Party coalition. This has meant working to purge some moderate Republicans: Senator Arlen Specter (PA) and Governor Charlie Crist (FL) left the

Republican Party in anticipation of difficulties in party primaries; this is surely happening at the rank-and-file level as well. Social conservatives, however, have pushed Tea Party activists to pay attention to their issues as well, demanding attention for their critical electoral role (Martin and Hohmann 2010). This means that Tea Party candidates who win Republican primaries oppose abortion rights and gay marriage, and activists who don't share those views must decide the issues they will be willing to place on the back burner.

Even more problematic in the current era is the issue of immigration. Populism in America has always contained a nativist streak, and nativists have mobilized across the country to promote a harsher immigration regime. At the same time, large business interests have historically supported relatively open borders and free labor. FreedomWorks, as a notable example, lists immigration reform among its lower priority issues, and calls for a guest worker program to facilitate the legal movement of labor across borders. In essence, the institutional conservative plan is to end illegal immigration primarily by providing a legal way for American employers to access the global labor market. This is not the position articulated by nativist groups at the grassroots, nor what specialist groups like the Federation for American Immigration Reform advocate.

Like many social movements, the positions articulated within the diverse Tea Party coalition create conflicts and contradictions. We've seen expressed concern with the deficit, but that concern is often overwhelmed by opposition to taxes in general, and opposition to government-run health care at the grassroots was notable for excluding Medicare. As an example, opposition to restoring tax rates to their pre-Bush levels is not a program to reduce the deficit. It is hard to imagine a focus on controlling federal deficits—a focus of some small specialist groups for several decades—animating populist mobilization for very long. Foreign policy may be even more problematic: The Tea Party includes both Ron Paul-style America-firsters on foreign policy, as well as traditional interventionist conservatives.

Activists have sought to find unifying issues, but since health care, the Obama administration has not helped by focusing on the sorts of issues that would link establishment conservatives with their (sometime) populist allies, like climate change. Presently, conservative critics like Senator Lindsey Graham charge that the Tea Party lacks any clear demands to focus mobilization or to use in pressing politicians. There is much antipathy to the government in the abstract, but there is a lot of support for many government programs. A large grassroots campaign to privatize Social Security, for example, is hardly imaginable.

Recently, in pursuit of restoring a government that embodies Constitutional principles, some advocates have argued for reforming the Constitution. Of course, campaigns to amend the Constitution are long, expensive, and rarely successful (see Mansbridge 1987). And then there's the content: Some Tea Party activists have called for repealing the 17th amendment, which provided for the direct election of Senators—rather than having state legislatures choose Senators, as outlined in the Constitution. It's hard to square this demand with a populist orientation or the democratic rhetoric the Tea Partiers employ.

As issues cycle through attention within government, the nature of alliances Tea Party activists can build, with both well-established, well-funded groups and other citizen groups, will change. Helpful analysis of emergent movement coalitions is dependent upon taking the interests of the organized seriously and paying careful attention to the policy process.

The Lure of Institutional Politics

If Tea Party partisans run risks in focusing on particular issues, it's not clear that candidates for office offer a much better chance for unity and sustained mobilization. The American political system offers frequent elections that essentially force advocates to compromise on issues in order to elect champions to office. For the Tea Party, the moment of potential influence arrived very early—in the 2010 midterm elections. Because Tea Party supporters are overwhelmingly concentrated in the Republican Party, and because they represent one of the most energized factions in contemporary politics, they are extremely well positioned to exercise influence in party primaries, where voter turnout is generally very low. Thus far, they have done so, helping to nominate favored candidates who are often opposed by the party's establishment. Many of these candidates, however, lost to Democrats who seemed beatable, for example Sharron Angle (Nevada), Christine O'Donnell (Delaware), and Ken Buck (Colorado) (Harris 2010). It's not that all of the Tea Party favorites lost, but they won in states that were already Republican (e.g., Utah and Kentucky).

And movement candidates virtually always disappoint in office. If they hold to the purist rhetoric, they will be unable to make inroads in Congress. If they eschew pork-barrel politics, they will disappoint constituents who *know* that other elected officials deliver earmarks to their districts. (Note that independent Socialist Bernie Sanders from Vermont has flourished in the Senate by legislating like a pragmatic Democrat.) If they compromise on principle to make deals, they will alienate many of the people who put them in office, because they will become the successful institutional politicians they railed against. This is a feature of the institutional design of the United States, and one that challenges all social movements.

The Outcomes of Social Movement Protest

The Tea Party has been extraordinarily effective at commanding media attention, but translating that attention into political influence is no easy matter. Like most social movements playing on the field of American politics, it is likely to be more successful in frustrating initiative than in taking it. The health care shout downs, followed by the election of Republican Scott Brown to the Senate in Massachusetts, were effective in slowing Democratic progress on the health care bill.

Paradoxically, however, the shout downs may have been more effective in warning Republicans off compromise with the Obama administration, and minimizing their direct influence on the resulting bill. Absent the prospect of cooperation with Republican allies, institutional Democrats had no real reason to trim their ambitions to gain votes, and sought compromises within their coalition, rather than across partisan boundaries.

It may well be that President Obama was unnecessarily timid in his health care stance (dropping insistence on a public option in the bill) or in his stimulus request (roughly half of what many economists said was necessary), but it's hard to credit the Tea Party with eliciting such concessions. By continuing to erode any space for moderates in the Republican Caucus in the primaries, and by helping to defeat conservative Democrats in conservative districts, the Tea Party allows Democrats in government to move a little further to the left.

Civility and Its Discontents

The most visible activism of the Tea Party has eschewed compromise or even a competition among politicians on anything less than an apocalyptic scorched earth landscape. President Obama and the Democratic Party are derided as socialist or even fascist, not as opponents in a democratic process. Ironically, officials elected through the constitutionally prescribed process—by majorities—are described as threats to American democracy, and therefore, not worth engaging in dialogue, much less negotiating compromises with.

The familiar processes of negotiating legislation inside mainstream political institutions, including, even, the Republican Party, are described as threats to American honor, heritage, and democracy. Patriots must give no quarter to such weak-kneed opposition to a threatening agenda. It is through this lens that we can understand the efforts to dismiss President Obama's claim to office and respect because of clearly false assertions about his birth or his religion.

If compromise and dialogue are anathema to some elements of the Tea Party, it bodes badly for the democratic resurgence activists seek to promote.

Conclusions

The Tea Party is another version of the sort of reactive politics that has animated social movements in America on both the left and right, and it embodies the routinization of protest predicted in the social movement society. Conservatives who have been shut out of government have adopted traditional progressive social movement tactics, taking to the streets to express their displeasure, and they've been aided by a weak economy and a few provocative initiatives from the Obama administration. Without doubt, an atmosphere of crisis has animated their efforts, and has aided activists in gaining both mass and specialized media attention.

Tea Party partisans have employed democratic rhetoric for obvious reasons. They claim that government has been unresponsive to their needs, values, and concerns (thus, non-democratic). They argue that citizens, like themselves, should play a critical role in making (or stopping) policies that affect their lives (thus, embodying democracy). They employ the Constitution as a justification for their claims, arguing that their efforts hark back to a better time for people like themselves. Without allies in power, the only meaningful expression for their concerns is through grassroots activism that, with increasing frequency, focuses on the electoral process.

However, the Tea Party has also engaged in decidedly undemocratic tactics, such as shouting down political opponents, and politicians have courted the Tea Party vote by vowing not to compromise with these opponents. With no prospects for a Tea Party Congressional majority on the horizon, these approaches make it unlikely that Tea Partiers will achieve the reforms they want, at least on a federal level.

In the contemporary social movement society, we've seen that substantial sponsorship is necessary to build the infrastructure of a movement. If those sponsors are comfortable with employing grassroots activism to serve their own ends, their willingness to allow the grassroots to define their efforts is not yet apparent. When social movement activism becomes widely diffused, used by the advantaged as well as the excluded, it may be that viable paths toward influence for the excluded become even harder to find and follow.

Meanwhile, Keli Carender has been reluctant to place her larger reform agenda at the mercy of the Republican Party. She has proposed working with the liberal group Moveon.org on a set of common issues: transparency in government, ending legislative earmarks, balancing the budget, reducing the influence of lobbyists, and protecting free speech (Ali 2010). For the most part, these are not the priorities of the large institutional sponsors who have made the meteoric growth of the Tea Party and the signal candidacies of Tea Party activists possible.

Successful mobilization has been contingent upon the linkage of populist anger with establishment resources. Absent the professional resources and funds of well-established groups like Americans for Prosperity or FreedomWorks, it is doubtful that frustration at the grassroots could have grown into a national movement so quickly. Absent real grassroots frustration with the economy and the Obama administration, it is unlikely that these groups could have bought a movement. The alliance negotiated between grassroots anger and frustration, partisan opportunism, and elements of elite interests is inherently unstable—as it has always been. Both successes and failures will strain these connections, and what emerges is likely to be more chaotic and unfocused than what has come before.

References

Ali, A. 2010. Inviting liberals to the tea party: Five areas where liberals and tea party members could find agreement. [Online]. Available at: http://www.congress.org/news/inviting-liberals-to-the-tea-party/ [accessed August 17, 2010].

Carender, K. 2009a. Blogger user profile: Liberty Belle. [Online]. Available at: http://www.blogger.com/profile/15903210730564785945 [accessed May 12, 2011].

Carender, K. 2009b. Come and take it. [Online]. Available at: http://www.youtube.com/watch?v=_IYLqtYEYeI&feature=player_embedded [Accessed May 12, 2011].

Carender, K. 2009c. Solution revolution. [Online]. Available at: http://redistributingknowledge.blogspot.com/2009_01_25_archive.html [accessed May 12, 2011].

Costain, A.N. 1991. *Inviting Women's Rebellion*. Baltimore: Johns Hopkins University Press.

Garcia Bedolla, L. 2010. A majority minority state. [Online]. Available at: http://www.nytimes.com/roomfordebate/2010/09/21/where-are-the-angry-california-voters/california-is-essentially-a-majority-minority-state [accessed September 23, 2010].

Haines, H.H. 1984. Black radicalization and the funding of civil rights: 1957–1970. *Social Problems*, 32(1), 31–43.

Haines, H.H. 1995. *Black Radicals and the Civil Rights Mainstream*. Knoxville: University of Tennessee Press.

Harris, J.F. 2010. Primary night yields good news for Obama, Dems. [Online]. Available at: http://www.politico.com/news/stories/0810/40941.html [accessed August 11, 2010].

Leibovich, M. 2010. Being Glenn Beck. [Online]. Available at: http://www.nytimes.com/2010/10/03/magazine/03beck-t.html?pagewanted=all [accessed September 29, 2010].

Lepore, J. 2010. *The Whites of Their Eyes: The Tea Party's Revolution and the Battle over American History*. Princeton: Princeton University Press.

McAdam, D. 1982. *Political Process and the Origins of Black Insurgency*. Chicago: University of Chicago Press.

McVeigh, R. 1999. Structural incentives for conservative mobilization: Power devaluation and the rise of the Ku Klux Klan, 1915–1925. *Social Forces*, 77(4), 1461–96.

Mansbridge, J. 1987. *Why We Lost the ERA*. Chicago: University of Chicago Press.

Martin, J. and Hohmann, J. 2010. "Values voters" tell Republicans: You still need us. [Online]. Available at: http://www.politico.com/news/stories/0910/42370.html [accessed September 18, 2010].

Martinez, L.M. 2008. Flowers from the same soil: Latino solidarity in the wake of the 2006 immigrant mobilizations. *American Behavioral Scientist*, 52, 557–79.

Mayer, J. 2010. Covert operations: The billionaire brothers who are waging a war against Obama. [Online]. Available at: http://www.newyorker.com/reporting/2010/08/30/100830fa_fact_mayer [accessed August 30, 2010].

Meyer, D.S. 1990. *A Winter of Discontent: The Nuclear Freeze and American Politics*. New York: Praeger.

Meyer, D.S. 2004. Protest and political opportunity. *Annual Review of Sociology*, 30, 125–45.

Meyer, D.S. 2006. Claiming credit: Stories of movement influence as outcomes. *Mobilization*, 11(3), 201–18.

Meyer, D.S. and Corrigall-Brown, C. 2005. Coalitions and political context: U.S. movements against wars in Iraq. *Mobilization*, 10(3), 327–44.

Meyer, D.S. and Staggenborg, S. 1996. Movements, countermovements, and the structure of political opportunity. *American Journal of Sociology*, 101(6), 1628–60.

Meyer, D.S. and Tarrow, S.R., eds. 1998. *The Social Movement Society: Contentious Politics for a New Century*. Lanham, MD: Rowman & Littlefield.

New York Times/CBS News. 2010. National Survey of Tea Party Supporters. [Online]. Available at: http://documents.nytimes.com/new-york-timescbs-news-poll-national-survey-of-tea-party-supporters [accessed April 9, 2013].

Okamoto, D.G. 2003. Toward a theory of panethnicity: Explaining Asian American collective action. *American Sociological Review*, 68(6), 811–42.

Parker, C.S. and Barreto, M.A. 2013. *Change They Can't Believe In: The Tea Party and Reactionary Politics in America*. Princeton: Princeton University Press.

Raban, J. 2010. At the Tea Party. [Online]. Available at: http://www.nybooks.com/articles/archives/2010/mar/25/at-the-tea-party/?pagination=false [accessed March 25, 2010].

Rauch, J. 2010. How Tea Party organizes without leaders. [Online]. Available at: http://www.freerepublic.com/focus/f-bloggers/2591379/posts [accessed September 11, 2010].

Thomas, A. 2010. Archived blog: The next move of the Alinsky left. [Online]. Available at: http://www.americanthinker.com/blog/2010/03/the_next_move_of_the_alinsky_1.html [accessed February 7, 2013].

Thrush, G. and Cogan, M. 2010. Republicans weigh costs of losing ugly. [Online]. Available at: http://www.politico.com/news/stories/0310/34838.html#ixzz0j0zCv3BH [accessed February 7, 2013].

Tilly, C. 1978. *From Mobilization to Revolution*. Reading, MA: Addison-Wesley.

Tomasky, M. 2009. Something new on the mall. [Online]. Available at: http://www.nybooks.com/articles/archives/2009/oct/22/something-new-on-the-mall/ [accessed October 22, 2009].

Van Dyke, N. and Soule, S.A. 2002. Structural social change and the mobilizing effect of threat: Explaining levels of patriot and militia organizing in the United States. *Social Problems*, 49(4), 497–520.

Vogel, K.P. 2010. Tea partiers air doubts about Armey. [Online]. Available at: http://www.politico.com/news/stories/0310/34990.html [accessed March 25, 2010].

Ward, D. 2010. American Revolution, part 2. [Online]. Available at: http://www2.canada.com/vancouversun/news/westcoastnews/story.html?id=c9c9297c-283d-49f0-b5be-ed35bf2bed17&p=3 [accessed October 9, 2010].

Weigel, D. 2010. Five myths about the Tea Party. [Online]. Available at: http://www.slate.com/id/2263063/ [accessed August 9, 2010].

Wright, S.A. 2007. *Patriots, Politics, and the Oklahoma City Bombing*. New York: Cambridge University Press.

Zernicke, K. 2010. *Boiling Mad: Inside Tea Party America*. New York: Time Books.

Zimmerman, E. 2010. Bachmann says Pelosi wanted to "incite" Tea Partiers. [Online]. Available at: http://thehill.com/blogs/blog-briefing-room/news/90347-bachmann-says-pelosi-wanted-to-incite-tea-partiers [accessed August 12, 2010].

PART II
Who Mobilized and Why? Ideology, Identity, and Emotions in the Tea Party

Chapter 5
The Tea Party Moment

Abby Scher and Chip Berlet

> The whole country is going socialist, higher taxes, slowly losing your liberty. It's liberty or socialism. It's not both ... Anytime you are taking from one group of people and giving to another, you are denying the rights of a group. Taking from the wealthy—you can't continue to take their money, give it to people who are less productive. What is part and parcel of the American spirit and what people don't understand is giving charity is not something you can demand from people.
>
> Nevada Tea Party activist and professional's wife

What is the Tea Party moment? When relatively privileged people rise up with economic grievances and reactionary solutions, can they be called populist, a happy word that suggests action for "the people" against robber barons? How can it be populist when beltway political entrepreneurs and economic royalists ally with local activists to short circuit weakened party structures in ways that elevate the role of big money in elections? Or is it a rebellion of elite individualists, secular and Christian, objecting to an administered society who want to be left alone; or of whites who feel blacks and Latinos get all the benefits of government? What about the small numbers of working-class supporters who feel unmoored from stable jobs and a predictable future, abandoned by government, and wondering why the big guys get the bailouts?

How about all of the above?

People analyzing the Tea Party movement stake out the significance of the right-wing insurgency based on their pre-existing theoretical tool kit, and all have something to offer us in understanding a very messy moment.

"Right-wing populism" is only one—very helpful—description of a diverse movement with clashing constituencies, and a range of critics rely on versions of this idea to try to understand the Tea Party. Unlike progressive populism (an upsurge of "the people" against monied interests), right-wing populism describes those whites of the middle class who identify themselves as the productive sector of society and scapegoat the poor, blacks, Jews, or other minorities as to blame for social ills while sneering at "elites" as being unproductive (Kazin 1995, Berlet and Lyons 2000). They may or may not be free market conservatives like Grover Norquist, Christian Rightists viewing their struggle through a biblical lens, or traditional conservatives standing "athwart history, yelling Stop," like the late William F. Buckley (1955). For Mark Lilla, the Tea Party is a populist movement of a special individualistic variety powered by a very American sense of narcissism: a blanket distrust of institutions and educated elites, and "an astonishing—and unwarranted—confidence in the self" (2010: n.p.). Most analysts using the concept, like Laura Miller of Salon.com, reach back to the cultural insights of historian Richard Hofstadter, who first formulated the idea of right-wing populism to help explain the conspiracy theorists of the McCarthy era and 1960s far right. He argued that this form of populism is driven by the status anxiety of a sector of the old middle class losing influence (Hofstadter 1965, Miller 2010).

Charles Postel, the historian and prize-winning author of the *Populist Vision* (2007), wonders why Tea Party analysts ignore the old right lineage of the movement. He is correct to point out that Tea Party arguments and even institutions can be traced to right-wing businessmen like Fred Koch from the National Association of Manufacturers who opposed the creation of the New Deal welfare state and government regulation as dangerous Communist "collectivism." Koch, the father of billionaire Tea Party backers David and Charles Koch, helped launch the conspiratorial John Birch Society in 1958. Birch arguments doubting the loyalty of their opponents and conflating the welfare state with dangerous communism have resurfaced in the Tea Party insurgency (Postel 2012).

Postel accurately points out that the Tea Parties are not a form of progressive populism such as the farmers and workers allied in the Peoples Party of the late 1800s (Canovan 1980, Kazin 1995, Postel 2010, 2012,). But as Michael Kazin, also a historian of progressive populism, recently reflected,

> There's not one populism. But one shared ideal is that the American people are a virtuous majority who believe the elites should be following through on their promises to make the country prosperous. If not, citizens must organize to humble the elite and dethrone it. It's somewhat of a fiction: There is no "American people," really, and there's no one elite. Conservative populists are exercised about cultural and political elites, and liberals about economical elites. (Kazin interview in Halloran 2010)

We argue that Tea Party mobilization is not solely driven by a right-wing populism that relies on creating racial scapegoats to mobilize. Instead, like Postel, we suggest that this diverse grassroots mobilization reflects longstanding modes of thinking in US politics, and shapes and is shaped by the mobilized middle class feeling that the power structure has betrayed them and undermined their rightful space at the center of civic life. That power structure includes the traditional Republican Party, the mainstream media, and government elites. The ideological themes the movement draws upon include libertarianism, apocalyptic Christianity, nativism, and white supremacy.

We interviewed a range of Tea Party activists in the Northwest, Rocky Mountains, Nevada, Ohio and other states at what was arguably the height of Tea Party mobilization in the 2010 election year when insurgents took over local and state parties and elected candidates to Congress. We found activists who fit every theory: right-wing populist, old right, Christian conservatives, ideological libertarians, monied defenders of wealth, and the worried little guy. They are all part of the Tea Party movement.

They joined with diverse fellows in the Tea Party. Before sharing their voices, we will quickly explore the broader economic and political context within which the movement developed.

The Rise of the Tea Party

The Tea Party movement gathered force starting in early 2009 with calls for reducing the $1.3 trillion federal budget deficit and stopping federal extensions of power to save the American auto industry and regulate health care. As discussed elsewhere in this volume, egged on by beltway organizers, Fox News (particularly Glenn Beck whose Fox television show began airing in January of that year), talk radio, and far right websites like WorldNet Daily, core activists called for further tax cuts on the rich to unleash economic growth, and also the rollback of the New Deal and Great Society safety net.

The Tea Party moment was a perfect storm bringing together five major political and economic trends of the last 20 years. The right-wing populists' scapegoating of minorities and "welfare cheats" is only one response to diverse trends.

First, rising economic inequality produces social and political isolation with some of the rich separating themselves from the rest of America (Massey 2007). They no longer see themselves as part of a civic community and have been powering a (legal) tax strike for the last 30 years or more. They have been funding efforts to promote their anti-tax ideology in both secular realms—seen in Jane Mayer's widely cited *New Yorker* article about David Koch (2010)—but also in religious arenas. It is bearing fruit as regional elites and small business people are having their grievances shaped by this ideology. Didn't someone once say the ruling ideas of an age are those of the ruling class? Well there's a battle raging. The Tea Partiers side with this part of the ruling class who they see as fellow producers and often show racial resentment of immigrants and blacks, scapegoating them as "tax eaters" who are taking their money, just like the ruling class resents their tax money going to the common good.

Second, the right-wing insurgency is a sign of a legitimation crisis. This is when the public loses faith in the government's ability to accomplish anything, including fixing the economy. The government may be unable to deal with contemporary economic problems for any number of reasons: partisan gridlock, counterproductive ruling class control, or the overwhelming nature of the economic problems (Habermas 1975). *New York Times* reporters Kate Zernike and Megan Thee-Brenan (2010) interviewed economically insecure Tea Partiers who feel abandoned by government and think that the government has already absented itself and proven to be unreliable in helping those who are not well off. So why give the government any more taxes or power? Larry M. Bartels (2008) tracked a similar sentiment even before the Tea Party emerged. He found that as Democratic and Republican officials alike failed to represent the views of their working-class constituents, these voters stopped expecting the government to do so.

Third, the Christian Right increasingly embraces a free market ideology. Free market Christianity predates the Tea Party of course, and is well studied (Kintz 1997, Moreton 2009). Postwar anti-communism was one crucible forging the link. Today, you see Christian free market ideas promoted by former Arkansas governor Mike Huckabee and Minnesota Congresswoman Michele Bachmann. The Heritage Foundation and today's Christian Right have been building ideology together since the 1990s (Meagher 2006) and it is bearing fruit, particularly since Glenn Beck used his Fox platform to popularize free market Christianity. Obscure Christian Right ideologues became regulars on the Glenn Beck show, like W. Cleon Skousen (the John Birch Society thinker who is now dead but whose books are high on Beck's reading list) and the Texas Republican and pseudo-historian David Barton (who argues Christian individualism undergirds the Constitution and promotes the free market).

Not that this linkage has everyone on the right happy. Koch and his allies created libertarian institutions to try to create a free market base to the Republican Party that counters its reliance on conservative evangelicals. While the Koch-founded Americans for Prosperity has accommodated the social conservatives, other institutions like the Cato Institute and FreedomWorks appear less happy with conservative Christian elements powering parts of the Tea Party and promoting the anti-Muslim story line.

Fourth, some classes think they respond better to a "flexible" economy than others. They feel they don't need or benefit from the larger infrastructure of government that regulates the economy and creates a social safety net for retirees and those the economy leaves behind. It seemed like everyone we interviewed in Nevada was a fairly privileged businessperson or retiree who had sold their successful business. Some said they were ready to do without Social Security or Medicare for the sake of the country.

Fifth, party institutions are becoming less important, as big money backs individuals rather than a party, but also because fewer and fewer Americans identify with political parties. The powerful elements of political parties are no longer the party regulars or central committees but campaigns. Campaigns rely on big donors to deliver soundbites through big advertising buys, bypassing party regulars. This opens the way for Tea Party influence. In the 2010 election, local Tea Party insurgents allied with beltway players to provide the grassroots power that party regulars generally provide. This was certainly true in Nevada; and the *New York Times*' Matt Bai (2010) documented the same dynamic in the campaign for the Delaware Senate seat in 2010 when the Tea Party candidate Christine O'Donnell defeated a moderate Republican congressman in the primary. While clearly the Tea Party has influence, the lack of formal structure within the movement only enlarges the power of GOP-oriented beltway organizations in agenda-setting.

Finally, the backlash against an administered society gives a libertarian edge to the movement. Bureaucratic efforts to rationalize an out of control economy and government bargaining with economic sectors can lead to complex and confusing reforms like the health care overhaul. While the political left opposes the complexity by supporting a government-sponsored single payer health care system, the right casts its lot with large insurance companies. Tea Party members voice concern about government overreach into the lives of citizens and business.

Tea Party Supporters and Ideological Lineages

Despite the political resonance created by Tea Party campaigners, a September 2010 poll found only 11 percent of Americans identified with the Tea Party movement (Public Religion Research Institute 2010, Jones and Cox 2010). A massive *New York Times*/CBS poll in April 2010 found that almost half of Tea Party supporters or a close family member relied on Social Security or Medicare. They were more likely to be evangelical Christians (39 percent, versus 28 percent of all people interviewed). They skewed older, wealthier, and more educated, with 20 percent in families earning more than $100,000 a year, compared to 14 percent of the general public. Sixty-five percent were older than 45. And they were 90 percent white (Zernike and Thee-Brenan 2010). We found various ideologies, frames, and narratives in the diverse Tea Party movement that matched the broad divisions found in national polling data.

Effective framing helps attract recruits to social movements (Goffman 1974, McCarthy and Zald 1977, Snow et al. 1986). Framing also helps explain ideologies to movement members (Oliver and Johnston 2000). A master frame serves as an umbrella under which different constituencies can work on the same issue (Snow and Benford 1992). For the Tea Parties, the master frame is that big government is out of control. Within that, there are many discrete frames and narratives as in other social movements (Ewick and Silbey 1995, Polletta 1998, Davis 2002). Libertarian free market individualists compete with the Christian Right activists to define the movement's goals. The perceived threat of big government to "religious freedom" helps unite them.

Fiscal Conservatives

The Tea Party is a truly grassroots force with existing free market-championing organizations like Americans for Prosperity and FreedomWorks trying to channel it. Zernike and Thee-Brenan (based on the *New York Times* poll and interviews) write that many Tea Party supporters do not want to cut taxes or dismantle Social Security or Medicare, and instead are most concerned about the size of the deficit. Tea Party supporters also seem to fear the prospect of being "administered" by an overreaching federal bureaucracy. The Tea Party activists and staffers, on the other hand, want to both cut taxes and dismantle Medicare and Social Security, unlike many Tea Party supporters. Nonetheless, the activist grassroots organizers, many of them older, get ideological training from youthful free marketers working for the beltway organizations.

Many Tea Partiers spout populist slogans, but some ally and identify with parts of the monied elite like David Koch, the oil industries billionaire, who view the "free market" as a realm of freedom injured by government action and see a redistributive tax system as a form of theft. "Why would I want to raise taxes on the rich when I want to be rich?" asked one retired small business owner.

The angry apocalyptic Tea Party mood fears the federal government's huge $1.3 trillion budget deficit presages America's collapse, and sees "ObamaCare" as a communist folly that will destroy health care in this country. The Tea Party activists we interviewed believed big government is gobbling up the "free market" and destroying the businesses it needs to rely on for its tax base. The Keynesian idea that there are times when the government must invest in the economy and jobs if the private sector is stuck, and even former Federal Reserve Chairman Alan Greenspan's support for tax hikes to reduce the deficit were dismissed as tired discredited theories, "socialist," or even class warfare. Embracing trickle-down economics like a life jacket, they saw cutting taxes as the only way to soothe the churning waters of an economy in trouble.

This is not the Silent Majority but a very vocal minority. More than 80 percent of Tea Party supporters oppose raising taxes on families making over $250,000, compared to the majority of all Americans who say raise taxes on the rich. In early August 2011, the specter of raising taxes on the rich galvanized the 70-plus strong Tea Party Caucus in Congress during the struggle over raising the debt limit, but we heard similar opposition to tax hikes on the wealthy in interviews at the grassroots.

The free market orientation of the Tea Party is consistent with the traditional Republican Party stance on economic matters. The movement can be understood within shifting party structures and alignments. Michael Rogin (1967), an influential critic of Hofstadter's interpretation of the conspiratorial right, pointed out that McCarthyism emerged within business-as-usual conflicts of party politics, as a new GOP establishment willing to accommodate the New Deal threatened to eclipse the right-wing forces which had been in charge. Many Tea Partiers are frustrated with the Republican Party establishment and feel that it has not stood by its traditional policy of fiscal restraint, and have turned to the Tea Party as an avenue for promoting their fiscal ideals.

In Nevada we met a well-off retired couple who attend church regularly and like Social Security and Medicare, who worried that the country would collapse under the weight of the federal deficit. But raising taxes on the wealthy to help with the deficit was class warfare, and Obama was a socialist, from their point of view. They are not right-wing populists, scapegoating immigrants or poor blacks, or "birthers" who believe President Obama is a secret Muslim, but former medium-sized business owners who identified with the elite. They, and others we met, are members of what sociologists used to call the "old middle class," a core base of traditional conservatism in the US with no sign of grievances against Wall Street.

While the Cato Institute, the Koch-funded libertarian think tank in Washington DC, and other Koch-funded beltway allies want to claim a libertarian, free market-loving coherence to the movement, many local Tea Partiers continue to support big government programs and just fear the feds have overreached, putting their own entitlements at risk. The small business owner we quoted who wants tax cuts for the wealthy also supports Medicare and Social Security, and thought media disinformation was to blame for statements to privatize the programs by Sharron Angle, his candidate of choice for Senate in his home state of Nevada in 2010.

Libertarians

Some of the beltway groups supporting local Tea Party activists, like Americans for Prosperity and FreedomWorks, seemed to be created in order to nurture a libertarian voting base so that the GOP would not be dependent on Christian conservatives to win office. But now many Tea Partiers are showing Christian conservative colors—only about a quarter of those polled who align themselves with the Tea Party say they are libertarians while 75 percent call themselves conservative Christians—and the two groups are split (Public Religion Research Institute 2011a, Montgomery 2012). Americans for Prosperity keeps supporting the free market Christian conservatives who take up the Tea Party banner, ignoring their religious arguments, while FreedomWorks seems uncomfortable with religious right Tea Partiers.

An exemplary ideological libertarian involved in Tea Party efforts is David Grabaskas, who arrived for an interview at the Ohio State University (OSU) student union in April 2010 as co-founder and president of the OSU chapter of Young Americans for Liberty (Grabaskas 2010a, 2010b, Young Americans for Liberty 2010a, 2010b). Grabaskas had just spoken at an April 15 tax day protest down the street at the state capitol building in Columbus. Grabaskas, at the time a PhD candidate studying nuclear engineering, squeezed in the interview in the midst of a flurry of organizing activities.

Grabaskas explained that Young Americans for Liberty (YAL) started as an outgrowth of students working on the Ron Paul presidential campaign. Grabaskas was also the Youth Outreach Coordinator for the Ohio Freedom Alliance which co-sponsored the April 15 rally along with the Columbus Tea Party and several other groups (Grabaskas 2010a, Young Americans for Liberty 2010b). A former socialist, Grabaskas came to believe "the whole financial system" in the United States was "a fraud." He also was against US wars in the Middle East. This drew him towards Ron Paul. Grabaskas said YAL was formed in part because the conservative "Young Americans for Freedom over the years basically had turned into the Young Republicans." YAL welcomes the participation of "limited government conservatives, classical liberals, and libertarians." Among the group's core beliefs are that "government is the negation of liberty ... voluntary action is the only ethical behavior [and] violent action is only warranted in defense of one's property (Young Americans for Liberty, 2010a).

The Christian Right

Nearly half of Tea Party supporters said they were conservative Christians in polling by the Public Religion Research Institute (2011a). Two-thirds say abortion should be illegal. Fewer than 20 percent support gay marriage. Similarly, Tea Party supporters "tend to have conservative opinions not just about economic matters, but also about social issues such as abortion and same-sex marriage" (Clement and Green 2011). Although some 27 percent of registered voters "expressed agreement" with the Tea Party Movement, Tea Partiers are much more likely than registered voters as a whole to say that their religion is the most important factor in determining their opinions on these social issues. And they draw disproportionate support from the ranks of white evangelical Protestants (Clement and Green 2011).

The studies suggest that "most people who agree with the religious right also support the Tea Party" but that "support for the Tea Party is not synonymous with support for the religious right." Forty-six percent of Tea Party supporters "had not heard of or did not have an opinion about" the Christian Right. Yet 42 percent "said they agree with the conservative Christian movement" (Clement and Green 2011). As has been true for roughly 30 years, some 16 percent of registered voters leaving polling places say they support the Christian Right.

Both Christine O'Donnell in Delaware and Sharron Angle in Nevada are among the new breed of right-wing Christian free marketers that includes Mike Huckabee, the former Arkansas governor who supports a flat tax, Sarah Palin, and Michele Bachmann, the Minnesota Congresswoman who launched the House Tea Party Caucus. O'Donnell and Angle were backed in their primaries by the anti-tax beltway group Club for Growth and Tea Party Express, a paper-thin front operated by Republican consultants in California (Brant-Zawadzki and Teo 2009, Burghart and Zeskind 2010).

Angle's primary win in 2010 does more than reveal the anti-federal government furor of the Tea Party moment. Her campaign, and that of O'Donnell, are ground zero in state-level party systems where local leaders fade further in importance as beltway players deploy corporate and other big money to promote "free market" ideologies among elected officials. And their Christian free market ideology shows the success of a 20-year strategy of free marketers to blend their ideology with the Christian Right, so that the social conservatives who make up much of the voting base of the Republican Party would embrace the low-tax, anti-New Deal politics of the economic conservatives. This made them compatible with the Tea Party moment and comfortable under its anti-government umbrella. However, plenty of Tea Partiers did not embrace their conservative Christianity.

A Southern Baptist who became politicized in the conservative Christian homeschooling movement of the 1980s, Angle spoke frankly to Christian broadcasters about the religious roots of her anti-federal government sentiment, even though her state is dominated by Roman Catholics and Mormons and keeps gambling and prostitution legal. Echoing an analysis promoted by the fundamentalist Christian Reconstructionist movement, she said in an April 2010 interview that Social Security and other parts of the government safety net are a form of idolatry that violates God's First Commandment:

> Entitlement programs ... make government our God. And that's really what's happening in this country is a violation of the First Commandment. We have become a country entrenched in idolatry, and that idolatry is the dependency upon our government. We're supposed to depend upon God for our protection and our provision and for our daily bread, not for our government. (Angle interviewed in Ralston 2010)

Angle's home state of Nevada, however, is a place where the Christian Right is notably weak so she raised some hackles. Her remark was just too much for Sherman Frederick, the libertarian-oriented publisher of the daily newspaper *Las Vegas Review Journal* who is a consistent champion of ever lower taxes:

> Angle spouts some religious stuff that not only makes her look politically bad, it gives people of faith—like, say our Founding Fathers—a black eye ... Our government was created by men who believed in God. And they crafted the government to provide a common protection. That wasn't idolatry. Expansion of that common protection to include things like Social Security, or even national health care (though I think it is a bad idea) is not necessarily idolatry. (2010)

So some people in Nevada shared a conservative Christian analysis that echoed Glenn Beck. Others fit Nevada's profile as not a very churchy place. Yet the tension between Tea Partiers and libertarians continued through the September 2012 Republican National Convention, where the libertarian Ron Paul delegates from the state led a protest against rule changes that consolidate future control of delegates in the hands of the winning candidate.

White Racial Antagonism

Tea Partiers show greater racial grievance than white evangelicals as a whole (a group that includes some liberals). Fifty-eight percent of Tea Partiers say minorities get too much government attention while the figure is 38 percent for white evangelicals (Public Religion Research Institute 2010). Other surveys by the Public Religion Research Institute (2011b, 2011c) reveal Tea Partier opposition to diversity and immigration. Studies by Parker (2010) and Keil and Keil (2012) found significant racial antagonism among Tea Party supporters toward blacks and Latinos.

This fit our experiences in the field. In Nevada we met a few Asian Americans who were Tea Party supporters, and listened to a handful of African Americans visiting from out of state. Otherwise everyone was white. Most were retired, since Nevada, as the lowest taxed state in the nation, attracts a lot of retirees. In Ohio, one Latino man carried a sign to a statehouse Tea Party rally noting his ethnicity and daring reporters to interview him. At a meeting in Idaho, everyone in the Fuddruckers restaurant private dining room looked white.

By using elaborate social science variable analysis, the Center for Social Inclusion (CSI) found a connection between economic issues, race, and voter support for Tea Party messages:

> Tea Party successes have been driven by a combination of economic insecurity and race. Our analysis shows that in congressional districts with economic insecurity, Tea Party candidates won 9 of 10 races where the White population is above 60 percent, while losing 7 of 10 races where the population of color is above 40 percent. Yet, in districts with higher economic security, Tea Party candidates failed in all but three races—[running against] incumbents representing White populations above 70 percent. (2010)

The *New York Times*/CBS poll in April 2010 found that "Tea Party supporters over all are more likely than the general public to say their personal financial situation is fairly good or very good" (Zernike and Thee-Brenan 2010). And this and other polls have shown that Tea Party supporters on average have higher incomes than most other Americans, although the degree of their higher income and wealth is often exaggerated by critics.

Fear and experiences of economic decline, however, are rampant among Tea Party supporters. The same *New York Times*/CBS poll found that "55 percent are concerned that someone in their household will be out of a job in the next year. And more than two-thirds say the recession has been difficult or caused hardship and major life changes" (Zernike and Thee-Brenan 2010).

The CSI study demonstrates how economic stress and racism among whites is linked. CSI found that "in congressional districts facing economic stress, the Tea Party used economic insecurity and growing racial fears to win in majority-White districts." Yet in predominantly white "congressional districts not in foreclosure distress" voters tended not "to support Tea Party candidates. Race was correlated with Tea Party victory, but not class." In those districts that had "large numbers of people of color and high foreclosure rates" there were few Tea Party candidate victories. According to the CSI report:

> The Tea Party's strategy of dividing voters along subtle, and not so subtle, references to race and ethnicity works in White economically distressed communities, but not necessarily White economically healthy communities or communities with sizable populations of color.

The purge of the Latino Caucus from the Nevada Republican Party after the Tea Party takeover made racial grievance visible. Tibi Ellis, the head of the state's Latino Caucus, was barred from participating in state party calls:

> The extreme conservatives say, well we're all Americans we don't have to cater to any group, but we do—we have a veterans' coalition, a business coalition, a Jewish coalition ... If anything will show how radical this new leadership is, it's things like that. Nobody is calling me to the table to see what my community is doing.

Other members of the Tea Party reveal what Joseph Lowndes called "a strong desire for racial innocence" (2012: 161). They affirm racial equality but overlook the practices that create inequality. And they assert a small government ethos that would explicitly leave the "less productive" behind. As the Nevada housewife said:

> Anytime you are taking from one group of people and giving to another, you are denying the rights of a group. Taking from the wealthy—you can't continue to take their money, give it to people who are less productive. What is part and parcel of the American spirit and what people don't understand is giving charity is not something you can demand from people.
>
> We are looking for our tax money being invested in our community. The small business owners who are creating the opportunity for 40 to 80,000 people to have a job—when tax policy comes down, we're taxed like the billionaires. We believe we should pay for certain infrastructure. We are not antitax. We are pro-home rule. If we're going to be taxed, I want that to be benefitting my community, not Detroit. Sorry Detroit.

Producerism and Race

Behind much Tea Party rhetoric is the claim that hard-working productive middle-class citizens are being squeezed in an economic vise—from above by high government taxes, onerous regulations, and monetary policies set by greedy bankers, and from below by lazy, sinful, and subversive parasites (Berlet and Lyons 2000, Berlet 2012). This narrative is called "producerism," and traces back to an essay by William Manning (1799). Republican Presidential candidate Mitt Romney invoked producerism in his videoed suggestion that 47 percent of the US population were government-dependent (Mother Jones 2012).

Michael Kazin (1995) explains that producerism is central to right-wing forms of populism, and involves white racial anger and resentment. Williams (1992, 1997) traces this to an organized right-wing campaign, dating back to the 1960s, to portray those receiving certain government benefits as the "undeserving poor," with a clear subtext that these people were predominantly non-white. Lo (1995) found similar subtexts in the tax revolt of the 1970s. Hardisty (1999) writes about the cynical use of racialized caricatures of the "undeserving poor" as "mobilizing resentment" among the white middle class to build right-wing social movements. The outcome has been devastating for poor families and welfare recipients (Morgen et al. 2010).

Clarence Lo (1995) has shown that the 1970s Anti-Tax movement sprang from the anger of white homeowners who resented state and federal initiatives to help poor and underemployed people—seen (inaccurately) as overwhelmingly composed of black people and other people of color. The scapegoats were "faceless bureaucrats," "tax and spend Democrats," "utopian social engineers," and "liberal elites." Racism was clearly involved, but so was fear of falling down the economic ladder. The economic distress in populist movements can be measurably real, realistically anticipated, or based on a sense of relative deprivation that is a blend of concrete and imaginary fears (Berlet 2012).

In researching the Klan of the 1920s, Rory McVeigh (2009) argues that shifting power dynamics disrupting traditional hierarchies in economic, political, and social power relationships launch the processes by which right-wing groups mobilize a mass base large enough to intrude into public debates in the larger society. The economic downturn of 2008 has left millions of people in the United States unemployed or underemployed. Even when still holding down a job, the mostly white, middle-class, Republican Tea Party activists are afraid of the possibility that their economic, political, or social status may drop—just as McVeigh theorizes (Berlet, 2010, 2012).

Past right-wing populist movements have been accompanied by the perception that economic security was being threatened. This has been shown with the progressive Prairie populists of the 1880s, the Ku Klux Klan of the 1920s, and the Patriot and armed citizen militias movements of the 1990s (Ostler 1993, Kaplan 1998, Van Dyke and Soule 2002). In her study of the Patriot and armed citizens militia movements Gallaher found that these mostly male and white activists stand on a fault line because they:

> occupy conflicting social positions. On the one hand, their class positionality, which leaves them captive to the ebb and flow of the global market, creates the context for their oppression as workers. On the other, their dominant racial and gender positions oppress by virtue of their normativity, even if the individuals in question do not set out to do so. (2002: 215)

One issue that stumped analysts for decades was that in the 1920s the Ku Klux Klan built a mass movement that attracted millions of white followers from relatively mainstream segments of the Protestant middle class, at a time when the economy was not just roaring but booming. McVeigh (2009) reviewed Klan literature and found that members feared losing economic power at a time of national prosperity due to their experience of threatened competition from upwardly-mobile Catholics and blacks.

It apparently is the perception of losing power, privilege, and status in economic, political, and social spheres (race, religion, gender) that matters, not statistical economic indicators. This gives new life to slightly revised versions of earlier theories seeking to explain right-wing movements such as Status Anxiety and Relative Deprivation (Gurr 1970, Tatlovich and Smith 2001). Even Hofstadter's theory of the Paranoid Style (1965) polishes up nicely if filtered through the lens of more recent scholarship on millenarian, millennial, and apocalyptic groups.

Economic power, however, acts independently from social power, because as Tatalovich and Smith note:

> values—not economics—lie at the heart of these disputes, and "status" claims are inherited by tradition and custom rather than defined through market forces. Governments intervene in the marketplace to achieve distributive goals, but status equalization looks toward the erosion of (largely private-sector) social hierarchies. These social interactions are fundamentally dissimilar from economic transactions. (2001: 6)

The Patriot Movement

A part of the Tea Party Movement that national polls do not capture is the way it builds on elements of the pre-existing Patriot Movement, especially those who also self-identify as supporting the Christian Right. The Patriot Movement is the umbrella name for a variety of historic right-wing populist groups that see themselves as defending the United States against subversion from without and within. In the 1950s and 1960s, their focus was stopping communism and pornography. In the 1990s, the Patriot Movement spawned a number of armed citizen militias across the nation, but most potently in the Northwest. The quintessential national Patriot (Americanist) organization is the John Birch Society. A central frame of the Patriot movement is right-wing populism mixed with conspiracy theories about betrayal. Historically, similar movements have been described in the social science literature as Nativist, 100% Americanism, Anti-Communist, Constitutionalist, Ethno-Nationalism, Middle-American Radicalism, and White Nationalism (Berlet and Lyons 2000).

Nevada Senate candidate Sharron Angle was seen as aligned with remnants of the Patriot Movement in her state, and armed, anti-immigrant border campaigners in the Southwest became associated with the Tea Party movement. The national Tea Party umbrella came to cover this regional far right phenomenon (Scher 2010a, 2010b).

Conspiracy Theories

Conspiracism as an ideological element of social movements appears episodically in American history. Robert Alan Goldberg explains:

> For generations, Americans have entertained visions of vast conspiracies that target their religion, race, and nation. Salem witches, British ministers, Catholic priests, slaveholders, Wall Street bankers, Jews, Bolsheviks, and black militants, all in their turn and among many other suspects, have been cast in the plotters role. (2001: x)

David Brion Davis argues that social and political movements to counter the "threat of conspiratorial subversion" gained strength early on because the country was "born in revolution and based on the sovereignty of the people" (1971: xv–xvi). He also observed that "crusades against subversion have never been the monopoly of a single social class or ideology, but have been readily appropriated by highly diverse groups" (Davis 1971: xvi). According to Goldberg "Conspiracism thrives when power is exercised at a distance by seemingly selfish groups zealous in their authority [and] all are susceptible to the prompting of conspiracy thinking, with class and gender lines offering no barriers" (2001: 188). Furthermore, conspiracist belief "demands confrontation and breeds activism and social movement mobilization" (Goldberg 2001: 188). In the past this has generated subversion, panics and countersubversive social movements.

Many Tea Party supporters have gained ideological training in the threat of liberal subversion from Glenn Beck, the loquacious former Fox network star and current talk radio host. Beck resuscitated old John Birch Society conspiracy writings to help make sense of the moment for many anxious Americans. Beck also teaches a fundamentalist view of the US Constitution that portrays it as a Christian individualist document undergirding the free market that has been distorted by liberal amendments such as that supporting a progressive income tax.

Conspiracy theories are widely believed in contemporary American society and dispersed through a dense national network of individuals, groups, and social movement organizations (Social Movement Study Network 2012). The villains identified include Freemasons, Jesuits, Jews, liberal elites, Muslims, and agents of Satan in the End Times (Goldberg 2001, Barkun 2003, Berlet 2004). Many scholars and journalists dismiss conspiracy claims as irrelevant, but this is a mistake because they can play a role in mobilizing political power struggles (Fenster 1999).

Right-wing conspiracy theorists appear not only on Fox News, but on a myriad of broadcast cable TV and radio programs and thousands of websites. The History Channel has a special series on conspiracies that outlines the alleged plot in detail and then gives a few comments from someone skeptical of the conspiracy theory. Conspiracy-oriented right-wing speakers continuously crisscross the United States appearing at local meetings of veterans groups, conservative and Republican clubs, and other brick and mortar social networks including local chapters of the Chamber of Commerce, Daughters of the American Revolution, the Federated Republican Women's Club, Hadassah, Kiwanis, and Rotary. Articles about subversion and liberal conspiracies appear in publications distributed to active and retired members of the armed services (Social Movement Study Network 2012).

Conspiracy theories about creeping socialism were being woven into the Tea Party collection of narratives from the very beginning. On February 15, 2009, nationally-known conservative blogger Michelle Malkin urged for tax protests to be scheduled nationwide. Her news peg was a Seattle protest scheduled for the next day. One of the organizers posted a comment thanking Malkin for the publicity. Other commenters worried that stopping federal "pork-barrel" spending was not enough. "We've lost our Constitutional Republic to the calls for Democracy, hence a socialistic oligarchy" read one comment. For one commenter both major political parties were to blame, complaining that "the Dems turned into Marxists and the Republicans turned into Socialists." A response added "due to the Marxist 'sensuality cartel' (e.g. the media and cinema) and the illiteracy cartel … (public schools), they will succeed. Most people will *ask* for socialism in the end, just watch" (Malkin blogsite 2009). Malkin's call for a national anti-tax protest movement and the subsequent comments about subversive conspiracies were made four days *before* the famed "Santelli Rant" widely reported as "launching" the Tea Party movement and framing it exclusively around government spending. We found, however, that exaggerated fears of socialism and conservative social issues were also important within the Tea Party movement from the beginning.

Repeating a story popularized by Glenn Beck, one Nevada woman says President Obama's family "belonged to the communist view" and attended a "little red church" during the 1950s, giving him "an experience of America that has nothing to do with me. He seems to see America as narrow minded, oppressive people. Everyone knows he's apologized all over the world with America being an oppressor." A *Chicago Tribune* reporter had quoted the Unitarian Church's present day pastor as joking that the Mercer Island church off the coast of Seattle was called the "little red church," liberal for its time. Based on little more than that, Beck has called Obama's grandparents Communists and un-American (Jones with Scharnberg and Loering 2007). With Obama's auto bailout and health care reform, this politics of demonization comes back to life as people reach for a framework that fits their sentimental predisposition (Scher 2010a).

One frame that spread among Tea Partiers combined Christian Right ideas with conspiracy theory. This frame presented an apocalyptic vision of Barack Obama as the Antichrist, an agent of Satan, coming disguised as a "man of peace." It was first heard during the 2008 campaign, and spread as Republican partisans generated suspicions of Obama's religion and foreign birthplace. In the grassroots and in the blogosphere, the frame of Obama as an imposter betraying America spread with increasing xenophobia and fear of immigrants and people of color (Berlet 2010, 2011, Duffy et al. 2012).

The conspiracism in Nevada was directed not just at President Obama, the socialistic imposter, but at fellow Republicans who didn't understand the danger. Thus Tea Partiers took control of the Nevada and Vegas area Republican Party in 2010, purging the establishment leaders who ran operations on the ground and wooed big local donors. While very conservative, these leaders raised local money and were willing to work with more moderate members of the party representing more liberal areas who the Tea Partiers, backed up by Fox television's Glenn Beck and right-wing websites, see as the enemy. Also the enemy was the then-Senate Minority leader, a Reno area Republican who backed tax hikes in this, the lowest-taxed state in the union, to save its budget from the recession-induced meltdown.

"Most of us who left are indeed fiscal conservatives and ardent supporters of constitutional rights, so the 'Marxist' accusation is a reflection of the deep paranoia and delusion within the current CCRP leadership," said the former chairman of the Las Vegas area Clark County Republican Party (CCRP) after he stepped down. "If we have to purge the RINOs (Republicans in Name Only) from power before we purge the fascists in power, so be it," replied an unrepentant Tea Partier. This echoes claims made on the national level. "The secular-socialist machine represents as great a threat to America as Nazi Germany or the Soviet Union once did," Newt Gingrich wrote in his book *To Save America* (2010: 4).

The overheated rhetoric in the Tea Party about Obama, liberals, and socialists destroying the "American Way of Life" is a form of demonization not uncommon in the bare-fist battles in political life throughout US history. Rogin (1987) refers to this in the public sphere as "episodes in political demonology." The demonization of an adversary involves well-established psychological processes (Lifton 1961, Noël 1994, Altemeyer 1996, Young-Bruehl 1996, Harrington 2004). This, however, does not imply any psychological dysfunction. Augusto, who studied the use of rhetorical demonization in opposing abortion-focused groups, found "the process by which one group cultivates a negative and oftentimes misleading image of an opposing group" actually "accounts for a great deal of the interaction between movements and counter-movements and plays an important role in how each side views itself and its opposition" (2009: 3).

Tilly (1978) suggested spreading fears of a serious threat was an effective way to build a social movement. Since the 1960s, right-wing movement leaders have skillfully exploited fears in the middle class and working class that their economic, social, and political stock was falling (Ehrenreich 1989, Kazin 1992, 1995, Hardisty 1999, Frank 2004). In the 1990s, Patriot movements and armed citizen militias formed around fears of an impending UN attack and the establishment of a socialist New World Order (Berlet and Lyons, 2000). Van Dyke and Soule (2002) found that different participation levels for these groups were explained in part by the presence of stressful structural social changes within each state. Once again this fits the power devaluation theory proposed by McVeigh (2009).

It is the perception of the threat that matters for mobilization, not the reality, although both can exist simultaneously. This demonstrates the Thomas Theorem, which observes that for movement actors, situations defined as real are real in their consequences (Thomas and Thomas, 1970 [1928]). When fears and anxieties are used in a movement mobilization they can be shaped by the use of demonization and scapegoating (Allport 1954). The way demonization intersects with conspiracism can produce apocalyptic timetables in which scapegoated groups are seen as poised on the brink of destroying the threatened idealized community (O'Leary 1994, Berlet 2011). Anthony and Robbins (1997, 1996) have explored the role of apocalyptic narratives that demonize an "Other" using a story line warning that time is running out to save the idealized community.

These apocalyptic warnings of impending doom are often part of a masculinist rhetorical strategy used to quickly mobilize action (Quinby 1994, 1997, 1999). But women embrace the demonization too. As the *Wall Street Journal* first reported, Sharron Angle was a member of the right-wing Christian, gun-toting, anti-government, income-tax-hating Independent American Party of Nevada during the 1990s while serving on a local school board in the Reno area

(Radnofsky 2010). This statewide party that thinks Republicans are "too corrupt and socialistic" still fields candidates and has 60,000 people on its voter rolls. It echoes larger Patriot Movement narratives warning archly of America losing its sovereignty to a North American Union encompassing Mexico and Canada, and calling for public lands to be transferred to private control or the United Nations (Berlet 2009).

Conclusions

Scholars, serious journalists, and other observers disagree as to what the Tea Party movement and moment represents. In fairness to us all, it is difficult to analyze a social movement in real time in the age of the internet, social media, and the hungry omnivorous 15-minutes-of-fame cable TV news cycle. Still, at the height of the Presidential campaign in October of 2012, Arun Gupta and Michelle Fawcet wrote "Romney appeals to white tribalism in Ohio," for the *Progressive* magazine. Citing Thomas Frank (2004) and Political Research Associates (2010), the authors identified the political moment and movement as built around right-wing "populist politics of resentment" and "invoking 'producerism,' telling Americans bruised by the downturn that your pain is due to social factors, which are presented as coded racial categories" (Gupta and Fawcet 2012).

The first wave of books on the Tea Party takes a variety of approaches to their examination of the movement. Jill Lepore provides an excellent corrective counterpoint to the Tea Partiers' revisionist history of the United States, and discusses the right-wing role in revising textbooks. Her main focus, however, is not the movement itself, although each chapter starts with a fascinating contemporary anecdote (Lepore 2010: esp. 3–16). Skocpol and Williamson treat the Tea Party and its participants as an instrumental social movement, but spend little space placing the Tea Party in analytical historic perspective. Street and DiMaggio (2011) contend that the Tea Party is not a real social movement at all, but a pseudo-movement fiction created by elites. They refer to "false" populism (Street and DiMaggio 2011: 141–4). Kate Zernike, a journalist by trade, provides the most detailed picture of the Tea Party as a form of social movement populism in her book *Boiling Mad: Inside Tea Party America* (2010). She cites Kazin (1995) on populism from the right (Zernike 2010: 53–4), McGirr (2001) on 1960s anti-communism providing the basis for Tea Party anti-collectivism (Zernike 2010: 54–5), and Warren (1976) on "Middle American Radicals" (Zernike 2010: 57–8). The value of using right-wing populism to describe the Tea Parties—or using different terms such as White Citizenship Movement, Precariat, Middle American Radicals, Anti-Statist Populism, or White Nationalism—is debated by scholars, and discussed in an edited collection on the Tea Parties (Rosenthal and Trost 2012; see esp. chapters by Berlet, Disch, Lowndes, and Postel).

While not all Tea Partiers are right-wing populists, we identify the Tea Party movement as a form of "right-wing populism" because we believe this terminology illuminates one of its most vital aspects. The ancient poet Heraclitus reminds us that "Everything changes and ... you cannot step twice into the same stream"; yet when he calls it a stream, we know of the fluid entity to which he refers. Right-wing populist movements always appear in different guises at different moments and different places, yet they share certain basic similarities.

The Tea Party illuminates and reflects the old cleavages of the 1950s—when some of the GOP accepted Roosevelt's New Deal, and those who didn't saw McCarthyism as an opportunity to roll it back. These clashes are being reinvigorated. This is promoted once again in part by a mass media phenomenon, and during the election race of 2012, a national Republican Party willing to ride the wave as long as it lasted.

In Nevada, at least, a few Republicans were uncomfortable as the election unfolded. That may not matter in the modern political world as campaign machines outstrip party structures in importance, and national groups led by political entrepreneurs like Karl Rove and Newt Gingrich ride in to shape up weakened local parties. Yet following the re-election of President Barack Obama there were voices inside the Republican Party urging the leadership to throw the Tea Party ideologues overboard, at least in terms of Republican Party institutional power and committee assignments in the House of Representatives.

The internal GOP struggles for power will be playing out long after this volume goes to press. Exactly when the Tea Party moment will pass is unpredictable; but when it does, another right-wing populist formation will start brewing.

References

Allport, G.W. 1954. *The Nature of Prejudice*. Cambridge, MA: Addison-Wesley.

Altemeyer, B. 1996. *The Authoritarian Specter*. Cambridge, MA: Harvard University Press.

Anthony, D. and Robbins, T. 1996. Religious totalism, violence and exemplary dualism: beyond the extrinsic model, in *Millennialism and Violence*, Cass Series on Political Violence, edited by M. Barkun. London: Frank Cass, 10–50.

Anthony, D. and Robbins, T. 1997. Religious totalism, exemplary dualism, and the Waco tragedy, in *Millennium, Messiahs, and Mayhem: Contemporary Apocalyptic Movements*, edited by T. Robbins, and S.J Palmer. New York: Routledge, 261–84.

Augusto, S. 2009. Lighting the fire inside: Vilification in the pro-life and pro-choice movements. Paper presented to the 104th annual meeting of the American Sociological Association, San Francisco, August 7–9. Available at: http://citation.allacademic.com/meta/p_mla_apa_research_citation/3/0/9/5/1/pages309519/p309519-1.php [accessed September 23, 2013].

Bai, M. 2010. Delaware race is a bellweather: All politics is national. *New York Times* [Online: September 29]. Available at: http://www.nytimes.com/2010/09/30/us/politics/30bai.html [accessed November 20, 2012].

Barkun, M. 2003. *A Culture of Conspiracy: Apocalyptic Visions in Contemporary America*. Berkeley: University of California Press.

Bartels, L.M. 2008. *Unequal Democracy: The Political Economy of the New Gilded Age*. Princeton: Princeton University Press.

Berezin, M. 2009. *Illiberal Politics in Neoliberal Times: Culture, Security and Populism in the New Europe*. New York: Cambridge University Press.

Berlet, C. 2004. Anti-Masonic conspiracy theories: A narrative form of demonization and scapegoating, in *Freemasonry in Context: History, Ritual, Controversy*, edited by A. de Hoyos and S.B. Morris. Lanham, MD: Rowman & Littlefield.

Berlet, C. 2009. Fears of fédéralisme in the United States: The case of the "North American Union" conspiracy theory, *Fédéralisme Régionalisme*, (9)1 [Online]. Available at: http://popups.ulg.ac.be/federalisme/document.php?id=786 [accessed December 12, 2012].

Berlet, C. 2010. The roots of anti-Obama rhetoric, in *Race in the Age of Obama*, Research in Race and Ethnic Relations 16, edited by D. Cunnigen and B.A. Marino. Bingley, West Yorkshire: Emerald, 301–19.

Berlet, C. 2011. Protocols to the left, protocols to the right: Conspiracism in American political discourse at the turn of the second millennium, in *The Paranoid Apocalypse: A Hundred-year Retrospective on the Protocols of the Elders of Zion*, edited by R. Landes and S. Katz. New York: New York University Press, 186–216. An earlier version, *Toxic to Democracy*, is online and available at: http://www.politicalresearch.org/wp-content/uploads/downloads/2012/11/Toxic-2D-all-rev-04.pdf [accessed January 12, 2012].

Berlet, C. 2012. Reframing populist resentments in the Tea Party Movement, in *Steep: The Precipitous Rise of the Tea Party*, edited by L. Rosenthal and C. Trost. Berkeley: University of California Press, 47–66.

Berlet, C. and Lyons, M. 2000. *Right-wing Populism in America: Too Close for Comfort*. New York: Guilford Press.

Brant-Zawadzki, A. and Teo, D. 2009. Anatomy of the Tea Party movement. *Huffington Post* [Online: December 11]. Available at: http://www.huffingtonpost.com/alex-brantzawadzki/anatomy-of-the-tea-party_b_380592.html [accessed December 12, 2012]. See also profiles of other groups linked at this page.

Buckley, W.F. 1955. Our mission statement. *National Review*, November 19 [Online]. Availiable at: http://www.nationalreview.com/articles/223549/our-mission-statement/william-f-buckley-jr [accessed January 5, 2013].

Burghart, D. and Zeskind, L. 2010. *Tea Party Nationalism: A Critical Examination of the Tea Party Movement and the Size, Scope, and Focus of Its National Factions*. Institute for Research & Education on Human Rights [Online: Fall 2010]. Available at: http://www.irehr.org/news/special-reports/item/443-tea-party-nationalism-report-pdf [accessed December 5, 2012].

Canovan, M. 1980. *Populism*. New York: Harcourt Brace Jovanovich.

Center for Social Inclusion. 2010. *Race Reaction: Voter Responses to Tea Party Messages in Economically Stressed Communities* [Online: November]. Available at: http://www.centerforsocialinclusion.org/race-reaction-voter-responses-to-tea-party-messages-in-economically-stressed-communities [accessed December 12, 2012].

Clement, S. and Green, J.C. 2011. *The Tea Party, Religion and Social Issues*. Pew Forum on Religion & Public Life, Washington DC [Online February 23]. Available at: http://pewresearch.org/pubs/1903/tea-party-movement-religion-social-issues-conservative-christian [accessed December 12, 2012].

Davis, D.B. 1971. Introduction, in *Fear of Conspiracy Images of Un-American Subversion from the Revolution to the Present*, edited by D.B. Davis. Ithaca, NY: Cornell University Press.

Davis, J., ed. 2002. *Stories of Change: Narrative and Social Movements*. Albany, NY: SUNY Press.

Disch, L. 2012. The Tea Party: A "white citizenship" movement?, in *Steep: The Precipitous Rise of the Tea Party*, edited by L. Rosenthal and C. Trost. Berkeley: University of California Press, 133–51.

Duffy, M., Page, J.T., and Young, R. 2012. Obama as anti-American: Visual folklore in right-wing forwarded e-mails and construction of conservative social identity. *Journal of American Folklore*, 125(496), 177–203.

Ehrenreich, B. 1989. *Fear of Falling: The Inner Life of the Middle Class*. New York: Harper Perennial.

Ewick, P. and Silbey, S.S. 1995. Subversive stories and hegemonic tales: Toward a sociology of narrative. *Law & Society Review*, 29(2), 197–226.

Fenster, M. 1999. *Conspiracy Theories: Secrecy and Power in American Culture*. Minneapolis: University of Minnesota Press.

Frank, T. 2004. *What's the Matter with Kansas? How Conservatives Won the Heart of America*. New York: Metropolitan.

Frederick, S. 2010. Oh my God! *Las Vegas Review Journal* [Online: August 5]. Available at: http://www.lvrj.com/blogs/sherm/Oh_My_God.html [accessed January 6, 2012].

Gallaher, C. 2002. *On the Fault Line: Race, Class, and the American Patriot Movement*. Lanham, MD: Rowman & Littlefield.

Gingrich, N. 2010. *To Save America: Stopping Obama's Secular-Socialist Machine*. Washington DC: Regnery.

Goffman, E. 1974. *Frame Analysis: An Essay on the Organization of Experience*. Cambridge, MA: Harvard University Press.

Goldberg, R.A. 2001. *Enemies Within: The Culture of Conspiracy in Modern America*. New Haven, CT: Yale University Press.

Grabaskas, D. 2010a. Interview with Chip Berlet, April, Columbus, OH.

Grabaskas, D. 2010b. *How a Pseudo-Socialist College Student Became a Tea Partier*. Student Free Press Association [Online: October 29]. http://www.studentfreepress.net/archives/4356 [accessed December 12, 2012].

Gross, N., Medvetz, T., and Russell, R. 2011. The contemporary American conservative movement. *Annual Review of Sociology*, 37, 325–54.

Gupta A. and Fawcett, M. 2012. Romney appeals to white tribalism in Ohio. *The Progressive* [Online: October 15]. Available at: http://www.progressive.org/romney-appeals-to-white-tribalism-in-ohio [accessed December 12, 2012].

Gurr, T.R. 1970. *Why Men Rebel*. Princeton: Princeton University Press.

Habermas, J. 1975. *Legitimation Crisis*. Translated by Thomas McCarthy. Boston: Beacon Press.

Halloran, L. 2010. *What's Behind the New Populism?* National Public Radio [Online: February 5]. Available at: http://www.npr.org/templates/story/story.php?storyId=123137382 [accessed December 12, 2012].

Hardisty, J. 1999. *Mobilizing Resentment: Conservative Resurgence from the John Birch Society to the Promise Keepers*. Boston: Beacon Press.

Harrington, E.R. 2004, The social psychology of hatred, *Journal of Hate Studies*, 3(1), 49–82. Available at http://journals.gonzaga.edu/index.php/johs/article/view/52/33 [accessed April 4, 2013].

Hofstadter, R. 1965. The paranoid style in American politics, in *The Paranoid Style in American Politics and Other Essays*, edited by R. Hofstadter. New York: Alfred A. Knopf.

Jones, R.P. and Cox, D. 2010. *Religion and the Tea Party in the 2010 Elections: An Analysis of the Third Biennial American Values Survey*. Public Religion Research Institute [Online: October]. Available at: http://tinyurl.com/prri-jones-cox-2010 [accessed December 12, 2012]. See also Public Religion Research Institute 2010.

Jones, T. with Scharnberg, K. and Loering, L. 2007. Family portraits: Strong personalities shaped a future senator, Barack Obama. *Chicago Tribune* [Online: March 27]. Available at: http://www.highbeam.com/doc/1G1-161068455.html [accessed December 12, 2012].

Kaplan, D. 1998. Republic of rage: A look inside the Patriot Movement. Paper presented to the 93rd annual meeting of the American Sociological Association, San Francisco, August 21–25.

Kazin, M. 1992. The grass-roots right: New histories of US conservatism in the twentieth century. *American Historical Review*, 97 (February), 136–55.

Kazin, M. 1995. *The Populist Persuasion: An American History*. New York: Basic Books.

Keil, T. and Keil, J.M. 2012. The characteristics of the congressional district and tea party victories in 2010. *Ethnicity and Race in a Changing World: A Review Journal*, 3(1) (Spring), 43–6.

Kintz, L. 1997. *Between Jesus and the Market: The Emotions That Matter in Right-wing America*. Durham, NC: Duke University Press.

Lepore, J. 2010. *The Whites of Their Eyes: The Tea Party's Revolution and the Battle over American History*. Princeton: Princeton University Press.

Levine, S. 2009. McCain's feminist mistake. *In These Times* weblog [Online: September 7]. Available at: http://www.inthesetimes.com/article/3890/ [accessed December 12, 2012].

Lifton, R.J. 1961. *Thought Reform and the Psychology of Totalism: A Study of "Brainwashing" in China*. New York: Norton.

Lilla, M. 2010. The tea party Jacobins. *New York Review of Books* [Online: May 27]. Available at: http://www.nybooks.com/articles/archives/2010/may/27/tea-party-jacobins/ [accessed December 12, 2012].

Lo, C.Y.H. 1995. *Small Property versus Big Government: Social Origins of the Property Tax Revolt*. Berkeley: University of California Press.

Lowndes, J. 2012. The past and future of race in the Tea Party Movement, in *Steep: The Precipitous Rise of the Tea Party*, edited by L. Rosenthal and C. Trost. Berkeley: University of California Press, 152–70.

McCarthy, J.D. and Zald, M.D. 1977. Resource mobilization and social movements: A partial theory. *American Journal of Sociology*, 82(6), 1212–41.

McGirr, L. 2001. *Suburban Warriors: The Origins of the New American Right*. Princeton: Princeton University Press.

McVeigh, R. 2009. *The Rise of the Ku Klux Klan: Right-wing Movements and National Politics*. Minneapolis: University of Minnesota Press.

Malkin, M. 2009. Taxpayer revolt: Porkulus protest in Seattle, Obama to sign Theft Act in Denver. Michelle Malkin blogsite [Online: February 15]. Available at: http://michellemalkin.com/2009/02/15/taxpayer-revolt-porkulus-protest-in-seattle/ [accessed November 10, 2010].

Malkin blogsite. 2009. Blogsite comments section [Online: February 15]. Available at: http://michellemalkin.com/2009/02/15/taxpayer-revolt-porkulus-protest-in-seattle/#comments [accessed November 10, 2010].

Manning, W. 1799. *The Key of Liberty, Shewing the Causes Why a Free Government Has Always Failed, and a Remidy against It, Written in the Year 1798 by William Manning*. Reprinted 1922, Billerica, MA: The Manning Association.

Massey, D.S. 2007. *Categorically Unequal: The American Stratification System*. New York: Russell Sage Foundation.

Mayer, J. 2010. Covert operations: The billionaire brothers who are waging a war against Obama. *The New Yorker* [Online: August 30]. Available at: http://www.newyorker.com/reporting/2010/08/30/100830fa_fact_mayer#ixzz2DGMDIvnT [accessed November 10, 2010].

Meagher, R. 2006. Tax revolt as a family value: How the Christian Right is becoming a free market champion. *Public Eye*, 21(1) (Winter), 8–16.

Miller, L. 2010. The paranoid style of American punditry. *Salon.com* [Online: September 15]. Available at: http://www.salon.com/2010/09/15/hofstadter/ [accessed November 10, 2010].

Montgomery, P. 2012. The Tea Party and the religious right movements: Frenemies with benefits, in *Steep: The Precipitous Rise of the Tea Party*, edited by L. Rosenthal and C. Trost. Berkeley: University of California Press, 242–74.

Moreton, B. 2009. *To Serve God and Wal-Mart: The Making of Christian Free Enterprise*. Cambridge, MA: Harvard University Press.

Morgen, S., Acker, J., and Weigt, J.M. 2010. *Stretched Thin: Poor Families, Welfare Work, and Welfare Reform*. Ithaca, NY: Cornell University Press.

Mother Jones. 2012. Full transcript of the Mitt Romney secret video, *Mother Jones* (web only) [Online: September 19]. Available at: http://www.motherjones.com/politics/2012/09/full-transcript-mitt-romney-secret-video#47percent [accessed November 10, 2012].

Noël, L. 1994. *Intolerance, A General Survey*. Translated by A. Bennett. Montreal: McGill-Queen's University Press.

Ohio Liberty Council. 2010. Political networking and overlay pages. Ohio Liberty Council website [Online: May 1]. Was available at: http://www.ohiolibertycouncil.org/?page_id=300 [accessed May 1, 2010, now offline].

O'Leary, S.D. 1994. *Arguing the Apocalypse: A Theory of Millennial Rhetoric*. New York: Oxford University Press.

Oliver, P.E. and Johnston, H. 2000. What a good idea! Frames and ideologies in social movement research. *Mobilization: An International Journal*, 5(1), 37–54.

Ostler, J. 1993. *Prairie Populism: The Fate of Agrarian Radicalism in Kansas, Nebraska, and Iowa, 1880–1892*. Lawrence: University Press of Kansas.

Parker, C. 2010. *2010 Multi-state Survey on Race & Politics*. University of Washington Institute for the Study of Ethnicity, Race and Sexuality [Online: March 2010]. Available at: http://depts.washington.edu/uwiser/racepolitics.html [accessed January 6, 2012].

Political Research Associates. 2010. *What is Producerism?* [Online: November 22]. Available at: http://www.publiceye.org/right_wing_populism/producerism.html [accessed January 6, 2012] (originally edited and posted by Chip Berlet while on staff).

Polletta, F. 1998. Contending stories: Narrative in social movements. *Qualitative Sociology*, 21, 419–46.

Postel, C. 2007. *The Populist Vision*. Oxford and New York: Oxford University Press.

Postel, C. 2010. Tea Party: Dark side of conservatism. *Politico* [Online: May 14]. Available at: http://www.politico.com/news/stories/0510/37217.html [accessed December 7, 2011].

Postel, C. 2012. The Tea Party in historical perspective: A conservative response to a crisis of political economy, in *Steep: The Precipitous Rise of the Tea Party*, edited by L. Rosenthal and C. Trost. Berkeley: University of California Press, 25–46.

Public Religion Research Institute. 2010. *American Values Survey: Religion and the Tea Party in the 2010 Elections*, overview page [Online: October 5]. Available at: http://tinyurl.com/prri-tea-2010 [accessed December 12, 2012]. See also Jones and Cox 2010.

Public Religion Research Institute. 2011a. *Fact Sheet: "Teavangelicals": Alignments and Tensions between the Tea Party and White Evangelical Protestants* [Online: November 6]. Available at: http://TinyURL.com/prri-tea-2011a [accessed December 12, 2012].

Public Religion Research Institute. 2011b. *Pluralism, Immigration and Civic Integration Survey* [Online: November 6]. Available at: http://tinyurl.com/prri-immigration-2011c [accessed January 2, 2013].

Public Religion Research Institute. 2011c. *What it Means to be American: Attitudes towards Increasing Diversity in America Ten Years after 9/11* [Online: November 6]. Available at: http://tinyurl.com/prri-diversity-2011b [accessed: January 2, 2013].

Quinby, L. 1994. *Anti-Apocalypse: Exercises in Genealogical Criticism.* Minneapolis: University of Minnesota Press.

Quinby, L. 1997. Coercive purity: The dangerous promise of apocalyptic masculinity, in *The Year 2000: Essays on the End*, edited by C.B. Strozier and M. Flynn. New York: New York University Press.

Quinby, L. 1999. *Millennial Seduction: A Skeptic Confronts Apocalyptic Culture.* Ithaca, NY: Cornell University Press.

Radnofsky, L. 2010. Angle, Reid and a crowded ballot. *Wall Street Journal*, Washington Wire, blog [Online: June 11]. Available at: http://blogs.wsj.com/washwire/2010/06/11/angle-reid-and-a-crowded-ballot/ [accessed January 9, 2012].

Ralston, J. 2010. Angle: "What's happening (in America) ... is a violation of the 1st Commandment,' entitlements 'make government our God'". Ralston's Flash, blog post, *Las Vegas Sun* [Online: August 4]. Available at: http://www.lasvegassun.com/blogs/ralstons-flash/2010/aug/04/angle-whats-happening-america-violation-1st-comman/ [accessed September 23, 2013].

Rogin, M.P. 1967. *The Intellectuals and McCarthy: The Radical Specter.* Cambridge, MA: MIT Press.

Rogin, M.P. 1987. *Ronald Reagan, the Movie: And Other Episodes in Political Demonology.* Berkeley: University of California Press.

Rosenthal L. and Trost, C., eds. 2012. *Steep: The Precipitous Rise of the Tea Party.* Berkeley: University of California Press.

Scher, A. 1996. *Cold War on the Home Front: Middle Class Women in Community Conflict in the Age of McCarthy.* Dissertation, New School for Social Research, June.

Scher, A. 2010a. The Tea Party's misinformation superhighway runs through Las Vegas. *Truthout* [Online: September 25]. Available at: http://archive.truthout.org/the-tea-partys-misinformation-superhighway-runs-through-las-vegas63538 [accessed December 12, 2012].

Scher, A. 2010b. Surprising Angle in Nevada, *The Progressive*, October. Available at: http://www.progressive.org/scher1010.html [accessed December 12, 2012].

Skocpol, T. and Williamson, V. 2012. *The Tea Party and the Remaking of Republican Conservatism.* Oxford and New York: Oxford University Press.

Snow, D.A. and Benford, R.D. 1992. Master frames and cycles of protest, in *Frontiers in Social Movement Theory*, edited by A.D. Morris and C.M. Mueller. New Haven: Yale University Press, 133–55.
Snow, D.A., Rochford, E.B. Jr., Worden, S.K., and Benford, R.D. 1986. Frame alignment process, micromobilization, and movement participation. *American Sociological Review*, 51, 464–81.
Social Movement Study Network. 2012. *A Dense Network: Spreading Conspiracy Theories through Subcultures* [Online: December 12]. Available at: http://www.socialmovementstudy.net/conspiracism/networking/dense.html [accessed December 12, 2012] (originally edited and posted by Chip Berlet while website curator).
Street, P.L. and Dimaggio, A.R. 2011. *Crashing the Tea Party: Mass Media and the Campaign to Remake American Politics*. Boulder, CO: Paradigm.
Tatalovich, S. and Smith, T.A. 2001. Status claims and cultural conflicts: The genesis of morality policy. *Policy Currents*, 10(4), 2–22.
Thomas, W.I. and Thomas, D.S. 1970 [1928]. Situations defined as real are real in their consequences, reprinted in *Social Psychology Through Symbolic Interaction*, edited by G.P. Stone and H.A. Faberman. Waltham, MA: Ginn Blaisdell, 154–5.
Tilly, C. 1978. *From Mobilization to Revolution*. Reading, MA: Addison-Wesley.
Van Dyke, N. and Soule, S.A. 2002. Structural social change and the mobilizing effect of threat: Explaining levels of patriot and militia organizing in the United States. *Social Problems*, 49(4), 497–520.
Warren, D.I. 1976. *The Radical Center: Middle Americans and the Politics of Alienation*. Notre Dame, IN: University of Notre Dame Press.
Williams, L.A. 1992. The ideology of division: behavior modification welfare reform proposals. *Yale Law Journal*, 102(3), 719–46.
Williams, L.A. 1997. *Decades of Distortion: The Right's 30-year Assault on Welfare*. Somerville, MA: Political Research Associates [Online]. Available at: http://www.publiceye.org/welfare/Decades-of-Distortion.html [accessed December 12, 2012].
Young Americans for Liberty. 2010a. *Mission Statement* [Online]. Available at: http://www.yaliberty.org/about/mission [accessed December 12, 2012].
Young Americans for Liberty. 2010b. *YAL Midwest Region*. [Online]. Available at: http://www.yaliberty.org/midwest-region [accessed May 1, 2010].
Young-Bruehl, E. 1996. *The Anatomy of Prejudices*. Cambridge, MA: Harvard University Press.
Zernike, K. 2010. *Boiling Mad: Inside Tea Party America*. New York: Times Books/Henry Holt.
Zernike, K. and Thee-Brenan, M. 2010. Poll finds Tea Party backers wealthier and more educated. *New York Times* [Online: April 14]. Available at: http://www.nytimes.com/2010/04/14/us/politics/15poll.html [accessed December 12, 2012].

Chapter 6
From Fervor to Fear: ICT and Emotions in the Tea Party Movement[1]

Deana A. Rohlinger and Jesse Klein

Emotion is pervasive in social life. It provides the fiery passion that motivates individuals to get involved in movements and lays the foundation for the commitment necessary to sustain activism over the long haul (Goodwin et al. 2001, Flam and King 2005). It is not surprising, then, that leaders try to cultivate emotions that will grow movement support and advance their political goals (Taylor 1996, Jasper 1998). Symbols and rhetoric that elicit pride, patriotism, fear, determination, hope, or anger can effectively mobilize individuals to action (Barker 2001, Goodwin and Pfaff 2001, Woehrle et al. 2008, Gould 2009, Jasper 2011). However, leaders alone do not control which emotions become relevant to a social movement. Emotion emerges through interaction and, at times, the affect expressed within a movement may have little resonance beyond an activist setting (Taylor 1996, Gould 2004). While activists can strategically choose the emotions they display to a broader public (Whittier 2001), leaders have incentives to try to maintain some control over emotional expression. A dramatic shift in emotion can alter movement goals and actions (Jasper 1998), something that leaders may want to avoid.

The ability of leaders to deploy emotions that move people from the armchair to the street and cultivate affect that is in line with movement goals may be easier in the digital age. New social movements are born and sometimes exist entirely online, which gives leaders some measure of control over the movement agenda as well as how individuals interact (Earl and Schussman 2003). In the 2000 strategic voting movement (aka "Nader trading"), for example, movement entrepreneurs adopted very different approaches to activism that either eased or undermined individual interaction with other users. While some leaders created automated sites that prohibited users from interacting, others developed open forums that encouraged individuals to negotiate a vote swap with one another in the real world (Schussman and Earl 2004). In the digital world, leaders literally shape how individuals engage an issue (Earl 2006) and, consequently, can moderate what emotions are expressed in a virtual forum.

---

1 We would like to thank Kyle Rogers for his research assistance on this project and the Department of Sociology at Florida State University for its research support.

Internet communication technology (ICT), however, is not a panacea for movement leaders. Movement dynamics shape the range of emotions available to a movement and, consequently, how leaders strategically employ emotions to maintain their political momentum (Goodwin et al. 2001). It may be easier for leaders to deploy positive emotions early in a "cycle of contention" (Tarrow 1998). Movement emergence requires leaders to mobilize support and action on behalf of a cause (Klandermans 1984, 1988), and cultivating positive emotions (e.g., pride) and associations (e.g., patriotism) may serve them well in this regard. The emotions implicated early in a cycle of contention may lose their motivational might once a movement achieves some level of success. In the wake of victory, some supporters head back to the proverbial armchair and leave the stalwarts to continue the fight in their absence. The problem of demobilization after success may be particularly troublesome for young social movements that want to capitalize on recent victories. The new political climate, ripe with opportunity and scant on activists in the street, may force leaders to adopt more ideologically driven positions and develop clear "us" versus "them" boundaries (Mansbridge 1986, Mansbridge and Morris 2001). The emotions expressed (and sanctioned) by leaders on- and off-line may become negative as they clearly define movement enemies and outline the threats that they pose to social, cultural, or political norms.

In this chapter, we draw on interviews, participant observation, as well as archival and newspaper sources, to examine how leaders use ICT to manage the emotional life of the Tallahassee, Florida, Tea Party movement. We find that leaders drew on different kinds of emotions and employed ICT in their emotional management efforts differently before and after the November 2010 election. Before the November elections, leaders drew on positive emotions that resonated with widely held American values. ICT played an important role in this initial mobilization because the local founder of the movement used Facebook to create a distinctly nonpartisan, but pro-America, forum for citizens to connect, learn about, and discuss local issues, candidates, activities, and events. The careful management of emotion in the virtual world attracted supporters across the political spectrum to the local movement and effectively complemented Tea Party groups organizing in the "real" world, which were explicitly conservative and often religious. The November election was a boon for the fledging movement and leaders quickly found that their success afforded them a great deal of political clout with the Republican-dominated legislature. However, support for the movement waned in the months following the election. Meeting and rally attendance in Florida dropped and Libertarians, Independents, and Democrats across the state began criticizing Tea Party support for the Republican's conservative agenda. In order to reengage the demobilized and disaffected, leaders began to stoke the fears of supporters casting Obama (and liberals more generally) as enemies of America who were destroying the country from the inside out. Fear, anger, and political hostility flourished on the Florida Tea Party Facebook page, as its founder turned his energy to policy instead of activism. This trajectory has important implications for the study of emotions, ICT, and social movements, as we discuss in the final portion of the chapter.

Emotion Management in the Digital Age

Although emotion has physiological and cognitive aspects, it also is a "cultural accomplishment" (Goodwin et al. 2004). Leaders try to develop "emotion cultures" (Hochschild 1979, 1983) that support political change efforts over the long haul (Taylor 1996, Jasper 2011). Emotional communication, or "emotives" (Reddy 1997), provide a foundation for emotion culture and, consequently, shape who participates in a social movement (Gould 2004). Cultivating an emotion culture that resonates broadly and motivates people to engage in a range of political activities (e.g., monetary contributions and participation in street protest) may be easier in the digital age. Leaders can create an array of forums that circumscribe emotional expression relative to movement ideas in virtual settings. Social media sites, discussion boards, and email all provide ways for supporters to connect with one another under the watchful eye of movement leaders, who can publicly sanction appropriate (and rebuke inappropriate) emotives at their discretion. Savvy leaders, then, will moderate online forums carefully, and reinforce emotional expression that can broaden the movement's public appeal and strengthen its political position. Leaders who want to mobilize broad swaths of the citizenry may draw on (and reinforce) symbols and rhetoric that elicit pride and patriotism, emotions that have a deep cultural resonance and the potential to cut across political divisions (Woehrle et al. 2008, Jasper 2011). In short, leaders can do more than represent and control the movement platforms in the digital age (Kretschmer and Meyer 2007). Savvy leaders will "leverage the affordances" (Earl and Kimport 2011) of ICT to cultivate and maintain an emotion culture that supports mobilization and advances movement goals.[2]

Social movements are not static. As movement dynamics shift, so do their emotion cultures and the ability of leaders to use ICT effectively in their emotion management efforts. There are at least three factors that affect whether leaders can use ICT in their efforts to create and maintain an emotion culture over time. First, the movement-controlled forum must serve as a central location for movement supporters to get information on issues, learn about opportunities to participate, and discuss strategies and goals. This is no small feat. Most social movement organizations have a virtual presence, but many group sites do little more than advertise an issue and solicit funds for campaigns (Earl 2006). As such, a movement-controlled site may espouse the emotions preferred by leadership but lack the ability to reinforce the desired affect with supporters. If leaders are to have the opportunity to sanction or rebuke emotional expression, then they must possess enough political skill and technological savvy to make online movement-controlled forums integral to organizing and decision-making processes, and maintain this importance over time.

---

2   We are not suggesting that new technology allows leaders to completely control emotions and emotional expression in social movements. Our objective is to take a first step at examining the role of ICT in how leaders cultivate and regulate emotional expression.

Second, leaders must be willing to cooperate with one another in the real and virtual worlds. Leaders do not always work together to achieve a common goal. Ideological conflicts, frame disputes, and competition for financial and human resources create obstacles to cooperation that must be negotiated by movement leadership (Staggenborg 1986, Benford 1993, Hathaway and Meyer 1997). The difficulties associated with cooperation and coordination do not necessarily disappear because a movement's presence (and consequently its supporters) are divided between the real and virtual worlds. Leaders must come to an agreement (explicit or implicit) regarding the broad goal of a movement and the emotions that are likely to mobilize citizens to this end.

Finally, leaders must actually take the time to manage emotional expression in movement-controlled forums. While this may seem obvious, individuals do not posses infinite reserves of time and energy. Leaders, particularly at the local level, rarely are professional activists and must juggle work and family in addition to their movement obligations (Wood 2002, Morris and Staggenborg 2004). Not surprisingly, the willingness and ability of leaders to moderate online forums may fluctuate over time and relative to a broader political context. For example, when a movement achieves some measure of success, leaders may let emotion management fall by the wayside as they focus their energy on affecting political change instead. Absent the presence of a moderator, new emotions may emerge as the motivation for activism and be reinforced in the virtual world.

Data and Methods

We employ several methods to examine the emotional life of the Tallahassee Tea Party movement before and after the November election. First, we monitored organizational websites, public forums (such as the movement Facebook sites) and emails for the local Tea Party groups on a daily basis.[3] Second, using Lexis Nexis, we collected all of the media coverage on the Tea Party movement in the state of Florida. Third, we attended more than a dozen meetings, rallies, and events hosted by local Tea Party groups between April 2010 and May 2011. Finally, we conducted semi-structured interviews with supporters of other Florida Tea Party groups. We used a variety of methods to locate respondents including email, online surveys, giving presentations at local meetings, handing out flyers at events, and posting flyers in a variety of locations on- and off-line. This strategy yielded a

---

3   The posts on public forums and Facebook were copied and pasted in a Word document. This information is organized chronologically so that we can see changes over time. Since emails are dated and are stand alone texts, they were archived and sorted by thematic topic. We further assessed our data using ATLAS.ti, a qualitative data analysis program that allowed us to analyze these themes systematically. These programs are beneficial insofar as they allow users to enter and analyze a variety of data (newspaper articles, archived online data, and interview transcripts, in this case) and verify the frequency and consistency of qualitative findings.

total of 46 movement supporters, who were interviewed between August 2010 and May 2011. Our respondents primarily lived in and around the Tallahassee area, although we also interviewed leaders and supporters from other parts of the state. Respondents were asked about their range of political experience (petitions, canvassing, protests, and so on), membership in other organizations, when and why they joined the Tea Party movement, the kinds of activities and events (on- and off-line) in which they had participated, their impressions of how the group affected their participation, and their feelings about activism and politics in the US more generally. The interviews ranged in length from 35 minutes to two and a half hours. All respondents are identified with pseudonyms.

Table 6.1 summarizes the demographics of the 32 respondents we interviewed formally (14 others we spoke with informally at events and rallies are not included). Our respondents are diverse in terms of their age, gender, relationship, parental, and employment status but relatively homogeneous in terms of their gender, race, and ethnicity. The gender, racial, and ethnic demographics are not representative of Tallahassee, in which 53 percent of the population is female, 60 percent is white, 34 percent is African American, 4 percent is Latino, and 2 percent is Asian.

The Tallahassee Tea Party Movement

As other chapters in this volume have discussed, the emergence of the Tea Party movement is attributable to many factors, among them Rick Santelli's now famous rant against President Obama's mortgage rescue plan and the rapid response from national conservative groups, answering his call to stage tea parties across the country. In Tallahassee, the first Tea Party event took place on March 17, 2009, after Anthony, a 32-year-old conservative activist, attended a Tea Party meeting organized by Brendan Steinhauser (the Director of Federal and State Campaigns for FreedomWorks and Anthony's friend), John O'Hara (vice president of external relations at the Illinois Policy Institute), Peter Flaherty (writer for the *American Spectator*), and Michelle Malkin (syndicated columnist and *Fox News* contributor) outside of the White House. Invigorated by the rally, Anthony decided to spearhead a similar effort in Florida's capital. He began by setting up a Facebook page for the movement and inviting conservatives to become a fan of the group. Within a week, the page had over 500 fans. Anthony then invited all the page fans to the first Tallahassee Tea Party. The event, which featured a keynote address by Dick Armey, attracted 300 Tea Partiers. Anthony capitalized on the "event buzz" and, using Facebook, grew the number of group supporters to nearly 1,000. He staged another rally the following month on Tax Day, April 15, 2009.[4]

---

4 According to Anthony, the number of fans for the Tallahassee Tea Party Facebook page fluctuated over time. He reports that at its height, there were nearly 1,500 fans. During the time we monitored the page, the number of fans fluctuated between 920 (in April 2010) and 830 (in April 2011).

Table 6.1 Overview of respondent demographics

	%	N
Gender		
Male	69	22
Female	31	10
Age		
18–35	31	10
36–50	31	10
51+	38	12
Race/Ethnicity		
White	81	26
Asian	0	0
Middle-Eastern	3	1
Latino	10	3
Multi-racial	6	2
Relationship Status		
Single	25	8
Partnered	6	2
Married	47	15
Divorced	19	6
Widowed	3	1
Employment Status		
Student	6	2
Employed	63	20
Unemployed	6	2
Retired	25	8
Parental Status		
No children	38	12
One child	22	7
2 or more children	40	13
Total Number of Respondents		32

Although this event was also well attended and included short speeches from three state legislators, Anthony, who also works full time at a fiscally conservative think tank, found he could not maintain the movement alone. He decided to coordinate and spread the movement online and asked other local conservatives to organize the movement on the ground. The result has been the creation of three additional local groups that support the Tea Party banner, but adopt different orientations to politics. The first group, which we call Citizens Holding Government Accountable, is a fiscally conservative, nonpartisan organization that works to "promote good conservative elected representatives to ALL levels of government." The group supports the Tea Party movement and specifically focuses on limiting government, fiscal responsibility, states' rights, and individual rights. The second organization, Christians for Responsible Government, also strongly supports the Tea Party platform but regards Judeo-Christian doctrine as critical to "uniting Americans" and "defending our country." The third group, Working for the American Way, integrates religious doctrine into its mission, which is to preserve "the rights and freedoms endowed by our Creator and guaranteed by our Constitution." Unlike the other groups, the primary goal of Working for the American Way is to provide a "bridge" between the Tea Party groups in order to increase the overall effectiveness of the movement's efforts in Florida.

In sum, during the period we studied, the Tallahassee Tea Party movement was characterized by cooperation. Although different local organizations operated on the ground, leaders were committed to working together to advance the Tea Party platform in local and state politics. Additionally, ICT played an important role in the local movement from its inception. Because Anthony decided to organize and coordinate the movement online, the group's Facebook page was the communication hub of the movement and, more specifically, a bulletin board where all the local leaders announced their activities as well as a democratic forum where movement leaders and supporters discussed the efficacy of different issues and candidates, strategies, and actions (Rohlinger et al. forthcoming). These factors put leaders at an advantage as they headed into the election insofar as they were able to create an emotion culture that emphasized pride and patriotism on- and off-line and to mobilize citizens across the political spectrum.

Pride and Patriotism: Mobilizing Across the Political Spectrum

The strategic deployment of emotion can engage a broader public and move them to action. Moral shocks, for example, create a "visceral unease" (Jasper 2011) and generate sufficient outrage to induce individuals to participate in social movements (Jasper and Poulsen 1993, Jasper 1997, Nepstad and Smith 2001). It is not surprising, then, that leaders of the Tallahassee Tea Party movement first capitalized on the burgeoning outrage over the size and reach of government to mobilize individuals to action. At a "Spending Revolt" rally, one leader attributed the growth of the local movement to the ability of the group to "capture the mood of the people in the moment and mobilize them." Indeed, virtually all of our respondents credited their involvement in the movement to their outrage over the actions of government. For example, a young African American woman interviewed at a Tea Party rally noted that as a Democrat she was "profoundly disappointed" with President Obama's decision to bail out the banks and auto industry and that it was time "to get the country back on track." Likewise, when asked why he joined the local Tea Party movement, Benjamin, a 59-year-old small business owner, exclaimed, "Government is out of control!" Connor, a 50-year-old retiree, agreed, adding, "It's happening in different ways for different people. They're not happy with the way their government has been working. And they're getting off the couch or out of their chairs and doing something about it."

Leaders cannot rely on anger, dissatisfaction, and frustration to mobilize supporters over the long haul. Leaders must manage emotions and cultivate affect that both legitimates the movement and provides sufficient inspiration to keep individuals involved (Taylor 1996, Jasper 1998, Goodwin et al. 2004). Emotions do not have to be positive to sustain mobilization (Jasper 2011). However, positive affect can be used to highlight the consonance between movement goals and societal values and make it easier for leaders to emphasize points of consensus among individuals holding a range of political perspectives. In the Tallahassee Tea Party movement, local leaders emphasized positive emotions in an effort to highlight a shared collective identity and mobilize across party lines (Klein and Rohlinger forthcoming). Drawing on pride and patriotism, leaders drew clear distinctions between their enemy (political parties dominated by "elite Washington insiders," who lack vision and ultimately are not accountable to their constituents) and themselves (average American citizens, who suffer the consequences of bad political decisions) and "transformed" "the boiling point of frustration and confusion" into motivation that transcended party politics.

In group meetings, at rallies, and on the Facebook page, leaders emphasized that the "great angry awakening" of the American citizenry meant new hope for the country and democracy. If citizens could "unite their voices" as Americans, than together they could "change the tide" of inside-the-beltway politics and make politicians accountable for decisions. This positive change, however, meant that supporters needed to undergo an emotional transformation so that the movement could make "smart decisions" regarding who they put into political office. For example, at a rally outside the capital a local leader explained to the crowd:

> Eighteen months ago when we first started the Tea Party thing, there were people showing up that were just mad as hell and they wanted to throw the bums out. I said, "Look here. You need to think about what bum you want to replace him with." [Crowd laughs]. I say this because they were just so mad that they wanted to throw everybody out. I said, "Wait a minute. The day after the election somebody else is taking their place and you need to trade up in this deal ..." They hadn't thought that far ahead.

The keynote speaker at the event, a middle-aged man who was riding across America asking politicians to reaffirm their commitment to the values outlined in the Constitution, echoed this sentiment and encouraged "Americans" and "patriots" to get involved in the democratic process in a positive way. He urged Tea Partiers to

> Be a part of the process and don't give up ... We can never go back to doing business the way we've done it. We can never not allow ourselves to be involved

in government again ... I talk to people like you in every state around this nation. They all feel the same way—they're so angry. We've got to get past that anger. We want to be better than what's there and the only way we can do it is if we go in with a positive attitude. Put down the anger. Let's focus all of our energy on changing our nation.

Anthony's decision to use ICT, and Facebook in particular, to organize and coordinate movement information and activities played an important role in both establishing and maintaining the emotions used during the Florida group's mobilization efforts leading up to the election. Although Anthony is conservative, and initially reached out to fellow conservatives through Facebook, he saw the potential to mobilize across party lines if the movement could maintain a "mainstream message," one that focused on the size, scope, and accountability of government rather than on political affiliation and cultural issues like abortion and gay marriage. He explained:

The [Tallahassee] Tea Party has not been focused on social issues or the cultural issues that divide America, but has been focused more on the issues that 70 to 80 per cent of the people agree with: a responsible government, accountable elected officials, and balancing the budget. Most people agree with that.

This sentiment was reflected on the Facebook page, which described the local Tea Party movement as explicitly nonpartisan:

This isn't a conservative or liberal thing. This is about government forking over billions of dollars to businesses that should have failed. This is about taking money from responsible people and handing it over to CEOs who squandered their own.

Citizens, the page added, need to "work together" to take back government from career politicians, who do not operate in the interest of "the people." Since the Facebook page served as the primary communication hub and discussion forum for the local movement leading up to the election and the page was monitored daily, Anthony was well positioned to cultivate (and reinforce) an emotion culture that emphasized pride and patriotism over partisanship.

Leaders' efforts to mobilize citizens by drawing on pride and patriotism were effective and supporters shared their stories online and at movement events. Patriotism generally and "love of country" specifically were often cited as a motivation for attending rallies and participating in local movement activities.[5]

---

5 Pride and patriotism are relevant to mobilization efforts in other movements as well, including the gay rights movement (Gould 2009) and the American peace movement (Woehrle et al. 2008). For a more general discussion regarding how these emotions affect the course of social movements, see Jasper (2011).

For example, one woman discussed her motivation for attending a rally and her experiences on the Facebook page:

> I went to express my love for my NATION and my hope for it. I was thrilled that there were hundreds there and it was all positive truth and uplifting LOVE of Country being expressed. I held an umbrella in one hand for protection from the sun, and waved my flag with the other hand and cried for joy. I had found people of like hearts!

Katherine, a 47-year-old state worker, agreed:

> It makes me feel good in my heart ... I think that it [the Tea Party movement] encompasses all that is good about humanity—helping your neighbor, working hard, being positive, working together to make things better for our communities, for our country, for our state... I feel very strongly about those things and the people involved in the Tea Party movement have very similar feelings. Because when I express my feelings, everybody nods and says, "yes, yes. That's how we feel too." So I think that it kind of goes back to this feeling of love of country—that sounds corny but it really is true. It really is what it comes down to, loving the ideal, loving America. That's what we're all striving for, to have a nice life and be free ... and to live in nice communities ... [where] people care about each other.

These emotions also successfully masked political divisions among movement supporters and promoted mobilization across party lines. The notions of individual freedom and rights, which are central to understandings of America identity, underscore that, while united by a love of country, America is composed of diverse opinions and people (Schildkraut 2002). As such, Tallahassee Tea Party supporters recognized that "being united" was different than "being in agreement" on every issue. In fact, supporters regarded differences among its members as a strength of the local movement and, therefore, something that should be embraced. A man recounting his first Tea Party rally on the Facebook page, for instance, noted that the movement valued differences of opinion. He explained that when some "rowdy protestors" arrived at the rally "they were not run off as might have been expected but, instead, invited in as neighbors and friends with differing opinions."

Using pride and patriotism as an emotional scaffolding for activism allowed leaders and supporters alike to avoid "hot button" issues, like abortion, immigration, and gay rights, which had the potential to undermine the diversity and, ultimately, the political power of the group. These issues were never discussed before the election for fear that the movement would be "torn apart" before it had a chance to affect change. For example, Nancy, a 49-year-old small business owner and long-time libertarian, warned that the movement would fail if these issues came to define the movement:

> I think it would be a big mistake for the Tea Party to focus on the immigration issue, on the abortion issue, on the gay rights issue. It's not something that would

unite the people who would perceive themselves associated with the Tea Party movement it's something that would be more likely to divide them ... Gay marriage is a non issue because the government has no business telling people whether they're married or not. Marriage is a business of a contract between two individuals or as a matter of religious practice. It's really not within the purview of government.

Even social conservatives agreed that these issues should be avoided in order to grow the strength and numbers of the movement. Logan, a retiree and a leader of a Tea Party group in rural Florida, expressed personal distaste for both abortion and gay marriage but added that it was important for him to "set these opinions aside" so that the movement could grow its strength and influence over local and state politics. Likewise, Deborah, a 55-year-old conservative activist who has picketed outside of abortion clinics, argued that controversial issues "could derail the central message ... and take down the Tea Party movement."

Political divisions, of course, did not completely disappear but, instead, were contained by ICT. Anthony moderated the Facebook page so that it served as a democratic forum where individuals holding various political beliefs could discuss candidates, issues, and movement goals (Rohlinger et al. forthcoming). Flaming posts were criticized or deleted by Anthony (and in some cases criticized by other supporters); actions that made it clear to visitors that the page was not simply a partisan forum. Thus, while divisions among area Tea Party supporters were clear, fans typically acknowledged a point of agreement with other posts before "respectfully" disagreeing. The existence of a forum encouraging nonpartisan discussion proved important in a local movement where most Libertarians, Independents, and Democrats were involved in the movement entirely online. Since these supporters primarily participated in online discussions, contributed money to political campaigns, and phoned/emailed legislators with their concerns, they were largely unaware that social, not just fiscal, conservatism had a strong presence in the real world. The ability of the Tallahassee Tea Party to mobilize across political difference was aided by the fact that the relatively diverse membership had little, if any, in-person contact.

Leaders of the Tallahassee Tea Party movement drew on culturally resonant emotions and common identities in order to mobilize politically diverse individuals to action. Pride, patriotism, and a shared enthusiasm that together, Tea Party supporters could turn the political tide, provided motivation for activism on- and off-line. As the founder of the local movement, Anthony not only set the emotional tone for the area movement but also maintained it in the virtual world. Taking a cue from Anthony, other leaders and movement supporters adopted this emotional framework, particularly in the virtual world. However, the emotions relevant to a movement are not static. Leaders make strategic decisions regarding what emotions to deploy relative to a broader political context. The next section examines the emotions leaders used in the wake of their electoral victory.

The Sting of Success: Stoking Fears over the Liberal Menace

The Tea Party movement was very successful during the 2010 election cycle. Movement-backed candidates swept races across the state giving Republicans a super majority in the state legislature. Even Republicans who had not gotten elected under the Tea Party banner embraced the movement's agenda and joined the Tea Party Caucus. It quickly became clear, however, that the Republican agenda was not just one of fiscal conservatism and smaller government. Legislators introduced bills that reflected social conservative ideologies. Among the most controversial were the 18 pieces of legislation designed to make legal abortion less accessible in the state, legislation giving politicians more control over the judicial system (and the Supreme Court in particular), legislation requiring TANF (Temporary Assistance for Needy Families) recipients to undergo mandatory drug testing at their expense, and legislation tightening control over voter registration procedures and voter rights at the polls.

These bills, which were signed by the governor, enraged many Democrats, Independents, and Libertarians—some of whom initially supported the movement. Libertarians and Independents, the two groups that regarded the Tea Party movement as holding great promise in American politics, were the most critical of Governor Rick Scott and the local movement. Libertarian and Independent discussion groups and websites were rife with condemnation, casting Scott as "a disaster," who "is killing Florida" and had "pretty much guaranteed Florida is gonna go Blue again the next election." Similarly, they blasted the Tea Party, arguing that the movement had been "infiltrated" by "Republicans," "neoconservatives," and "extremists." One person posting on a Florida Libertarian website argued that neoconservatives had taken over the Tea Party movement and condemned supporters for allowing the movement to be co-opted for political purposes. He argued:

> Because Beck and Palin infiltrated the movement it is full of neo-cons. Lenin once said "the best way to silence the opposition is to lead it." We are back to solving non-existent problems while the country goes to hell in a 'Bama basket!! ... Florida Republicans seem to be doing everything in their power to get themselves kicked out next time around. Maybe someday fiscally responsible voters will realize that the Republicans aren't the answer. At some point the people are going to catch on, the Libertarian Party is the only party of principle, and the only ones who are going to say what they mean and do what they say. Keep the government out of my personal life. You CANNOT have government regulation of morality. Lower our taxes and stop wasting all of our money on bullshit! Why aren't the Tea Party and conservatives complaining? In a time where there is a budget crunch everyone is tightening their belts—no pet projects should be accepted.

On an Independent website, one poster argued that the Tea Party movement in the state of Florida never existed. He claimed:

> The Tea Party is a fake astroturf "movement" brought to you by the corporate shills at Americans for Prosperity and the Koch brothers who make their living economically raping your country. They claim to stand for the "taxpayers over moneyed special interests" but rigorously defend the likes of Exxon and Bank of America.

Not all Libertarians and Independents abandoned the movement. However, of those supporters we interviewed in the wake of the movement's electoral victory, the majority of Libertarians and Independents identified the Republican Party as an "enemy" of the movement. Animosity toward party politics, and the Republican Party in particular, was inherent to the Tallahassee area movement. Supporters blamed the Republicans for abandoning their core fiscally conservative ideals and growing too comfortable in their political careers. As George, a 60-year-old attorney, explained, Republicans "fell ill to the same disease that affects everybody apparently that goes up there. They drank the Washington Kool-Aid. They got in the business of earmarks and pork politics." This skepticism of party politics skyrocketed in the wake of the Tea Party movement's electoral victory.[6] Area Tea Party supporters became "distrustful" of the Republicans who embraced the movement platform and, specifically, viewed it as an effort to "co-opt" the Tea Party for their own political purposes. Joseph, a 61-year-old unemployed electronics technician, explained:

> Most people in the Tea Party Movement have just about given up on the Republican Party. They're compromised and they're entrenched power ... There's almost as much corruption in the Republican Party as there is in the Democratic Party.

Hayden, a 33-year-old soldier in the US Army, agreed, noting that he was even more skeptical of the Republican Party since his involvement in the Tea Party movement:

> I'm a lot more skeptical of how true really conservative they [Republicans] are ... I've noticed this over the last 8 to 10 years, truly with the exception of a couple social issues, the Republican Party and the Democrat Party are largely the same thing.

Mathew, a 55-year-old insurance salesman, added that his involvement with the Tea Party movement had made him "even less tolerant of mainstream Republicans. I'm more nauseated by them, by the typical Republican hash and gobbledygook. Just I'm less tolerant and less patient with it. It's just Democrat-light." Nancy

---

6   For a more detailed discussion regarding the relationship between the Tea Party movement and the Republican Party, see Rohlinger et al. (forthcoming).

agreed with this assessment and warned that if the movement was not careful it would be taken over by the party.

> What you'll get is, eventually the message of the Tea Party being diluted down and being represented by people who are professional politicians and entrenched in the establishment ... [These politicians] won't really represent the interests of the people who were attracted to the Tea Party's idea of removing power from the entrenched political establishment.

In short, local leaders faced criticism from current and former supporters alike, many of whom believed that the movement had been (or was in danger of being) diluted and taken over by the Republican Party and career politicians.

Disaffected and suspicious supporters were not the only problem the Tallahassee Tea Party movement faced after the election. Social movement victories often come at a price. When the battle is over, a once aggrieved population demobilizes, leaving the committed few to keep up the fight until the next crisis emerges and the cycle of protest begins again (Taylor 1989, Tarrow 1998). Indeed, in the Tallahassee area, many satisfied supporters seemed to have resumed their lives shortly after the election. Attendance at group meetings fell and finding ways to reengage supporters in order to keep the Tea Party agenda prominent in the minds of elected officials became a regular topic of conversation. Likewise, activity on the movement's Facebook page plummeted after January 2011 and, when there was a post, it generally stood without being "liked" or commented upon. For example, James, a fan, alerted Tallahassee Tea Party supporters to one activist's unruly behavior in April. He posted:

> Today a person identifying himself as a Tea Party member cursed and became verbally disrespectful to a Law Enforcement Officer at The Capital; saying "why are you letting these illegals run the halls of The Capital." 1st- Understand that the LEO are there to protect ALL PEOPLE gathering at the Capital. Come on folks ... show a little common sense. An LEO assigned to protect you doesn't need ignorant rude abuse, especially when they are not the ones to complain to. The person with this ignorant question needs to know that you make us all look bad when you make such out-bursts. Long Live The Tea Party but get out of the faces of the LEO that are simply doing their jobs.

Several weeks later another fan asked, "Are we sure it was actually a Tea Party member?" James replied, "I posted this weeks ago, and this is the first response. What I thought I would have heard was people saying, that's right folks, support law enforcement as they put it on the line daily for all of us. Yes, the person was a Tea Party'er. That wasn't the point."

As the dynamics of the local movement changed, so did the emotion culture of the movement. In order to mobilize supporters anew, local leaders on the ground began to tighten their ranks, identify their enemies, and outline the threats that need redress. In the new movement environment, leaders argued that the Tea Party movement is engaged in a "war for the soul of America" and warned supporters that without their involvement the country may collapse. The biggest threat to America is Obama and his liberal ilk, who have brought the country to the brink of collapse by making it vulnerable to terrorist attacks and financial ruin. These themes were prevalent at the area Tea Party rallies held during the opening week of the legislative session. For example, one leader stoked fears over another terrorist attack to highlight the importance of the Tea Party and the need for it to remain visible:

> Friends, this administration is quickly doing what Osama Bin Laden and Al Qaida were not able to do. And, that is to bring this country to her knees! And speaking of Al Qaida, do not believe for a second that our enemy is not aware of what is going on. While our nation is drowning in debt, radical Islamic groups quietly build their massive infrastructure within the USA, secretly awaiting our demise. Let's not give them hope. If we care anything for this nation, we must not let that occur!

He then urged Tea Party supporters to think about how "radical liberals" were undermining freedoms in ways that would affect future generations and the country's history.

> Soon my wife Emily and I will be trying to get pregnant. I do not want to leave my son or daughter with a country that is saddled with a debt that cannot be repaid. With a country that cannot be fixed. With a nation that is being built by our enemies from within. I don't want my future grandchildren to have to ask why Americans stood by and did nothing while they watched their country disintegrate. The United States was an experiment that went right. Let's not see it go up in flames. Our children's future is at stake. Let's fight to keep our country the bastion of freedom that we have been used to.

The threat Obama and Democrats pose to America is fully developed in a book sold by conservative author Dr. Truth, called *The New Democrat: A Parody in Celebration of the Tea Party Movement*, which was sold at area Tea Party events after (but not before) the November election. The book, which is a parody of Dr. Seuss's *The Cat in the Hat*, features Obama wearing the red star (a symbol of socialism), Glenn Beck as the fish, Nancy Pelosi as Thing 1, and Harry Reid as Thing 2. In this rendition, the self-aggrandizing Obama "grovels" to dictators and "derails" the country by saddling it with debt. The threat to America grows when Pelosi and Reid are released from their box and promote Obama's destructive agenda. On page 42, "Dem 1" and "Dem 2" are shown ripping the Constitution and then flying it like a kite through the White House. The accompanying text reads:

> Those Dems got to work, And they got to work quick. Tore up the Constitution and then gave it a kick! They banged it around from the ceiling to floor. And

said "It's a living document!" Glenn [the fish] said "Not any more!" They undermined the freedom on which our republic depends. And took tax payer's money to spend on their friends.

As Election Day approaches, however, Dem 1 and Dem 2 grow nervous that they might lose their power. Obama soothes their fears:

> "Have no fear," said the cat, "The voters love me. They're just like the press. I'm their Messiah, you see. He said, sounding flat, "Want my 'hope' and my 'change.' I'm their new Democrat! And I've been working so hard to change everything, and be their sole source of hope! I'm their Socialist king! Nothing will stop me from being their hero! Why I bet I could come out for a mosque at ground zero!"

Casting liberals as the enemy in a war over American freedom (and conservative Christians as "real" Americans) was quickly picked up by area Tea Party movement supporters (Klein and Rohlinger forthcoming). In fact, all of the respondents interviewed between January and May 2011 alluded to "wrong headedness" of liberals and their "socialist" tendencies. Riley, a 49-year-old political consultant, warned that liberals were destroying the country by creating an "overwhelming, overbearing state, socialist state that's going to take away people's rights and drive us into bankruptcy." Diane, a 56-year-old sales representative added that the Obama administration is attacking American freedoms:

> Freedom. You can't find that anywhere else, this is the last place for it. Once it's lost here, it's gone. And a lot of young people don't realize that, and they get very idealistic. They start following the people on the left and it's almost like liberalism and socialism. It's almost like a fad. They don't realize how devastating it is. If you haven't served in the military, you don't know what it is to go out and fight for freedom. Everybody takes the freedom for granted and it's just stupid because it's the most valuable thing that there is. These brave people that go out and die for their country and it really ticks me off when people sit around and talk about, "Oh we ought to be a socialist country, and punish people working hard." It makes me sick to my stomach.

Kenneth, a 55-year-old ROTC (Reserve Officers' Training Corps) instructor, agreed:

> I grew up in a different country than we're living in now and I was just really really upset with the way we were being forced to go by people I think that don't understand what makes this country great. When all this legislation started, about forcing people to buy things, literally I could read the paper and almost get physically ill thinking about which way we were going and what has happened to this country.

Joseph concluded that the Tea Party Movement was "the only viable means of change, real change for the better ... in a government moving toward socialism."

The shift in emotions—from pride and patriotism to fear—was palpable during the meetings we attended after the election as well. Because we had an established presence within the groups, the local leaders continued to support the research project while recognizing that we were different and should be regarded with some suspicion. For example, at the February meeting of the Citizens Holding Government Accountable, Richard, the leader of group, introduced us to a newcomer noting that we had spent time with the group and its members. He added that even though we may be "enemies" he still "loves us." Another member, Oliver, added that he thought that we were "born again [conservatives] and just won't tell" them. Similarly, at the March meeting of Christians for Responsible Government, one of the authors was verbally attacked by the leader of the College Republicans, who wanted her ejected from the meeting. He argued that her intent was to make the Tea Party movement "look bad" and cited the "overwhelming liberalism" of the Sociology Department as evidence. While Katherine, the group's leader, approved her presence and referred to her as a "special guest" conducting scholarly research on the Tea Party movement, the College Republican retorted that the social science departments, especially Sociology, "are honestly like Democrat factories. Really. Something more has to be done [about her presence at the meeting]."

The absence of Anthony on- and off-line fueled this dramatic shift in the area movement's emotion culture after the election. The once vibrant Facebook page became a virtual ghost town. Few fans posted to the page in the wake of the election and Anthony rarely posted news or moderated the discussion that did exist. Without his presence as an active moderator, the posts and dialogue became more strident and partisan. This was clear in a heated exchange over whether the movement should support the attack on unions in Florida. During the 2011 legislative session, the Republican majority launched an attack on state workers arguing that they were unfairly compensated relative to those working in private industry. While there were a number of ways that Republicans suggested that state workers could be weaned from the tax payer's teat, the legislature took aim at unions which, they argued, undermined competition in the marketplace and guaranteed inflated wages in unionized industries. Because the right to unionize is part of the state constitution, the legislators proposed three separate bills designed to remove the political teeth of unions. The first bill would decertify unions that did not have at least 50 percent of the workers signed as members, the second bill would prohibit union dues from being automatically deducted from members' pay checks, and the final bill would require unions to obtain written permission from members to use their dues for political purposes. While many area Tea Party supporters vocally supported the bills, some argued that this moved away from the movement's primary goals.

For example, Kenny posted that "The Tallahassee Tea Party should not support the union busting bills being forced through our state government!!!!!!!!!!!! It has nothing to do with the principles of the Tea Party" on the Facebook page. Chuck, another fan, responded, "Telling people that they don't have to pay union dues is not union busting. It does remove considerable money for the pockets of organized crime!" Chuck went on to explain that he spent two decades working at the Department of Justice and knew how corrupt unions really are. Kenny replied:

> Thanks for responding Chuck. I do not know why any of what you wrote about has a bit to do with the Tallahassee Tea Party, which is what I mentioned I disagreed with. I understand that some unions have issues, well tell me what doesn't? Cops, firefighters or politicians. They all have their good and bad. All I wanted was the Tallahassee Tea Party to work on local matters like why the city and county have raised and wasted tax payer money. Unions are not the problem. Too much flippin' government is the problem. I was at a political function tonight in which I was told by a state rep that the dues bill was payback and nothing else.

Another fan, George, agreed and asked:

> Chuck, isn't Florida a right-to-work state?? Doesn't that mean that no one has to join a union if they don't want to?? What the current legislation does is prevent those who want to join a union from having their dues automatically deducted from their paychecks ... Most employers use direct deposit now instead of issuing a paycheck ... if you want 10% of your paycheck to go to a church, all you need to do is supply the routing number and the account number. Why is it that union dues cannot use this same process? ... Chuck, you've shown yourself to be the typical Tea Partier: completely uninformed about the situation and so full of hatred that you can't help but compare all of your "enemies" with criminals.

Not surprisingly, Chuck took offense at the comments and challenged George to meet him "face to face" for presumably a physical confrontation. He posted:

> George, we both live in Tallahassee and I take great offense to the comments you made about me so I want to give you a chance to say them to my face. Name the time and the place. I will be waiting ... I am going to give you a chance to tell me face to face how sorry and full of hatred I am. Don't you want to have it out with a typical Tea Partier instead of on the other end of a computer!!

Kenny tried to moderate the discussion and refocus the debate on the issues rather than personal attacks. He interjected:

> WOW, guys lets chill a little. Chuck, I respect your opinion but still disagree. I would have more respect for the Tallahassee Tea Party if they would start to focus more on local tax issues. For example, I haven't seen any mention of the

fact that our county commission wants to raise the gas tax by 5 cents per gallon. I am a democrat and a union member but still cannot stand the way our local governments waste the heck out of our tax dollars and do it for political reasons. We need to consolidate our government. That's the topic I would like to see our tea party focus on! What do you'll think?

In his response, Chuck tempered his opinion, but insisted that unions required government regulation:

Kenny, I got a little carried away but the union dues thing does not bust unions or stop workers from joining unions. Every worker has the right to join or not to join at least in this state. The tea party should stay involved and make sure that legislators in this state do not become beholden to the unions as they have in other states. I bet the state rep you talked with was a democrat!

Chuck concluded his post with a veiled threat, "George, it's easy to talk crap on a computer, but I am the wrong one [to taunt]. I never forget!"

The emotional culture and mobilization efforts of the Tallahassee Tea Party dramatically changed in the wake of the November 2010 elections. Leaders no longer worked to unite supporters by their love of country and hope to change America for the better. Instead, they defined the movement along ideological lines and stoked fears of the liberal threat. This dramatic shift was made possible, in part, by the absence of Anthony. Before the election, Anthony used ICT and Facebook in particular to organize and connect Tea Party supporters across their political differences. Absent Anthony's authority and moderate message, the Facebook page became a forum for political strife that fuels, rather than counters, the emergence of activism couched in fear.

Conclusions

Emotions provide the passion that fuels activism and leaders try to cultivate affect that will mobilize broad swaths of citizenry and sustain movement support over the long haul. Clearly, ICT can help leaders in this regard. Online platforms like Facebook provide a setting where supporters interact with one another under the watchful eye of movement leaders. Thus, in addition to setting the emotional tone of a webpage, leaders can moderate interactions and effectively reinforce the desired emotions in the real and virtual worlds. Of course, the Tallahassee Tea Party movement had distinct advantages in this regard. Because the movement was initially set up on Facebook, the page played an important role in mobilization efforts and made it easier for Anthony to reinforce his mainstream message. Likewise, local leaders operating on the ground cooperated with one another and ultimately adopted, rather than challenged, Anthony's emphasis on pride and patriotism.

While not all local movements may experience this level of cooperation, divisions in local movements where some supporters participate entirely online are a growing reality that may have benefits. Savvy leaders that can cast their causes as mainstream and draw on emotions and collective identities that simultaneously acknowledge and downplay political differences may be able to effectively broaden their movement support. This point is particularly interesting because it stands in opposition to how scholars typically think about effective recruitment. Rather than coming to a cause via face-to-face communication, friendships, and group affiliation (Snow et al. 1980, McAdam 1988, Klatch 1999), individuals may shop movement causes and participate in those that seem of interest and representative of their beliefs. While the ability to maintain ICT recruits over the long haul is up for debate, it is clear that having activists operating in both the real and virtual worlds can benefit a local movement—and, in this case, make it seem far more representative than it is.

Of course, movements and the emotions relevant to mobilization change. As movement claims are co-opted and institutionalized, supporters herald their victory and head back to their armchairs to revel in their success. However, when a political climate is ripe with opportunity and the movement is not ready or willing to be absorbed by Party machinery, the lack of supporters in the street and in the halls of legislature create a dilemma for leaders. They may be able to reinvigorate some of the movement's base, but, to do so, must rely on negative emotions (like fear) and cast former allies as enemies. These shifts may create rifts within local movements and undermine the political effectiveness of the movement. The shift in Tallahassee did not create rifts, because online leader Anthony did not challenge this changing emotion culture on- or off-line.

The utility of ICT in a local movement also depends upon its leaders (Staggenborg 1988). Anthony's use of Facebook required time, motivation, and some level of political skill, a resource that is not equally distributed across the population. Similarly, local leaders rarely are full-time activists, which, given other demands, makes online efforts difficult to sustain. When leaders are absent, supporters can commandeer a movement page for their own purposes. In the case of the Tallahassee Tea Party, absent Anthony's authority, fans used the Facebook page to define the movement along political lines—a message that was reinforced at Tea Party meetings and events. ICT, in short, is an important tool in the repertoire of contemporary social movements (Earl and Kimport 2011). In skilled hands, ICT can help a movement bridge political divides and build the political might of a movement. However, in less skilled hands, ICT becomes a blunt instrument that in the end may do more harm than good.

References

Barker, C. 2001. Fear, laughter, and collective power: The making of solidarity at the Lenin Shipyard in Gdansk, Poland, August 1980, in *Passionate Politics:*

Emotions and Social Movements, edited by J. Goodwin, J. Jasper, and F. Polletta. Chicago: University of Chicago Press, 175–94.
Benford, R. 1993. Frame disputes within the Nuclear Disarmament Movement. *Social Forces*, 71(3), 677–701.
Earl, J. 2006. Pursuing social change online: The use of four protest tactics on the internet. *Social Science Computer Review*, 20(10), 1–16.
Earl, J. and Kimport, K. 2011. *Digitally Enabled Social Change: Activism in the Internet Age*. New York: MIT Press.
Earl, J. and Schussman, A. 2003. The new site of activism: On-line organizations, movement entrepreneurs, and the changing locations of social movement decision making. *Research in Social Movements, Conflicts and Change*, 24, 155–87.
Flam, H. and King, D. 2005. *Emotions and Social Movements*. New York: Routledge.
Goodwin, J., Jasper, J., and Polletta, F. 2001. *Passionate Politics: Emotions and Social Movements*. Chicago: University of Chicago Press.
Goodwin, J., Jasper, J., and Polletta, F. 2004. Emotional dimensions of social movements, in *The Blackwell Companion to Social Movements*, edited by D. Snow, S. Soule, and H. Kriesi. Malden, MA: Blackwell, 413–32.
Goodwin, J. and Pfaff, S. 2001. Emotion work in high-risk social movements: Managing fear in the US and East German Civil Rights Movements, in *Passionate Politics: Emotions and Social Movements*, edited by J. Goodwin, J. Jasper, and F. Polletta. Chicago: University of Chicago Press, 282–302.
Gould, D. 2004. Passionate political processes: Bringing emotions back into the study of social movements, in *Rethinking Social Movements*, edited by J. Goodwin and J. Jasper. New York: Rowman & Littlefield, 155–76.
Gould, D. 2009. *Moving Politics*. Chicago: University of Chicago Press.
Hathaway, W. and Meyer, D.S. 1997. Competition and cooperation in movement coalitions: Lobbying for peace in the 1980s, in *Coalitions and Political Movements: The Lessons of the Nuclear Freeze*, edited by T. Rochon and D. Meyer. Boulder, CO: Lynne Rienner, 61–79.
Hochschild, A. 1979. Emotion work, feeling rules, and social structure. *American Journal of Sociology*, 85(2), 551–75.
Hochschild, A. 1983. *The Managed Heart: Commercialization of Human Feeling*. Berkeley: University of California Press.
Jasper, J. 1997. *The Art of Moral Protest: Culture, Biography, and Creativity in Social Movements*. Chicago: University of Chicago Press.
Jasper, J. 1998. The emotions of protest: Affective and reactive emotions in and around social movements. *Sociological Forum*, 13(3), 397–424.
Jasper, J. 2011. Emotions and social movements: Twenty years of theory and research. *Annual Review of Sociology*, 37, 285–303.
Jasper, J. and Poulsen, J. 1993. Fighting back: Vulnerabilities, blunders, and countermobilization by the targets in three animal rights campaigns. *Sociological Forum*, 8(4), 639–57.

Klandermans, B. 1984. Mobilization and participation: Social-psychological expansions of resource mobilization theory. *American Sociological Review*, 49(5), 583–600.

Klandermans, B. 1988. The formation and mobilization of consensus. *International Social Movement Research: A Research Annual*, 1, 173–96.

Klatch, R. 1999. *A Generation Divided: The New Left, The New Right and the 1960s*. Los Angeles: University of California Press.

Klein, J. and Rohlinger, D. Forthcoming. Constricting borders: Collective identity in the Tea Party Movement, in *Border Politics, Social Movements and Globalization*, edited by N. Naples and J. Bickham-Mendez. New York: New York University Press.

Kretschmer, K. and Meyer, D.S. 2007. Platform leadership: Cultivating support for a public profile. *American Behavioral Scientist*, 50(10), 1395–412.

McAdam, D. 1988. *Freedom Summer*. New York: Oxford University Press.

Mansbridge, J. 1986. *Why We Lost the ERA*. Chicago: University of Chicago Press.

Mansbridge, J. and Morris, A. 2001. *Oppositional Consciousness: The Subjective Roots of Social Protest*. Chicago: University of Chicago Press.

Morris, A. and Staggenborg, S. 2004. Leadership and social movements, in *The Blackwell Companion to Social Movements*, edited by D. Snow, S. Soule, and H. Kriesi. Malden, MA: Blackwell, 171–96.

Nepstad, S.E. and Smith, C. 2001. The social structure of moral outrage in recruitment to the US Central America Peace Movement, in *Passionate Politics: Emotions and Social Movements*, edited by J. Goodwin, J. Jasper, and F. Polletta. Chicago: University of Chicago Press, 158–74.

Reddy, W. 1997. Against constructionism: The historical enthnography of emotions. *Current Anthropolgy*, 38(3), 327–51.

Rohlinger, D., Bunnage, L., and Klein, J. Forthcoming. Virtual power plays: Social movements, ICT, and party politics, in *The Internet and Democracy: Voters, Candidates, Parties and Social Movements*, edited by B. Groffman, A. Trechsel, and M. Franklin. New York: Springer.

Schildkraut, D. 2002. The more things change: American identity and mass and elite responses to 9/11. *Political Psychology*, 23(3), 511–55.

Schussman, A. and Earl, J. 2004. From barricades to firewalls? Strategic voting and social movement leadership in the internet age. *Sociological Inquiry*, 74(4), 439–63.

Snow, D., Zurcher, L., and Olson-Ekland, S. 1980. Social networks and social movements: A microstructural approach to differential recruitment. *American Sociological Review*, 45(5), 787–801.

Staggenborg, S. 1986. Coalition work in the Pro-choice Movement: Organizational and environmental opportunities and obstacles. *Social Problems*, 33(5), 374–90.

Staggenborg, S. 1988. The consequences of professionalization and formalization in the Pro-choice Movement. *American Sociological Review*, 53(4), 585–606.

Tarrow, S. 1998. *Power in Movement: Social Movements and Contentious Politics*. New York: Cambridge University Press.

Taylor, V. 1989. Sources of continuity in social movements. *American Sociological Review*, 54, 761–75.

Taylor, V. 1996. *Rock-A-By Baby*. New York: Routledge.

Whittier, N. 2001. Emotional strategies: The collective reconstruction and display of oppositional emotions in the movement against child sexual abuse, in *Passionate Politics: Emotions and Social Movements*, edited by J. Goodwin, J. Jasper, and F. Polletta. Chicago: University of Chicago Press, 233–49.

Woehrle, L., Coy, P., and Maney, G. 2008. *Contesting Patriotism: Culture, Power, and Strategy in the Peace Movement*. New York: Rowman & Littlefield.

Wood, R. 2002. *Faith in Action: Religion, Race, and Democratic Organizing in America*. Chicago: University of Chicago Press.

Chapter 7
Who are "We the People"? Multidimensional Identity Work in the Tea Party[1]

Ruth Braunstein

From "Silent Majority" to "We the People"

In the large back room of a popular restaurant, 30 members of the Patriots[2] stand and face the flag to recite the Pledge of Allegiance before starting their monthly meeting. They have just shared their outrage that President Obama omitted the words, "endowed by their Creator," when he quoted the Declaration of Independence earlier in the week. Now we place our hands over our hearts and our voices merge as we recite from memory words I have not called forth in years. When we get to the phrase, "under God, indivisible," people shout—a small act of resistance against what they see as the steady erosion of core American values. As she calls the meeting to order, Linda, the Patriots' founder and leader, directs us to a handout. She has broken The Preamble down into seven segments, with commentary on each piece, followed by discussion questions. She asks if anyone can recite it by heart, as she had to do when she was in school. Everyone laughs as Pete, who is in his late sixties, races through the long memorized words, his eyes pinched closed to show he is not reading it from the paper. When he finishes, he takes a dramatic breath and smiles, "I guess I still remember it!" Now Linda turns to John, a longhaired mechanic in his late twenties, and asks him to read the first passage aloud. He begins, "We the People of the United States...."

As "we the people," the Patriots and other Tea Partiers around the country seek to stake a claim to the rights and privileges associated with membership in the category of the American citizenry. They have rallied around this collective identity as a constant reminder (to themselves and their public audiences) that ordinary men and women like them are legitimate participants in public debates about the decisions that shape their lives. They have organized in order to hold their elected officials accountable, a duty many regret they failed to uphold for

---

[1] I would like to thank David Meyer and Nella Van Dyke for their helpful editorial suggestions, as well as Courtney Bender, Hana Brown, Craig Calhoun, Jeff Manza, Rory McVeigh, Ashley Mears, Harel Shapira and David Snow for their valuable feedback on previous drafts. I would also like to thank the audience at the 2012 Young Scholars in Social Movements Mini-Conference at Notre Dame for their criticisms and suggestions.

[2] The names of all groups, individuals and places are pseudonyms.

many years. Addressing a local "taxpayers" watchdog group, Linda recounted her conversion story from a stay-at-home mom to a "politically crazed woman": "I was busy living the American Dream. I am sorry for that, because I wasn't paying attention." She cites the debate over ObamaCare—the Tea Party's term for the Affordable Care Act—as the moment when she sat up and took notice. This bill was concrete proof that President Obama was willing to legislate against the will of the people. This signaled a seismic shift: the world was shifting beneath her feet; the country was hurtling toward socialism. Although she used to be in the Navy, where she was taught not to question the President, she knew she needed to stand up and demand to be heard now, or her children's futures were at stake.

Others tell similar tales of awakening from decades of complacency and, armed with little or no knowledge about the political process, setting out to become informed citizen activists. While some joined through ties to local Republican networks or community groups, others showed up alone (and often in defiance of liberal friends and family members). Although some had previous political experience, many truly were novices. Linda, for example, had served on her local school board, while others had been privately honing their political chops for years—on internet message boards and around the dinner table—before timidly joining others in public. Some were small business owners concerned about overregulation; some were religious conservatives concerned that God was being "shoved out" of public life; and some were libertarian-leaning loners concerned about the erosion of individual liberty. They all sought to become the kinds of citizens who could keep government in check. They had long felt marginalized within a society obsessed with political correctness, maligned by a media biased toward the left, and ignored by political elites obsessed with their own power. They had been a "silent majority," but not for long; they were about to become "we the people."

This collective identity has empowered the Patriots to dig out their pocket Constitutions, call forth the Preamble from their middle school memories, and reclaim their voices as active citizens. They are fed up with "politics as usual," and blame both the Republican and the Democratic parties for failing to represent the American people. In theory, by shedding their partisan affiliations and rallying around a unifying collective identity as "we the people," they seek to reassert the rightful authority of all ordinary citizens. Yet this idea—that they are "we the people"—has little meaning in itself until it is enacted in the course of their collective activities.

Understanding the complex, and often contradictory, ways in which the Patriots define "we the people" in practice offers key insights into this movement, which we would miss by interpreting their collective action as a straightforward expression of conservative ideology. After all, to be conservative can mean a variety of things—it can signal an orientation against progress, a commitment to free market capitalism and limited government, or a traditionalist moral worldview, among other things. The qualities that characterize movements identifying as conservative have shifted over time, fail to adequately predict adherents' policy goals at any given time, and are perpetually contested by the diverse set of groups identifying as conservative (Gross et al. 2011). In order to situate this movement within the broader political field and understand its appeal to its members, it is necessary to examine the process through which actual groups of Tea Partiers act, interact, and define themselves in relation to a constellation of other political actors.

Drawing on ethnographic fieldwork with the Patriots, I show that when they actually set out to enact their collective identity as "we the people," they engage in identity work on two different fields of struggle. These fields are organized around two different goals, which are also in constant tension with one another—asserting their voices as citizens, on one hand, and advocating for particular policies, on the other. In the course of pursuing one goal or another, they map themselves in relation to different constellations of actors on each of these identity fields. The implicit meaning of the category of "the people" shifts as they align themselves with, and position themselves against, these different groups. Yet the meaning of "we the people" cannot be reduced to either of these dimensions alone. Indeed, when faced with contradictions or conflicts over their collective identities or goals, they also engage in identity work that helps them to navigate between and across these different identity fields.

Understanding Multidimensional Identity Work

A proliferation of research on New Social Movements and identity politics in the 1970s and 1980s led social movement researchers to take seriously the role of collective identity in political action (Laraña et al. 1994, Polletta and Jasper 2001). Although this early work focused on progressive movements, more recently scholars have shed light on the role collective identity plays in *all* movements (Bernstein 2005), including conservative and right-wing movements (McVeigh et al. 2004, Blee and Creasap 2010, Gross et al. 2011, Calhoun 2012).

Collective identity is "a shared sense of 'one-ness' or 'we-ness' anchored in real or imagined shared attributes and experiences among those who comprise the collectivity and in relation or contrast to one or more actual or imagined sets of 'others'" (Snow 2001). Collective identity is distinct from personal or social identity, although these often inform each other. Moreover, collective identity is something that people "carry and speak" in public (Lichterman 1999: 105). While some collective identities are rooted in interpersonal relationships, others are shared by groups of individuals who understand themselves as equivalent members of the same category, whether or not they know each other (Calhoun 1994). Some categorical identities are based on individual characteristics that all group members share—like gender, race, or class. But others are based on claims to membership in a political category—like the American citizenry—and the rights that come with this membership (Calhoun 1997, Taylor 2004, Anderson 2006).

Although groups often speak as if the bounds of such categories are fixed, they in reality infuse these categories with meaning through the collective definition of their boundaries and the modes through which they distinguish insiders from outsiders (Taylor and Whittier 1992, Schwalbe and Mason-Schrock 1996). This process also involves defining the other actors that comprise the political field on which a group operates (Bourdieu 1991, Calhoun 2012). This field includes not only adversaries—the "them" to a group's "us" (Gamson 1992)—but also allies, audiences, and relevant institutions (Hunt et al. 1994, Melucci 1995). Rather than approaching this "multiorganizational field" (Bernstein 1997) as something that objectively exists, however, we must observe how groups work together to construct different representations of one or more fields on which they imagine their collective action playing out. This approach implies an understanding of collective identity as both constructed (Snow and McAdam 2000) and intrinsically relational (Melucci 1995).

The process of constructing these fields and embedding one's group within them is achieved through a form of identity work called *mapping*. Although the concept of identity work refers to a much wider range of practices (Snow and Anderson 1987, Schwalbe and Mason-Schrock 1996, Reger et al. 2008), the concept of mapping specifically "highlights two distinct dimensions of identity work—the simultaneous definition of a group and its relevant social surroundings" (Lichterman 2008: 86). Although these social surroundings could consist of specific actors operating in a tangible local setting, they could also consist of more abstract categories of actors on a constructed identity field.[3]

This conceptual framework provides the tools necessary for understanding the complex process through which groups maintain multidimensional collective identities. Although previous research has found that groups pivot between different collective identities in different situations or contexts (Pulido 1996, Lichterman 1999), or as they pursue multiple goals (Melucci 1995, Bernstein 1997), less is known about the particular kind of identity work this requires. I propose that multidimensional identity work involves situating one's group simultaneously (or alternately) in multiple identity fields, each of which is organized around a different set of stakes, involves a different set of actors, and operates according to a different set of internal rules and criteria for inclusion and exclusion (Bourdieu 1984, 1991).

Mapping *within* each identity field should resemble the general model of identity work outlined by Schwalbe and Mason-Schrock (1996: 122):

> (1) *defining*, or the creation of a social representation that brings an identity into existence; (2) *coding*, or the creation of a set of rules for signifying an identity; (3) *affirming*, or the creation of opportunities for enacting and validating claims to an identity; and (4) *policing*, or the protection of the meaning of an identity and enforcement of the code for signifying it.

---

3 Hunt et al. (1994) conceptualize separate "identity fields" of protagonists, antagonists, and audiences, each of which consists of "constellations of identity attributions" associated with each set of actors. In contrast, I use the term "identity fields" to refer to representations of entire fields of action on which all of these groups and their relationships to one another are mapped.

Although much of this is achieved through identity talk (Hunt and Benford 1994, Lichterman 1999), we can also observe these processes in a variety of other group practices. For example, groups may signify and affirm their identities by selectively associating with or distancing from certain people, by wearing certain clothing or listening to certain kinds of music, or by engaging in certain rituals and activities (Snow and Anderson 1987, Bernstein 2008).

Yet groups must also reconcile conflicts and bridge differences *across* different identity fields. While Bernstein (2008) offers insights into how movements contend with *individuals'* multiple and intersecting identities, the challenges of managing conflicts between multiple or multidimensional *collective* identities remains untheorized. Extending the concept of mapping, we might think of the type of identity work this requires as akin to *navigating*. Although this navigational identity work could take a number of forms, it is likely to involve the definition of an overarching identity that is abstract enough to contain each subsidiary dimension; the creation of signifiers that are transposable onto each of the identity fields on which a group maps itself; and/or the use of criteria for inclusion and exclusion within each field that are flexible enough not to contradict the criteria used in other fields (Lamont and Fournier 1992, Jasper 1997).

In the following sections, I show how in the course of enacting their identity as "we the people," the Patriots map themselves onto two different identity fields, each of which implies a different definition of "the people." I then show how they reconcile tensions and contradictions by navigating across these two dimensions of their identity. They do so by constructing an overarching narrative identity that affirms their authenticity as the true protectors of America's founding principles and, thus, as model representatives of "we the people." Moreover, they extract from this narrative a set of behaviors associated with good citizenship that they use as flexible criteria for inclusions and exclusions within each identity field. In so doing, they are able to make necessary distinctions within *each* identity field, while maintaining the potential inclusivity of the category of "the people" across *both* identity fields.

Data and Methods

This analysis is based on data collected through ethnographic fieldwork in a handful of Tea Party groups in New York State between 2010 and 2012. The Patriots are one of the largest and most active of these groups, and where I focused my time and attention. During this time, I attended the majority of their monthly meetings and rallies, as well as occasional social gatherings. During election seasons, I volunteered alongside them and attended candidate "meet and greets" and debates sponsored by area groups. Following the shooting of Rep. Gabrielle Giffords (D-AZ), I accompanied 30 of them to a local shooting range for "some good old American Pistol/Rifle Shooting" and a group discussion about gun rights. I spent a weekend with volunteers staffing the group's informational tent at a local flea market, joined the early risers among them to pass out their group newspaper to morning train commuters and traveled with them to Glenn Beck's Restoring Honor Rally in Washington DC. I also attended meetings of other community groups with which Patriots members cross-pollinate: the local Republican club's Friday night "Pizza and Politics" discussions, a meeting of a local taxpayer watchdog group, and a regular gathering of veterans. Excerpts of all conversations and interactions are drawn from detailed field notes or transcripts of interviews with core group members.

I supplement my field notes with material drawn from the group's extensive online communications, which I have systematically collected since beginning fieldwork. Many of the Patriots post regularly on social networking platforms like Meetup, Facebook, and Twitter, and receive regular email communications from national organizations supporting Tea Party activism—the Tea Party Patriots, Tea Party Nation or FreedomWorks, for example. I, too, have plugged into most of these outlets during my time with the Patriots. I receive 20–30 emails on average per day from different local and national groups, and my RSS reader captures nearly that many blogs and comments posted daily by Tea Partiers I know personally. Most significant to the internal life of the group, however, is a daily email called the Must Know News. When newcomers add their name to the group's clipboard sign-in sheet or register through their website, they are essentially joining its email list. Each morning at 5:30 am, Linda sits down at her computer and drafts this lengthy email digest, which she sends to her growing list of subscribers. When I first met Linda, she had around 1,500 people on her list; it has since swelled to over 5,000. This list is a point of pride for the group. Disagreements with neighboring Tea Party leaders are often chalked up to jealously that her list is bigger than theirs.

At the end of each email is a comprehensive listing of events of interest to Tea Partiers across the tri-state area: from group meetings to public rallies to candidate fundraisers. While some of her subscribers never attend these face-to-face events, the more active among them attend several each week during busy periods. During periods in which there are few face-to-face activities scheduled in the area, the constant flow of online communications helps to keep participants connected to one another. Indeed, while meetings and rallies were sparse during the first half of 2012, Linda reported one summer morning that she had received 6,318 emails in response to her previous day's email in which she had asked: "Is ANYONE paying attention?" This, she announced, was "a[n] inbox record for me ... I am thrilled to know so many Patriots!" Although thousands of people immerse themselves in this online community, there are only between 50 and 100 regular participants in the group's face-to-face activities. Of these, around ten are considered core members who, along with Linda and her husband, steer the group's major strategic decisions.

Although the Patriots consider themselves part of the national assemblage of groups known as the Tea Party movement, no single group is representative of the movement as a whole. Despite some commonalities, there are also significant differences between groups identifying with this movement (Skocpol and Williamson 2012). It is thus necessary to consider how the Patriots compare to other Tea Party groups around the country. In demographic terms, the Patriots generally resemble other Tea Party activists (Williamson et al. 2011; Skocpol and Williamson 2012) and Tea Party supporters around the country (Zernike and Thee-Brenan 2010). Most of the Patriots are white, middle to upper-middle class, and slightly better educated than the general public. Many are small business owners. Many are veterans. All say they are concerned about the direction in which the country is headed.

Yet the political and economic context in which they operate differs from many other Tea Party groups. First, although the statewide and congressional districts from which the Patriots draw most of their members are nearly evenly divided between registered Democratic and Republican voters,[4] New York State as a whole leans heavily Democratic.[5] Meanwhile, most Tea Party activity in the country has been observed in Red states (Skocpol and Williamson 2012: 91). During the 2010 election cycle, however, the Patriots and other area groups injected new energy into several "swing" races, supporting non-establishment candidates first during tightly contested Republican primaries and then during the general election. They successfully sent candidates to both Congress and the statehouse.

At the same time, the economic position of their communities in relation to the urban center of the state drives a continued sense of marginalization. Whereas the city's economy has thrived even during the economic downturn, the rest of the state has been weakened by decades of deindustrialization. Even though most of the Patriots reside in relatively affluent suburbs, the widespread perception of an imbalance in power between the city and the rest of the state fuels resentments that permeate the statewide political landscape. Taken together, these factors could shape the group's collective identity in ways that may not be shared by Tea Party groups in different political and economic contexts.

Studying the Patriots as an outsider who does not share their collective identity raises a number of questions that cannot fully be addressed here, but some brief comments are necessary. I introduced myself to them as a researcher interested in citizen activism. Because Linda is in the process of completing her bachelor's degree—having returned to school after raising her four kids—she was particularly supportive of this research. They knew I was from "the City" and attended a university most of them automatically associated with "liberal elites." Whenever asked, I told them that my personal politics were more to the left, but that I was there with an open mind to learn about the issues that concerned them and spurred them to action. Most responded that that they were open to people of all political stripes who sought to be informed participants in the political process. With few exceptions, they have welcomed me into their activities, and I have maintained a friendly and respectful stance toward them. By welcoming a researcher who does not identify as part of their movement, they have shown their willingness to be scrutinized as public actors and to accept that an outsider might portray them fairly.

---

4   As of November 1, 2008, New York State Board of Elections.
5   The governor, both Senators and two-thirds of the Congressional delegation are Democrats. In 2008, 63 percent of New Yorkers voted for President Obama.

There are limits, of course, to what I am able to represent about their identities. I do not purport to have access to the thoughts or experiences that might inform their personal identities. What I have been able to document is how they "wear identities in public" (Lichterman 1999): the ways in which group members discuss, debate, reflect upon, and represent a sense of commonality with other group members and allies; as well as a sense of embattlement with illegitimate authorities and imagined rivals in their community and beyond. Throughout these interactions I have listened closely to the way the Patriots identify themselves individually, as a group, and in relation to a constellation of other actors operating at the local and national scales. I took note of each of these reference points, which are perpetually in flux, in order to map the fields in which they position themselves in any given situation.

Multidimensional Identity Work in the Patriots

When the Patriots set out to enact their identity as "we the people," they engage in identity work on two different fields of struggle. These fields are organized around two different goals, which are also in constant tension with one another—asserting their voices as citizens, on one hand, and advocating for particular policies, on the other. In the course of pursuing one goal or another, they map themselves in relation to different constellations of actors on each of these fields. The implicit meaning of the category of "the people" shifts as they align themselves with, and position themselves against, these different groups.

The Informed Citizen and the Taxpayer

It is 6 am when two middle-aged men stride toward me across the empty train station parking lot. They both carry unwieldy stacks of paper under each arm; they both wear khaki pants and button down shirts. "Business casual" was the term Gilbert had used to describe how I should dress this morning to distribute copies of their newspaper, *The Informed Citizen*, to commuters as they boarded their trains into the city. "This is just the type of activism the Patriots look for," he had written in his email the day before. "For me the days of yelling at the TV are over!" He said that after we finished handing out the papers, he would also be happy to talk to me about how he got involved in the group. "We call it the Ah-Ha moment!" As they approach, it is clear which one of them is Gilbert; his greeting, like his email, is punctuated by exclamation points. "There she is!"

He introduces me to Jamie and runs into the shop to buy a large coffee, which he sips even as drops of sweat drip from his forehead, forcing him to wipe them away with the back of his hand every few minutes during the next two hours. It is over 80 degrees and humid. They chat about how they should approach the station, and whether Jamie should take some of the papers and hit another station down the street soon. They agree he should, and keep looking around for someone named

Phil. Without finding him we head upstairs to the covered area people must pass through between the parking lot and the tracks. We situate ourselves at the top of the stairs. They explain that they have selected this spot so they are not in the way but are still able to catch most people. They say they have not had any trouble with the staff for passing out the newspapers, and they assume that as long as they are not bothering anyone they should be fine here. Jamie mentions having had only one run in so far. Truth be told, he seems a bit excited to have this war story to tell (and I have heard him tell it several times since). He says that he has seen the same guy twice while handing out the papers. He knows it's the same guy because he called him a racist both times. As he delivers this punch line, they both lower their eyes and shake their heads, noting it is unfortunate for someone to make such a snap judgment.

They show me the stack of a few hundred "newspapers," which are photocopied and stapled along the sides. The pages are all askew and stapled crookedly so they appear a bit amateurish. Over the next few months, *The Informed Citizen* would evolve from this stapled newspaper into a professionally laid out paper printed on newsprint. They explain that because the group is composed of many small business owners—including both of them—they are able to pool their skills and resources to write and produce these types of materials. Gilbert tells me that he and his wife Rebecca (also an active Patriot) own a small business that is tied to the real estate market and has suffered in recent years. They have had to make a number of difficult decisions, including laying off some of their employees and selling their retirement savings accounts, in order to keep their business afloat. Although they had never been politically active before, they started paying attention to politics because they believed that the requirements imposed on small businesses by "ObamaCare" would mean the end of their livelihoods. They think that government should be required to make the same kinds of sacrifices they have had to make during tough times. Now he and Rebecca are involved in a number of Tea Party groups in the area. Despite having a young child, they manage to show up at multiple events each week.

Just standing in this train station triggers Gilbert's frustration about a new payroll tax intended to help the state transit authority balance its budget. Several times over the next few hours, he complains that business owners in the suburbs are being asked to pay for a system that they use less frequently than people in the city, and sometimes not at all. Although this specific tax is on his mind, he does not see it as an isolated issue. He transitions seamlessly from talking about the transit tax to talking about ObamaCare, citing both as evidence of a broader pattern of "unconstitutional" infringements by an overactive government on the rights of "we the people." Linda expressed a similar sentiment on her blog a few months later:

> The truth of the matter is our government and their friends no longer believe they are answerable to our laws or to We the People, but is very much answerable to 'some'. Make no mistake—what we are witnessing is a runaway and unlawful

federal government and its allies that are damn close to destroying the United States of America. Their unconstitutional actions are countless.

This statement, like Gilbert's complaints in the train station, defines a set of actors and their relationships to one another. In both cases, they portray a government in breach of its contract to "we the people." Its crime: reaching into their pockets, extracting tax money, and redistributing it against their will. Although Gilbert primarily associates this radical redistributive agenda with President Obama and the Democratic Party, he also expresses frustration with Republicans in Washington and Albany. "They should be really enthusiastic about serving the public," he says of his representatives from both parties. But he worries that most of them are mainly interested in keeping their jobs and their generous government benefits. By this account, even most Republicans have been unwilling to curtail government's expanding reach into the lives of the hardworking people who pay its bills.

Linda acknowledges that there are "some" citizens who support this form of government action, yet this category is defined as outside of and in opposition to "we the people." A few months after we handed out newspapers, Gilbert's wife Rebecca spoke at a local rally. Her comments clarify the way in which the Patriots distinguish themselves from those who support redistributive policies, and the grounds on which these others are excluded from "we the people." After telling the crowd about her own experiences as a small business owner and as part of a family struggling to get by, she launched into a critique of the Obama administration's redistributive agenda. She concluded by distinguishing herself and the rest of the people gathered from those who receive benefits from these policies: "There is a difference between those who produce something and provide for themselves, and those who produce nothing and brag about it!" The crowd burst into applause.

When they speak about redistributive policies in this manner, they effectively divide "the people" into two categories: hardworking taxpayers like themselves and lazy, undeserving others who are taking more than their fair share. Of course, they ignore the extent to which middle-class and wealthy Americans also receive government benefits that may outweigh their net contributions to the system (Steuerle and Rennane 2011). Still, by defining themselves as "payers," the Patriots distance themselves from "takers" by highlighting the moral value of work and personal responsibility. In so doing, they also align themselves, somewhat uneasily, with the Republican Party and other elites advocating on behalf of wealthy and corporate "taxpayers."

For Gilbert and the rest of the Patriots, it is not just about the transit tax or ObamaCare; it is about the quiet destruction of a country that values thrift, autonomy and entrepreneurialism, a country where small businesses and middle-class taxpayers are celebrated rather than crushed. As a small business owner himself, Jamie agrees with this sentiment. But he also makes a point to preface any criticism of the government with an acknowledgement that the people have failed to uphold their end of the bargain, too. The group's resident economic expert and a self-proclaimed "capitalist," Jamie is also a "reformed hippie." He told me on that first day we met that the protestors of the 1960s (himself included) did a lot of work to keep the government in check, and then everything started going well and people stopped paying attention. People got comfortable going to work every day and driving big cars and living in big houses, and they stopped paying attention to the government. Now everything has gotten out of control again, and it's up to those same citizens to push back to preserve everything they have worked for. That the Tea Party is an older, wiser and wealthier incarnation of 1960s protest movements is not, for him, a contradiction in terms.

Similarly, Linda insists, "It's no longer a right–left thing." Rather, it is about being informed and engaged. She compared the dilemma facing Americans to that facing the hero of the movie *The Matrix*. She had started writing the Must Know News for the following morning, so she gave me a preview of the question she planned to pose to the group:

> Morpheus, the leader of a small but growing movement (today's equivalent to the Tea Party) seeks to challenge the contemporary power structure (our government). Neo is believed to be "the chosen one" who will lead humans out of captivity (That's us individually). Early in the film Morpheus gives Neo a choice between a red pill and a blue pill. If he takes the red pill he can see the world as it truly is. If he takes the blue pill he will wake up at home, remember nothing, and continue to live in a mirage. As you read the following, I ask you just one question—which pill will you take—the blue or the red?

The Patriots, she explains, have chosen "to have our eyes wide open. And then there's 50% of Americans that are taking the other pill and they don't want to know anything. They say, the government's got it, you know, we're good and we're busy raising our kids, and we don't have time for this. It's a choice."

These comments map their group onto a field in which the Tea Party is framed as the vanguard of a "small but growing movement" against government and elite domination, which has the potential to one day include *all* of "the people." With their eyes wide open, they are working tirelessly to scratch the surface of an opaque political process, peer inside, and report back what they have seen. They are confident that if only people take the time to listen to the "facts," they will join their efforts. Of course, Linda worries aloud that some people may be beyond their reach. Technically, to qualify as an "informed citizen" requires that one gather the "facts" from multiple sources, set aside one's biases, and approach each policy question with an open mind. *The Informed Citizen* and the Must Know News are intended to aid people in this process, by offering a wider range of views than the mainstream media provides and empowering group members to develop the knowledge required to evaluate alternative claims. The problem, Linda notes, is that "it's not going to matter to the people on the Left that want socialism, who want communism, that want all this kind of crap. Because *you're never going to open their eyes, because they believe it*." With this logic, she deems people on "the Left" incapable of fulfilling their responsibilities as citizens. She claims this is not because she disagrees with their conclusions, but because she believes their ideological commitments render them incapable of open-minded deliberation and rational debate.

But the Patriots assert that the majority of *reasonable* Americans would agree with them, if only they too opened their eyes. After all, the Patriots do not believe they are demanding anything controversial: they want only to safeguard those values that make America the greatest country on earth, which the founders enshrined in the Constitution and which the military has sacrificed time and again to protect. Their task is therefore not only to confront government elites, but also to convince others to join their fight. While Gilbert and Jamie do their part by distributing the newspaper, other members of the group contribute in their own ways. Josephine, who has been part of the group since its earliest days, produces homemade pamphlets that she drops off at local businesses in her town to be distributed to their customers. The glossy pamphlets feature a clipart image of an American flag rippling in the wind. Underneath the flag, she has printed the title, "Seeds of Liberty," followed by a list of three "seeds":

> **Faith** in the Lord God our Creator
> **Knowledge** of the History of the United States and the World Around Us
> **Courage** To Speak Out and Fight to Defend The Founding Fathers' Gift to Us ... The Constitution of These United States.

She also regularly submits letters to the editor of her local newspaper and posts at her blog on the group's website. In her blog, she often acknowledges that she is overwhelmed by the task ahead of them. After all, she explains in a post on the group's website, the Patriots and other Tea Party groups can only do so much without the rest of their fellow citizens lending a hand:

> There is so much to pay attention to if WE THE PEOPLE want to protect Our Country, Our Constitution, Our Liberty ... WE ARE IN TROUBLE and right now, I'm not sure those of us who have been tirelessly on top of it all can continue without a majority of the country helping. In the words of Abraham Lincoln ... "America will never be destroyed from the outside. If we falter and lose our freedoms, it will be because we destroyed ourselves."

It is this sense of urgency to spread the word that drives Josephine to write pamphlet after pamphlet and print them up at her own expense; sends Linda to her computer every morning at 5:30 am; and sends Jamie and Gilbert to the train station hours before their long workdays begin. And it is this desire to convert "a majority of the country" that structures Gilbert's interactions with passersby.

As we stand on the train platform, Gilbert is above-average friendly to everyone who passes. He extends a newspaper to each person, saying, "Just a little something put together by a group of concerned citizens in the area." He is careful to identify them each time as "concerned citizens," not as business owners or conservative citizens or members of the Tea Party (although the newspaper identifies them clearly as such). Just "concerned citizens," a broad identity that is accurate in some sense, and likely shared with many people who passed. While each person's concerns are likely different, it is as if those differences are less relevant this morning than the need for all of them to come together, inform themselves, and become the type of citizenry that can hold government accountable to its constitutional mandate.

He goofily struggles to balance the newspapers and his coffee while wiping sweat from his brow, often chuckling and offering self-deprecating jokes to the people who reach for the sweaty papers. He asks if I am there to help or just observe. I waver, but watching him struggle I eventually take the stack of newspapers and hold them while he passes them out. Most people take them without looking. Some flatly refuse. Others scan the front to determine what it is all about, and many do not take it at all. One man lingers nearby at the top of the stairs as he reads it. When he finishes reading, he looks up at me and shakes his head. Saying nothing, he hands the newspaper back to Gilbert and descends the stairs. The man named Phil eventually arrives, and Jamie leaves with him to tackle another station down the road. Gilbert comments that this is just the sort of thing he loves about working with these guys. No one has to tell them to do anything. They just want to get stuff done.

The significance of this practice was confirmed when I discovered that this was one of the activities that the Patriots highlighted when a local journalist profiled the group. Upon reading his description of Jamie and Gilbert distributing newspapers in the local newspaper months later, I was struck by the similarities to my own experience. They brought him to the same train station they brought me, and gave him nearly the same spiel they gave me. The quotes he ran could have been copied from my own field notes. Their practiced repetition revealed this was a performance that had been staged: for my benefit, for the journalist, and for the broader public in which they imagine themselves as participants. But this activity was not *only* about promoting a careful public image of their group. They went to the train station to hand out newspapers before the journalist or I arrived, and continued going after. They handed the newspaper out at rallies and information booths, posted it on their website and left it in the vestibules of local shops and restaurants. Josephine and others followed suit in their own ways, barely aware that anyone might be watching. These practices are as meaningful for participants in the group as they are central to the image they project beyond the group.

Sitting in a diner near her home months later, Linda told me that of all of the things the group had done together, the newspaper was what she was most proud of. I had expected her to point to recent electoral victories by the candidates they had supported or the increase in the size of the group. But she explained that it was the newspaper, "because we got it into people's hands that were not part of the Tea Party. The Tea Party, you know, you're preaching to the choir … They're the ones already doing their homework." She told me, "everybody that handed out that newspaper came back with at least two conversations, where people had read it, had already gotten it and were saying, 'I didn't know this, or I didn't know that.'" She recalled that I had been with them and asked if I was there the day they had "gotten their heads handed to them," referencing the man who had called them racists. I said I had heard about it. She nodded and shrugged, "Yeah, but they read it. It doesn't matter what they outwardly said. They left with it. They read it." The waitress interrupted us. "You want more coffee?" Linda signaled for her to refill my cup. She continued, "I don't need to be right. I just need people to think, and know. That's my thing. I hope I'm wrong ... I swear to God I hope I'm wrong!"

Struggling over Identities and Goals

I have shown that in the course of enacting their collective identity as "we the people," the Patriots map themselves onto two different identity fields, each of which implies a different definition of the people. On one hand, they define themselves as the vanguard of a potentially broad-based group of informed citizens struggling to reclaim their rightful democratic authority from elites. On the other hand, they define themselves as payers against takers (and their "socialist" allies) in a struggle for control over government spending. Yet the meaning of "we the people" cannot be reduced to either of these dimensions alone. Indeed, in this section, I show how the group struggles to maintain a precarious balance between both dimensions, while also maintaining distance from a partisan identity.

It was 42 days and counting until the 2010 midterm elections, and tonight's meeting would be about the Patriots' strategy during the weeks leading up to Election Day. After we recited the Pledge of Allegiance, Linda pulled a small book from her stack of materials and began reading aloud. She sat at one of six large banquet tables that had been shoved into the corner of the large back room of the restaurant. Over the sound of forks clinking and people whispering, she read about ordinary citizens who joined civic organizations, wrote letters, and staged rallies. When she was done, she looked around for dramatic effect and explained that what they were doing here today is just like what people were doing earlier in our country's history. People looked around their tables, nodding to one another knowingly.

It is not uncommon for the Patriots to connect their activism to earlier episodes in American history. Linda did so explicitly here, but this continuity with the past is also signaled more subtly each time they refer to their movement as the Tea Party, reference their duty to protect the Constitution, quote the Founding Fathers, or stand to recite the Pledge. These references are drawn from a deep well of political and religious symbols that are woven into a sweeping narrative of ordinary people standing up to protect a particular vision of American greatness. A standard version of the Patriots' narrative starts with the Sons of Liberty quietly organizing their neighbors and preparing for the event that would later be called the Boston Tea Party. Declaring the system of "no taxation without representation" illegitimate, they stood up to their distant and illegitimate rulers and the corporation that was benefitting (with the government's blessing) off the backs of ordinary people.

The narrative continues with the drafting of the Declaration of Independence, when Thomas Jefferson enshrined the notion that "all men are created equal, that they are endowed by their Creator with certain inalienable rights." These words serve as the textual basis for their claims to democratic authority. Recall their anger at President Obama when he allegedly omitted the phrase "endowed by their Creator" from his reading of this document. For most of the Patriots, these words—like the phrase "one nation under God" in the Pledge of Allegiance— also confirm America's heritage as a nation founded on Judeo-Christian values, and justify continued adherence to these values even as the United States grows increasingly value-diverse.

The next chapter in their narrative is the drafting of the Constitution and Bill of Rights, and the tales of conflict and compromise among the Founding Fathers engaged in negotiating these foundational documents. Not only do they hold up these men as models for what public figures in a democracy should look like, but they site these documents as contracts that contemporary elected officials are duty-bound to uphold. In this way, Tea Partiers often speak of the Constitution as an inerrant text akin to a fundamentalist's Bible. As Linda explained in an interview, the job of elected officials is quite simple:

> Uphold the constitution. Do what the Constitution allows you to do. Nothing more, nothing less. They can't even do that. Document's been around for 200 years. Watching them read it, you would swear to God they'd never read it once ... But stick with the Constitution. You can't go wrong. Can't go wrong!

This logic requires they subject policies to the test of whether they are consistent with the "intent of the Founders." Concerns about the transit tax and ObamaCare, for example, were framed in terms of how these policies breached the government's contract with "we the people."

Finally, they trace their lineage forward, through the men and woman of the armed forces who have protected these Constitutional values again and again, against threats ranging from socialism to radical Islam. Because so many of the Patriots have served in the military, at one time or another, this represents the ultimate expression of what it means to be an American patriot. By extension, to disrespect the Constitution is to disrespect the considerable sacrifices of these men and women. When they refer to themselves as "we the people," they call forth this entire narrative of faithful stewardship of America's founding principles. As selective as it is sweeping, this particular telling of America's history is nonetheless familiar to most of the Patriots, and provides context for their group practices.

After closing her book, Linda calls upon everyone to do what they can to contribute to the upcoming general election. A number of the candidates that people in this room had supported have emerged victorious from their Republican primaries the previous week, and this group of newly minted politicos is feeling confident. She reminds everyone that the Patriots will not be endorsing a candidate in the general election. It is *up to each of them* to select a candidate to support—

based on their own research and individual priorities. Once they have done this, the most important thing they can all do is put up a lawn sign. From the other side of the room, someone chimes in: "It's all about organizing. But the problem is that the Republicans aren't organized." Next to me, one of the group's youngest members, John, starts shaking his head.

The first time I met John he was wearing a black t-shirt with large white letters across the front saying, "Who is John Galt?" a reference to the protagonist in Ayn Rand's novel *Atlas Shrugged*. We were at a large rally in the parking lot of this same restaurant about a month earlier, and Linda had dragged him to meet me. She introduced him as her "absolute #1 favorite Tea Partier." He blushed, and she asked how everything was going with his family. He said that they are still fighting about everything. Apparently, they are not supportive of his newfound political views. She turned to me and said, "Family is the hardest part." She was called away to deal with something on stage, and he told me that a few years ago he had not been political at all, but that in the last year he had started reading more and more about politics and sought out a local group that thought about things the way he did. When a friend forwarded Linda's email to him, he had gotten in touch with her and started attending events. In his late twenties, he was one of the youngest people there. He works as a mechanic, and said he is often too tired after a long day at work to socialize. "So here I am talking to you!" he laughed, seeming embarrassed.

I can tell he is growing increasingly frustrated tonight as he listens to the group strategizing about the election. He tries to interject: "But we're not the Republican Party!" But no one hears him. Meanwhile, Gilbert (who is about 6'5 to John's 5'10) stands up so he can get everyone's attention. Echoing John's point, he says, "The thing about the Tea Party is that there's no central leadership. It's like herding cats." He says that part of why he likes the Tea Party is that it is made up of people who are very individualistic, strong-minded, small-business owner types. Frankly, he acknowledges, it's hard to get those people to work together or toward any common purpose. "And that's ok."

Changing the subject, Linda asks everyone to turn to a 1934 *Chicago Tribune* cartoon that has been circulating in the Tea Party blogosphere. She has printed it out for everyone to discuss. It is called "Planned Economy or Planned Destruction" and it depicts a horse-drawn wagon carrying "young pinkies from Columbia and Harvard" throwing bags of money into the street. On the back of the wagon are the words "Depleting the resources of the soundest government in the world." In the bottom left-hand corner, a bearded man writes, "Plan of Action for U.S.: SPEND! SPEND! SPEND under the guise of recovery—bust the government—blame the capitalists for the failure—junk the Constitution and declare a dictatorship." In the distance, a cross-armed Stalin remarks, "How red the sunrise is getting!"

It only takes a moment for people to start commenting aloud about how similar it is to their current situation. John raises his hand and notes that it shows how close we came before to destroying the country. Yet, he notes hopefully, they somehow managed to come together and pull themselves out. Someone in the back of the room shouts, "The difference though, is that Roosevelt loved America!" It is not uncommon for Tea Partiers to question opponents' love for and loyalty to America as grounds for delegitimizing their positions. Another Patriot once told me, "You know, I honestly do believe that for the first time we have a president in the White House who I feel in my heart and soul is a traitor to this country." But tonight, Linda cuts this man off and says sternly, "It's not just about Obama. And it's not about Democrats and Republicans. This is about us not being vigilant and letting our political leaders take too much power." She reminds them that even if they feel like they win this time around, they have to stay vigilant or they will just slip back into the way things were. The man backs down. "It's true," he responds. "You know what they say? We get the government we deserve. People are people. Everyone's a crook at heart. If we stop watching, it will go right back."

An older woman agrees. "We've won the battle," she said, "but we have a long war ahead of us." In a somber tone, the woman next to her says she is not sure how they can ever fix things. "I mean, how do we get rid of all of these regulations? All of these huge agencies, the EPA [Environmental Protection Agency]." While she speaks, Linda's son, who is around 30 and an active member of the group himself, starts to get visibly agitated. As she rattles off a list of federal agencies and insists that we simply need to get rid of all of them, he grows impatient and cuts her off. "But we need some of those!" he snaps. He reminds everyone that a few decades ago, the EPA stopped companies that were dumping chemicals into their water. He says he understands her point that they have gotten too big, but "we need *some* regulations."

There is a lull in the otherwise riotous conversation. No one else speaks on the topic. An older woman across the room suddenly says, "What we really need is to teach our children." She explains that she has recently adopted a new grandchild, and has been teaching her the Pledge of Allegiance, "including the 'under God' part!" Everyone laughs, the awkwardness of their other disagreements set aside for now. Linda is nodding in vigorous agreement with this point. She mentions that Josephine could not be there tonight, but that she had called to tell her she had been reading her grandchild's history book and was outraged to find that in an entire chapter, "There were only two pages on Christianity. The rest of it was on Islam!" The room erupted in nods and groans and murmurs of "Two pages?!" and "Yes, I know!" and "Islam ... of course." "She is beside herself," Linda says. "She said last year she *never* would have looked at the child's book, but now." A number of them have sat on their town school boards, and they begin trading war stories. These stories, like the cartoon, are all delivered with the same moral: the need for "we the people" to be vigilant in the face of these mounting threats to American values.

Identity Work Within and Across Identity Fields

Mapping Within Identity Fields

I have shown that the Patriots have organized around a collective identity as "we the people." When they set out to enact this collective identity in practice, however, they engage in identity work on two different (and sometimes conflicting) identity fields. Each of these fields is organized around a different set of stakes, involves a different set of actors, and operates according to a different set of internal rules and criteria for inclusion and exclusion. I have introduced the concepts of mapping and navigating in order to explain the ways in which they engage in identity work *within* and *across* these different identity fields. In this section, I review the specific practices they use to map their group *within* each identity field.

On one level, the Patriots imagine themselves engaged in a struggle to assert their voices and claim their rightful democratic authority as part of the American citizenry. On this field of struggle, they define themselves as the vanguard of a broad-based movement against elite domination, which could eventually include all of "the people." Membership in this category requires informing oneself and becoming the kind of active citizen capable of engaging in reasoned public debate with both neighbors (defined as potential recruits to this effort who have not yet "opened their eyes") and elites (defined as distant, out of touch and in breach of their responsibility to represent the people).

They have developed a variety of practices that members use to map themselves onto this identity field. When Linda says that it is not about left versus right, but about being informed or not, she explicitly defines the criteria for membership in "the people." By naming their newspaper *The Informed Citizen*, they align their group with this category. By handing out this newspaper to their neighbors, identifying themselves as concerned citizens, recounting their disappointment about being called racists, and welcoming members of all political stripes (including me) they publicly affirm the potential inclusivity of this category. Meanwhile, when they refer to the government and elected officials as distant, out of touch, corrupt or unaccountable to the people, they position themselves in opposition to these illegitimate authorities.

On another level, however, the Patriots imagine themselves engaged in a struggle for control over government spending. On this field of struggle, the category of "the people" no longer comprises all informed citizens positioned against illegitimate elites. Instead, they encode "the people" as the hardworking yet exploited "payers" in a redistributive system of excessive taxation and spending, and align themselves with this category. In so doing, they position themselves against a group of "takers" who are not paying their fair share, yet are being aided and abetted by a "socialist" government. Moreover, because they primarily associate Democratic Party elites with these "socialist" policies, this positioning also brings them into uneasy alignment with Republican Party elites. This mapping thus operates in tension with their efforts to maintain critical distance from both parties, and to resist domination by all elites.

Mapping on this identity field is achieved through a variety of practices. They carefully develop practiced accounts of the ways in which individual policies unfairly burden some citizens, while benefitting others who are less deserving. At the same time, they abstract away from the specific details of each policy by embedding each in a broader pattern of what they consider "unconstitutional" action by an overactive government. When they identify these policies as unconstitutional and as breaches of the government's contract with "we the people," they delimit the category of "the people" to the overburdened "payers." They then signal their alignment with this group by: introducing themselves as small business owners; mentioning in passing how hard they work and the sacrifices they make to get by (contrasting this to the unwillingness of both government and the recipients of government aid to make the same sacrifices during tough times); suggesting volunteers dress in "business casual" when interacting with neighbors; and demonstrating through their volunteerism a "can-do" spirit that they associate with entrepreneurialism and personal responsibility.

This process of mapping themselves within each identity field looks similar to identity work observed in many groups (Schwalbe and Mason-Schrock 1996). Through a variety of different kinds of group practices, they define the category in which they seek to claim membership and situate it in a particular field of action; they specify a set of criteria for membership in the category; they enact this identity by engaging in practices that affirm their membership; and they police the boundaries of the category using various strategies of distinguishing insiders from outsiders. Where I go beyond existing theorizing is in showing that groups engage in this process on *multiple* identity fields simultaneously, and that they must constantly work to manage tensions between them. In order to reconcile contradictions and bridge differences across identity fields, they use a form of identity work I call *navigating*. This concept builds on the idea of mapping (Melucci 1995, Lichterman 2008), but refers specifically to the identity work required of groups balancing multiple or multidimensional collective identities. The Patriots' navigational identity work takes two main forms, discussed in the following section.

Navigating Across Identity Fields

Overarching Narrative Identity First, the Patriots construct an overarching "narrative identity" (Somers 1994). Although previous research has identified narrative as a common form of identity talk, it has typically focused on what Somers (1994: 618) calls "ontological narratives"—stories that individual social actors tell to define who they are, what they are doing, where they have been, and where they are going (Hunt and Benford 1994, Tilly 2002, Polletta 2006). The Patriots, on the other hand, have constructed a narrative identity that draws on, transforms, and embeds their group within a "public narrative" (Somers 1994: 619): namely, a history of America's founding and perseverance. When the Patriots study the Preamble, adorn their pamphlets and newspapers with American flags, quote the Founding Fathers, recite the Pledge of Allegiance together, and read aloud from histories of citizen activism, they signal their connection to a long line of American patriots who have protected the country and its foundational values from destruction.

This narrative identity facilitates their navigational identity work in the following ways. First, the narrative is *abstract* enough to contain both subsidiary dimensions of their identity. In this single narrative, they see reflections of themselves as both informed citizens standing up to distant and unresponsive decision-makers, and as aggrieved taxpayers standing up for their right to individual liberty from the tyranny of collective obligations. Within the context of this narrative, these identities are not contradictory, but mutually reinforcing. Second, the narrative contains *modular symbols* that the group is able to draw upon, in different ways, within both identity fields. For example, the Constitution serves as the basis for their claims to democratic authority and as a tool for assessing the legitimacy of policy. These symbols thus serve as threads that maintain continuity between both dimensions of their identity.

Third, the narrative offers *characters and plot lines* that help the Patriots make sense of their own contradictions. The drafters of the Constitution, for example, are portrayed as enmeshed in struggle over competing interests and goals, which they transcend only due to their larger shared love for their country. When the Patriots explicitly reference disagreements among the Founding Fathers or declare with pride that getting the group to agree on any single strategy is like "herding cats ... and that's ok," they draw on this narrative in order to code their own group *struggles* as signifiers of their patriotism and authenticity as the true protectors of the vision of the Founding Fathers and, thus, as model representatives of "we the people." This allows them to smooth over conflicts within group settings and to maintain commitment to one another and their shared project amidst myriad disagreements.

Finally, the narrative not only situates them in relation to other actors, but also in *time*. While individual narratives help activists to make sense of their action by "locating" them in biographical time (Hadden and Lester 1978), public narratives locate groups in historical time. Specifically, the narrative on which the Patriots draw links together a series of pivotal moments in which the actions of patriotic men and women like them have determined whether America thrives or declines. When they speak ominously about the country's imminent destruction, they refocus the groups' attention on the urgency and historical import of their action. This not only helps them to overcome disagreements within the group over how to balance competing identities and goals, but also represents an effort to lift their group above the partisan fray. Such petty squabbles are cast as insignificant; after all, the very soul of America is at stake, and it is up to them to protect it.

Flexible Criteria of Inclusion and Exclusion In their second form of navigational identity work, the Patriots employ criteria for inclusion and exclusion within each identity field that are *flexible* enough that they do not explicitly contradict the criteria used in other fields. On each of the fields on which they map their identities, they simultaneously claim inclusivity and assert their differences from groups of opponents and unworthy "others." Because they justify these inclusions and exclusions on different grounds within each field of struggle, in some cases it may appear that the two dimensions of their identity conflict. For example, their alignment with Republican elites and conservative ideologues when pursuing policy goals operates in tension with their simultaneous efforts to maintain critical distance from both parties and all elites. Their vilification of welfare recipients—who are disproportionately coded as African Americans or Hispanic immigrants in national Tea Party rhetoric (Zernike 2010, Williamson et al. 2011, Skocpol and Williamson 2012)—operates in tension with their rejections of accusations of racism and their efforts to align themselves with *all* citizens across the political divide who seek to inform themselves and hold elites accountable.

They manage these tensions by avoiding criteria rooted in static group *characteristics*, whether these are partisan, ideological, racial, ethnic, or religious. Instead, they define "the people" in terms of *behaviors* they associate with good citizenship. These behaviors—including being informed, hard working, and patriotic—are extracted from their overarching narrative identity as "we the people." Because these behaviors are hypothetically available to *all* citizens, the Patriots argue that distinctions made on these grounds are acceptable. After all, they are only excluding those individuals who *choose* not to educate themselves about issues and engage in public debates with an open mind; those who *choose* not to work hard and instead take handouts; and those who hate America and wish to destroy the Constitution. If the individuals effectively excluded on these grounds happen to be disproportionately Democrats, liberals/leftists, Muslims, African Americans or Hispanic immigrants, for example, this is simply attributed to the fact that members of these groups are not behaving as good citizens. By drawing on these flexible tools of distinction, they maintain the potential inclusivity of the category of "the people" across *both* identity fields, while still making those distinctions necessary within *each* identity field to define the group in relationship to opponents or unworthy "others."

On the surface, this style of identity work resembles "civic" nationalism (Brubaker 1999), a form of national identity work that is often characterized as *inclusive*, and contrasted to more *exclusionary* forms of national identity work that code the categories of "American" or "the people" in explicitly racial, ethnic, or religious terms (Gerteis and Gooslby 2005, McVeigh 2009). But this case reveals that this distinction is not so clear. Indeed, while the Patriots make *explicit* distinctions on civic grounds, they *implicitly* exclude groups of racial, ethnic, and religious minorities, as well as Democrats and people they associate with the ideological left.

Moreover, even the seemingly inclusive civic criteria they use are exclusionary in some ways. While being informed, open-minded, and reasonable are qualities associated with a widely accepted liberal model of citizenship (Habermas 1989, Schudson 1998), critics have called attention to the ways in which even these criteria tacitly exclude a number of groups from full participation in public life (Calhoun 1992, Fraser 1992). Moreover, the behaviors associated with good citizenship have changed over time and are perpetually contested by different groups within American society today (Schudson 1998, Lepore 2010). By selectively associating some behaviors and not others with their definition of "the people," they assert the moral superiority of their particular vision of American citizenship, while dismissing other visions as anti-American.

By drawing on behaviors rather than group characteristics as their criteria of inclusion and exclusion, the Patriots are able to reconcile conflicts between the two different dimensions of their identity. Moreover, this allows them to derive the internal group-making benefits of exclusion (McVeigh et al. 2004), while associating themselves with a more inclusive and publicly acceptable style of identity work.

Conclusions

Observers of social movement groups often seek to decode these groups' true identities, and interpret multidimensionality as either a failure to achieve consensus or an effort in duplicity. Yet many groups, like the Patriots, do not have a single stable identity. The conceptual framework proposed in this chapter offers insights into how such groups balance multidimensional identities in practice. This involves identity work on two separate but interacting levels: *mapping* within each identity field, and *navigating* across multiple identity fields. More research is required to determine whether similar practices are found within other groups working to balance multiple or multidimensional identities, and whether the form that mapping and navigating takes varies systematically across different kinds of groups. But the benefit of such a framework is that it allows researchers to account for apparent contradictions within collective identities that might otherwise be interpreted as group failures, or worse, organized out of explanations. Instead, this framework offers insights into how these contradictions themselves may actually play a role in constituting collective identity. In this light, the management of multidimensionality must be understood as an ongoing achievement of collective action.

An analysis of the Patriots as a straightforward expression of conservative ideology would be unable to account for a number of the contradictions that run through this group, and the broader Tea Party movement of which it is a part. By analyzing the way in which the Patriots enact a multidimensional identity as "we the people," this chapter offers deeper insights into the complex and sometimes conflicting ways in which these activists understand their collective action and their relationship to other actors on the political field. To be "we the people" is not only to identify as informed citizens or payers, to confront elites or takers, to demand a voice as citizens or advocate for constitutional policy arrangements. It is also to struggle over these identities and goals, just as their revolutionary forebears and the Founding Fathers did. It is to be engaged, to be vigilant, and above all to be critical (always, of everyone, even the Tea Party). The Patriots' association with America's revolutionary history serves as a narrative thread that connects each of these dimensions of their identity, while also justifying exclusions within each of the fields on which they imagine their collective action playing out. On their journey of transformation from being a member of the "silent majority" to becoming "we the people," this narrative identity has served as a source of guidance, strength, and commonality for many of the Patriots. It anchors participants to the movement and to each other, despite other differences they may have. While people can argue over whether or not they live up to the standards of good citizenship they associate with their identity as "we the people" (or whether these standards are in fact democratic), associating themselves with this vision of democratic practice has given the Patriots a sense of purpose and commitment that has outlived their critics' expectations.

References

Anderson, B. 2006. *Imagined Communities: Reflections on the Origin and Spread of Nationalism*. 3rd ed. New York and London: Verso.
Bernstein, M. 1997. Celebration and suppression: The strategic uses of identity by the lesbian and gay movement. *American Journal of Sociology*, 103(3), 531–65.
Bernstein, M. 2005. Identity politics. *Annual Review of Sociology*, 31, 47–74.
Bernstein, M. 2008. The analytic dimensions of identity: A political identity framework, in *Identity Work in Social Movements*, edited by J. Reger, D.J. Myers, and R.L. Einwohner. Minneapolis: University of Minnesota Press, 277–301.
Blee, K.M. and Creasap, K.A. 2010. Conservative and right-wing movements. *Annual Review of Sociology*, 36, 269–86.
Bourdieu, P. 1984. *Distinction: A Social Critique of the Judgment of Taste*. Cambridge, MA: Harvard University Press.
Bourdieu, P. 1991. *Language and Symbolic Power*. Cambridge, MA: Harvard University Press.
Brubaker, R. 1999. The Manichean myth: Rethinking the distinction between "civic" and "ethnic" nationalism. In *Nation and National Identity: The European Experience in Perspective*, edited by H. Kriesi, K. Armingeon, H. Siegrist, and A. Wimmer. Zürich: Ruegger, 55–72.
Calhoun, C.J. 1992. *Habermas and the Public Sphere*. Cambridge, MA: MIT Press.
Calhoun, C.J. 1994. *Social Theory and the Politics of Identity*. Oxford: Wiley-Blackwell.
Calhoun, C.J. 1997. *Nationalism*. Minneapolis: University of Minnesota Press.
Calhoun, C. 2012. *The Roots of Radicalism: Tradition, the Public Sphere and Early Nineteenth-century Social Movements*. Chicago: University of Chicago Press.
Fraser, N. 1992. Rethinking the public sphere: A contribution to the critique of actually existing democracy, in *Habermas and the Public Sphere*, edited by C.J. Calhoun. Cambridge, MA: MIT Press, 109–42.

Gamson, W.A. 1992. *Talking Politics*. Cambridge and New York: Cambridge University Press.

Gerteis, J. and Goolsby, A. 2005. Nationalism in America: The case of the populist movement. *Theory and Society*, 34(2), 197–225.

Gross, N., Medvetz, T., and Russell, R. 2011. The contemporary American conservative movement. *Annual Review of Sociology*, 37, 325–54.

Habermas, J. 1989. *The Structural Transformation of the Public Sphere: An Inquiry into a Category of Bourgeois Society*. Translated by T. Burger. Cambridge, MA: MIT Press.

Hadden, S. and Lester, M. 1978. Talking identity: The production of "self" in interaction. *Human Studies*, 1(1), 331–56.

Hunt, S.A. and Benford, R.D. 1994. Identity talk in the peace and justice movement. *Journal of Contemporary Ethnography*, 22(4), 488–517.

Hunt, S.A., Benford, R.D., and Snow, D.A. 1994. Identity fields: Framing processes and the social construction of movement identities, in *New Social Movements: From Ideology to Identity*, edited by E. Laraña, H. Johnston, and J.R Gusfield. Philadelphia: Temple University Press, 185–208.

Jasper, J.M. 1997. *The Art of Moral Protest*. Chicago: University of Chicago Press.

Lamont, M. and Fournier, M. 1992. *Cultivating Differences: Symbolic Boundaries and the Making of Inequality*. Chicago: University of Chicago Press.

Laraña, E., Johnston, H., and Gusfield, J.R. 1994. *New Social Movements: From Ideology to Identity*. Philadelphia: Temple University Press.

Lepore, J. 2010. *The Whites of Their Eyes: The Tea Party's Revolution and the Battle Over American History*. Princeton: Princeton University Press.

Lichterman, P. 1999. Talking identity in the public sphere: Broad visions and small spaces in sexual identity politics. *Theory and Society*, 28(1), 101–41.

Lichterman, P. 2008. Religion and the construction of civic identity. *American Sociological Review*, 73(1), 83–104.

McVeigh, R. 2009. *The Rise of the Ku Klux Klan: Right-wing Movements and National Politics*. Minneapolis: University of Minnesota Press.

McVeigh, R., Myers, D.J., and Sikkink, D. 2004. Corn, Klansmen, and Coolidge: Structure and framing in social movements. *Social Forces*, 83(2), 653–90.

Melucci, A. 1995. The process of collective identity, in *Social Movements and Culture*, edited by H. Johnston and B. Klandermans. Minneapolis: University of Minnesota Press, 41–63.

Polletta, F. 2006. *It Was Like a Fever: Storytelling in Protest and Politics*. Chicago: University of Chicago Press.

Polletta, F. and Jasper, J.M. 2001. Collective identity and social movements. *Annual Review of Sociology*, 27, 283–305.

Pulido, L. 1996. *Environmentalism and Economic Justice: Two Chicano Struggles in the Southwest*. Tucson: University of Arizona Press.

Reger, J., Myers, D.J., and Einwohner, R.L. 2008. *Identity Work in Social Movements*. Minneapolis: University of Minnesota Press.

Schudson, M. 1998. *The Good Citizen: A History of American Civic Life*. New York: Free Press.

Schwalbe, M.L. and Mason-Schrock, D. 1996. Identity work as group process. *Advances in Group Processes*, 13, 113–47.

Skocpol, T. and Williamson, V. 2012. *The Tea Party and the Remaking of Republican Conservatism*. Oxford: Oxford University Press.

Snow, D. 2001. Collective identity and expressive forms, in *International Encyclopedia of the Social and Behavioral Sciences*, edited by N.J. Smelser and P.B. Baltes. Oxford: Elsevier, 2212–19.

Snow, D.A. and Anderson, L. 1987. Identity work among the homeless: The verbal construction and avowal of personal identities. *American Journal of Sociology*, 92(6), 1336–71.

Snow, D.A. and McAdam, D. 2000. Identity work processes in the context of social movements: Clarifying the identity/movement nexus, in *Self, Identity, and Social Movements*, edited by S. Stryker, T.J. Owens, and R.W. White. Minneapolis: University of Minnesota Press, 41–67.

Somers, M.R. 1994. The narrative constitution of identity: A relational and network approach. *Theory and Society*, 23(5), 605–49.

Steuerle, C.E. and Rennane, S. 2011. Social Security and Medicare taxes and benefits over a lifetime. *Urban Institute* [Online: June 20]. Available at: http://www.urban.org/publications/412281.html [accessed August 1, 2012].

Taylor, C. 2004. *Modern Social Imaginaries*. Durham, NC: Duke University Press.

Taylor, V. and Whittier, N.E. 1992. Collective identity in social movement communities: Lesbian feminist mobilization, in *Frontiers in Social Movement Theory*, edited by A. Morris and C. McClurg Mueller. New Haven: Yale University Press, 104–29.

Tilly, C. 2002. *Stories, Identities, and Political Change*. Lanham, MD.: Rowman & Littlefield.

Williamson, V., Skocpol, T., and Coggin, J. 2011. The Tea Party and the remaking of Republican conservatism. *Perspectives on Politics*, 9(1), 25–43.

Zernike, K. 2010. *Boiling Mad: Inside Tea Party America*. New York: Henry Holt.

Zernike, K. and Thee-Brenan, M. 2010. Poll finds Tea Party Backers wealthier and more educated. *New York Times* [Online: April 14] Available at: http://www.nytimes.com/2010/04/15/us/politics/15poll.html [accessed August 1, 2012].

Conclusion

Nella Van Dyke and David S. Meyer

Perhaps the most interesting paradox about the Tea Party movement's dramatic and frustrating trajectory is that it was largely defined—and stymied—by the actual functioning of the Constitution Tea Partiers like to romanticize. Tea Party activists consistently extolled Constitutional government, even as they sometimes expressed opposition to particular amendments that provided for the collection of income tax and the direct elections of Senators. At the same time, the core innovations of the US Constitution, the separation of powers and staggered direct elections, provided severe obstacles preventing movement activists from achieving their aims. Although the centrality of the Constitutional romance is hardly universal among American social movements, the institutional blocks it creates are. The chapters presented here set the stage for a serious examination of the experiences of the Tea Party movement, exploring which are particular to the movement and which are endemic to social movements in America. Summing up these chapters and looking to the future, we can think about similarities and differences.

Like most movements in American history, the ostensibly rapid emergence of the Tea Party belied the long effort to organize and mobilize that helped produce it. The movement's overnight success took more than a decade of investment. And like most movements in American history, its influence is likely to continue to develop well beyond its peak of mobilization.

The chapters in this book provide a number of views of the early portion of the Tea Party movement's life. They provide a basis for developing trusted verities about social movements generally and in America particularly, as well as a helpful portrait of a movement's early emergence, which should ground and direct subsequent analyses of its development.

The Tea Party movement's emergence was facilitated by a dramatic infusion of financial resources early on, and extensive promotional coverage from widely accessible news media. Fox News and talk radio provided a massive public voice for the movement to an extent rarely enjoyed by social movements, and certainly never within months of the movement's emergence. Republican Party operatives were heavily involved in Tea Party organizations and protests early on, also a rare phenomenon. These compelling characteristics make the movement a puzzle, both to the public as well as to academics. Further, although the Tea Party appeared as a new force in American politics, it was animated by ideologies and movements that have deep roots in the American past, roots that activists sometimes worked to camouflage. The contributors to this volume situate the movement within existing theories of social movements, and provide theoretical developments that take into account the movement's distinct qualities.

At the same time, the Tea Party shares a great deal with other social movements we have seen in the US. More and more, citizens from every walk of life protest to make themselves heard and attempt political influence; it should be no surprise to see those who typically engage in more institutional politicking, such as lobbying or working within Congress, participating in a social movement. This offers support for an argument Meyer and Tarrow (1998) advanced under the name "social movement society." The Tea Party also underscores a question they raised but did not develop: if social movement politics become increasingly attractive to interests that should be able to compete effectively in mainstream politics, might the interests of the less advantaged be further crowded out? The early reports here suggest a disturbing conclusion, one that was only partly answered by the emergence of a kind of countermovement, Occupy Wall Street, in 2011. But much is yet to come.

And, for other aspects of the movement, the jury is still out on whether or not the dynamics that appear within this movement are unique or characteristic of other contemporary mobilizations. The ideological conundrums experienced by the Tea Party group Ruth Braunstein studied are hardly unusual; the strategies her informants used to negotiate complex and differing identities and ideologies are also unlikely to be peculiar to the Tea Party. Rohlinger and Klein show us how leaders can use internet technology to control a group's rhetorical and emotional message, and suggest that movements may rely more on positive emotions to generate mobilization early on in a movement. This may or may not be a characteristic common to other contemporary social movements.

The scholarship presented in this volume is like all good scholarship in that it raises as many questions as it answers. Every chapter raises questions that call for further research. In addition, while the chapters cover a wide territory, there are many questions about the Tea Party that remain unanswered. We discuss a few in the following pages, while also considering the Tea Party's trajectory.

Questions for Further Exploration

Resources and Mobilization

In early coverage and treatment of the Tea Party, much was made of the large investment made in mobilization by outside interests, particularly large corporate interests that funded institutionally-oriented advocacy groups, like FreedomWorks and Americans for Prosperity. But outside investment by well-heeled interests is hardly peculiar to the Tea Party. Of course, most movements are not explicitly concerned with the travails of the best-educated and wealthiest fraction of America (but see Martin 2013), but affluent interests have supported movements for civil liberties, against the death penalty, for nuclear arms control, for environmental protection, and for welfare benefits.

When faced with the charge that the Tea Party movement really represents only the interests of its generous benefactors, the Koch brothers, Tea Partiers like to cite George Soros, the billionaire currency speculator who has bankrolled political efforts for civil liberties generally. The easy equivalence is deceptive; it's hard to see how decriminalizing drugs, for example, serves Soros's business interests in the way relaxing environmental regulation supports the Kochs' businesses; the scope and scale of the Tea Party's dependence on large capital may indeed be unique. Nonetheless, the relationship of funders to causes and movements is something that merits more serious attention from scholars of social movements.

Fetner and King argue that the Tea Party is unique because of the massive infusion of cash early on that facilitated the movement's emergence. They suggest that all social movements have three levels of resources, and that while most movements begin initially drawing primarily on resources from the bottom tier, or grassroots, the Tea Party started with massive resources from the top tier. Their work raises the questions of whether other movements have started with top tier resources, and how do top tier driven movements differ from others? Several contributors suggest that resources from the top make the movement vulnerable to cooptation—do resources from the top always make a movement vulnerable to cooptation or does the timing of those resources influence this dynamic?

In addition, while the media have provided a fair amount of information on the national-level funding of the Tea Party, we still know very little about the funding of local Tea Party mobilization. While it seems clear that the resources provided to local groups for mobilization have been important, we still don't know to what extent local groups have relied on the substantial resources of the national organizations. How does resource mobilization play out at the local level in a movement enjoying substantial top tier resources? Have local groups received significant financial donations?

Political Context, Opportunities, and Threats

Several of the chapters here note the relationship of the Tea Party's trajectory to the political context, what scholars refer to as the structure of political opportunities (Meyer 2006). At once, the emergence of the Tea Party as a social movement, in the wake of the 2008 elections, a devastating defeat for conservative interests, underscores the recognition that opportunities for mobilization are not always aligned with opportunities for policy influence. The appeal of the grassroots strategy was underscored by those unfavorable political opportunities in mainstream politics. The money, know-how, and connections of high level conservative operatives were worth less than usual at the moment of the movement's emergence, and activists mobilized by emphasizing the threat represented by the new Obama administration. At the same time, the movement clearly enjoyed political access and the benefit of political know-how. Republican

Party insiders were highly involved in the movement's early days to an unusual degree, as noted by Almeida and Van Dyke. Thus, the movement was born in a context of both opportunity and threat.

Synthesizing exclusion and threat, McVeigh argues that his power devaluation theory explains the movement's timing. Power devaluation theory claims that threats to some combination of political power, economic power, or social status explain why middle-class individuals may be inspired to mobilize. McVeigh (1999) and others (Olzak 1992, Soule 1992, Van Dyke and Soule 2002) have demonstrated that the timing of other right-wing mobilizations can also be explained by threat, but few studies consider to what extent left-wing or progressive movements are motivated by threats. While scholarship is beginning to suggest that threats also inspire progressive mobilization (Meyer 1990, Martin and Dixon 2010, Johnson and Frickel 2011), this work suggests that different types of threats, such as threats to the environment or potential negative policies, may inspire progressive versus conservative mobilizations. The question remains whether middle-class citizens are sometimes inspired to join progressive movements in response to threats to economic or social status.

The Tea Party's place in history is shared, at least in terms of timing, with the Occupy Movement, which emerged in the fall of 2011, following the untitled occupation in Madison and selected protests against authoritarian governments and/or inequality spreading around the world. In the United States, both movements were responses to the slow economic recovery following the great recession of 2008. Both movements express frustration with the politicians in Washington, with government, and with politics as usual. However, the funding of these movements at their onset was very different, as was their relationship with the media, their ties to national political parties, their approach to mobilization, most of their issues, and their decision-making process (hierarchical, or non). How do we make sense of the broader wave of activism during this period? Is it a protest cycle, and if so, to what extent does it look like other protest cycles that have occurred nationally? It seems unusual to have both left- and right-wing mobilizations, which are not directly in a movement–countermovement relationship, operating simultaneously. Certainly this was not the social movement dynamic seen during the 1960s protest wave in the US or internationally, which was dominated by left-wing or progressive movements such as the civil rights movement and women's movement nationally, and a wave of anti-colonial uprisings internationally. Future work should analyze the movement's place within the broader political moment and theorize the constellation of contemporary mobilizations.

Tea Partiers must grapple with a way to manage the institutions of American politics effectively. More quickly than most social movements, much of the Tea Party directed substantial efforts to elections, raising and spending a great deal of money for the 2010 midterm elections at both the national and the state level. The most visible vehicle for movement efforts—and conflicts—was the Republican Party. Tea Partiers supported primary challengers to incumbent Republicans deemed insufficiently conservative or resolute, sacrificing some likely general election victories in the process (e.g., Christine O'Donnell in Delaware, Ken Buck in Colorado). Although the Republicans did very well in the elections, regaining control of the House of Representatives and winning large numbers of state legislative and gubernatorial elections, the focus on ideology created a rift between committed Tea Partiers, who wanted strong advocates, and establishment Republicans, who wanted to win elections. The focus on elections also meant the general atrophy of the grassroots groups and an even more intensified focus on raising and spending money for those elections. The American political system offers frequent elections to entice, institutionalize, and divide social movements (Meyer 2006), and it appears to have worked in this case.

At the same time, Republicans in power, in the House of Representatives and in the states, faced with the difficulties of governing, provoked opposition within their party and beyond. Inside the party, Republican regulars had difficulties translating Tea Party enthusiasm into a meaningful legislative agenda. John Boehner, for example, the new Speaker of the House, had a hard time getting his caucus to agree on much—aside from repealing Obama's health care reform. They voted to do so dozens of times, but faced the obstacle of the US Senate as well as a certain presidential veto. Big electoral gains didn't translate into policy. In the states, where Tea Party-supported governments could implement policy, there was a backlash in the streets. Most notably, citizens in Wisconsin mobilized to try to prevent the passage of new laws that would weaken public sector unions and collective bargaining. In Madison, Wisconsin protesters marched through the streets, slept in parks, and descended upon the Capitol for more than a week, drawing national attention—but losing the policy battle.

These provocations, however, were helpful to Democrats in mobilizing opposition to the Tea Party, including in the following 2012 elections. President Obama, the movement's prime target, won re-election relatively easily, campaigning against a Republican candidate, former Massachusetts governor Mitt Romney, who had sought, largely unsuccessfully, the movement's blessing. This followed a very long Republican primary season in which Tea Partiers rallied around successive alternatives to Governor Romney (Michele Bachmann, Herman Cain, Newt Gingrich, Rick Santorum in turn), each of whom represented only a slice of the Tea Party agenda. Once the final election was held, Republicans fared poorly, losing seats in the House of Representatives and across the states; the Tea Party imprimatur had become an electoral albatross in many places. The Republican establishment has continued to explore ways to maintain the energy of the enthusiastic activists without allowing the Party to be defined by them. It's been difficult.

The question of institutionalization, and how it plays into intramovement debates about strategies, claims, and tactics, is a recurrent one in the study of social movements, but one in which there is a great deal of room for progress. It will be interesting to see whether the Tea Party remains closely tied to institutional politics, and if it does, how these ties continue to shape movement issues and actions.

Individual Recruitment, Identity, Ideology

The Tea Party enjoys, or at least did during its 2009–2010 heyday, a wide-ranging and somewhat diverse membership (although not in terms of racial diversity). Scher and Berlet identify six ideological strands of the Tea Party movement, and their chapter clearly illustrates that individuals have been drawn to the Tea Party for a variety of reasons. A couple of the Tea Partiers interviewed and quoted in this book describe effectively recruiting themselves by connecting to the movement online, not through already established personal connections; they talk about this as their first foray into social activism. At this point, we don't know the extent to which these individuals reflect a recruitment process and history common to this movement. Most research on recruitment to activism finds the opposite—that individuals are more typically drawn to protest through their personal connections (Snow et al. 1980, McAdam 1986, Gould 1991, McAdam and Paulsen 1993). Those ties allow someone to be asked personally to participate. In any given event, most people participating will not be new to activism; participants often have a long history of prior activism (McAdam 1988, Meyer and Whittier 1994, Taylor et al. 2009). The personal connections that invite early mobilization may often precede political commitments and even the new activists' stances on issues (see Munson 2009). The question remains whether Tea Party activists share these attributes as well. As the internet and social media become increasingly important to mobilization, it is possible that these forms of connection have been more instrumental in drawing participants to the Tea Party than have the personal connections that drove earlier mobilizations.

Additional questions also remain regarding local variation in Tea Party mobilization. Though we know that Tea Party organizations formed widely across the US (see Figure 3.2), we know very little about how ideological resonance and identity management within the movement vary depending on geographic location. Binder and Wood (2012), in their study of college student conservatives, demonstrate that different locations have different political cultures which shape the ideologies adopted by locals. Thus, it is likely that there is variation in the extent to which particular ideological elements are embraced by residents in different locations in the US.

In addition, the extent to which different groups formed a similar collective identity and managed any emergent identity conflicts remains a question for further study. In her contribution to this volume, Ruth Braunstein explores how the inclusive ideology used by the Tea Party group she studied, focusing on citizen rights to a voice in politics and emphasizing an expansive "we the people" identity, comes in conflict with the more narrowly defined group identity deployed by the same group when discussing specific policy matters. The group negotiates the shifting boundaries of their group identity and the conflicts it creates by referring to an overarching narrative identity, which is abstract enough to encompass both conflicting identities, and provides familiar plot lines and a sense of history and the importance of the group's work. While we know that other movements have experienced similar conflicts between group identities deployed in different instances (Armstrong 2003), we don't know whether other groups employ the same means of negotiating these conflicts. Perhaps there are multiple strategies that vary depending on the local context.

Identity, of course, is closely related to claims. Organizing the Tea Party around trying to prevent unwanted political initiatives from the Obama administration, particularly the passage of financial stimulus legislation, a financial bailout for the financial industry, followed by a bailout of the automobile industry, and perhaps most significantly, health care reform, produced hundreds of ideologically diverse groups like the one that Braunstein profiled. Ideological differences were managed both within groups and between the thousands of local groups and the fewer national groups that comprised the Tea Party. "No" is a simple and powerful political claim, but Tea Partiers lost the large policy battles on virtually all that initially unified them: a stimulus bill was passed, albeit one that was smaller and more heavily weighted to tax cuts than liberal advocates would have liked; the financial and automobile industries received financial bailouts; and Obama's health care reform was passed, and has begun to come into force. Tea Partiers must now negotiate their alliances based on new issues and, perhaps, new identities; as Meyer and Pullum note, these negotiations face serious obstacles, including ideological differences on social issues, like abortion and gay marriage, foreign and military policy, and immigration. There are distinct differences among most grassroots groups on such issues, and between the grassroots and the well-resourced national groups.

Meanwhile, all of the groups faced questions about their subsequent existence when the peak of attention and salience had passed. Many grassroots groups disappeared, as activists turned to other more focused issues, often locally, or just to private pursuits. At the national level, some of the most visible Tea Party groups managed disruptive leadership changes. Amid much bad publicity, Mark Meckler, a co-founder of the Tea Party Patriots, quit the group as it worked to oust him and develop a more stable source of funding (Lee 2012). More dramatically, accusing FreedomWorks CEO Matt Kibbe of personal corruption, former Rep. Dick Armey, who had served as chair of the group since its inception in 2004, arrived in FreedomWorks' Washington offices with a pistol at his waist, leaving only when the terms of a large buy-out from his contract were negotiated (Drum 2012). Armey received $8 million to sever his ties with the group and keep his differences with Kibbe private. Less dramatically, social movement groups often have to deal with the challenges of leadership when the peak moment of mobilization has passed.

Conclusions

We have illustrated but a few examples of the theoretical questions raised by the chapters in this book. We hope this book will encourage further research on these important questions. In addition, while the book answers some important questions regarding the Tea Party, it is clear that there are a great number of questions that remain unresolved. We hope that the material presented here will present a good springboard for further research on the movement.

Readers will wonder what will become of this Tea Party movement, and what that fate tells us about American politics. The history of social movements in the United States suggests, strongly, a few clear points in the way of outcomes. First, we expect several Tea Party organizations to survive, at least on the national level, and we expect at least some politicians to give rhetorical deference to the movement. Both the number of organizations and the number of deferential politicians are likely to decline with time.

Organizations survive because organizers commit to their survival, often at the expense of the movements that gave rise to them in the first place, neglecting grassroots mobilization. In order to survive, political organizations need to negotiate a stable relationship with mainstream politics, secure a flow of resources, and generally develop institutions and procedures that make it easier to carry on (Staggenborg 1988). Once an organization with the appellation "Tea Party" has been established in Washington DC, everything we know about politics in America suggests that it will persist (Wilson 1973); there are currently several. In pursuit of survival, these organizations will tailor their agendas to issues that allow them to survive, that is, issues that will maintain a flow of funding. For the most part, this means neglecting grassroots supporters in favor of funders. The large funders who seeded the Tea Party activism were interested in promoting a non-religious, limited government, pro-business campaign, even as the Tea Party cultivated a somewhat different profile. We expect a continuing struggle over defining just what the Tea Party is.

References

Armstrong, E.A. *Forging Gay Identities: Organizing Sexuality in San Francisco, 1950–1994*. Chicago: University of Chicago Press.

Binder, A.J. and Wood, K. 2012. *Becoming Right: How Campuses Shape Young Conservatives*. Princeton: Princeton University Press.

Drum, K. 2012. Dick Armey leads armed coup of Tea Party group, gets bought off with $8 million. *Mother Jones* [Online: December 26]. Available at http://www.motherjones.com/kevin-drum/2012/12/dick-armey-leads-armed-coup-tea-party-group-gets-bought-8-million [accessed June 10, 2013].

Gould, R. 1991. Multiple networks and mobilization in the Paris Commune, 1871. *American Sociological Review*, 56(6), 716–29.

Johnson, E.W. and Frickel, S. 2011. Ecological threat and the founding of U.S. national environmental movement organizations, 1962–1998. *Social Problems*, 58(3), 305–29.

Lee, M.J. 2012. Mark Meckler, Tea Party founder, quits. *Politico* [Online: February 24]. Available at http://www.politico.com/news/stories/0212/73255.html [accessed June 20, 2013].

McAdam, D. 1986. Recruitment to high-risk activism: The case of Freedom Summer. *American Journal of Sociology*, 92(1), 64–90.

McAdam, D. 1988. *Freedom Summer*. Oxford: Oxford University Press.

McAdam, D. and Paulsen, R. 1993. Social ties and activism: Towards a specification of the relationship. *American Journal of Sociology*, 99(3), 640–67.

McVeigh, R. 1999. Structural incentives for conservative mobilization: Power devaluation and the rise of the Ku Klux Klan, 1915–1925. *Social Forces*, 77(4), 1461–96.

Martin, A. and Dixon, M. 2010. Changing to win? Resistance, threat and the role of unions in strikes, 1984–2002. *American Journal of Sociology*, 116(1), 93–129.

Martin, I.W. 2013. *Rich People's Movements: Grassroots Campaigns to Untax the One Percent*. New York: Oxford University Press.

Meyer, D.S. 1990. *A Winter of Discontent: The Nuclear Freeze and American Politics*. New York: Praeger.

Meyer, D.S. 2006. The Politics of Protest: Social Movements in America. New York: Oxford.

Meyer, D.S. and Tarrow, S.R., eds. 1998. *The Social Movement Society: Contentious Politics for a New Century*. Lanham, MD: Rowman & Littlefield.

Meyer, D.S. and Whittier, N. 1994. Social movement spillover. *Social Problems*, 41(2), 277–98.

Munson, Z.W. 2009. T*he Making of Pro-life Activists: How Social Movement Mobilization Works*, Chicago, University of Chicago Press.

Olzak, S. 1992. *The Dynamics of Ethnic Competition and Conflict*. Palo Alto: Stanford University Press.

Snow, D.A., Zurcher, L.A. Jr., and Ekland-Olson, S. 1980. Social networks and social movements: A micro-structural approach to differential recruitment. *American Sociological Review*, 45(5), 787–801.

Soule, S.A. 1992. Populism and black lynching in Georgia, 1890–1900. *Social Forces*, 71(2), 431–49.

Staggenborg, S. 1988. Consequences of professionalization and formalization in the Pro-Choice movement. *American Sociological Review*, 53(4), 585–606.

Taylor, V., Kimport, K., Van Dyke, N., and Andersen, E. 2009. Culture and mobilization: Tactical repertoires, same-sex weddings, and the impact on gay activism. *American Sociological Review*, 74(6), 865–90.

Van Dyke, N. and Soule, S.A. 2002. Structural social change and the mobilizing effect of threat: Explaining levels of patriot and militia mobilizing in the United States. *Social Problems*, 49(4), 497–520.

Wilson, J.Q. 1973. *Political Organizations*. New York: Basic Books.

Index

African Americans
    activists, political opportunity theory 80
    social movements 83
    Tea Party movement, negative views by 26
American Legislative Exchange Council 76
American Majority group 59, 86
Americans for Prosperity 64, 86, 88, 93, 102, 105
    Tea Party, links 66, 103
    Texas Defending the American Dream, summit 66
Angle, Sharron 87, 91, 105, 106–7, 111, 114
Anti-Tax movement 109
Armey, Dick 40, 58–9, 86, 88–9, 129, 181

Bachmann, Michele 60, 85, 102, 106, 179
Bartels, Larry M. 101
Barton, David 102
Beck, Glenn 42, 48, 65, 81, 101, 102, 107, 113, 139
    9/12 Project 88
    ideological training, provision of 112
    Restoring Honor Rally (2010) 154
Bill of Rights 88, 163
Black Congressional Caucus 84
Boehner, John 49, 179
Bolivia, social movement partyism 58
Boston Tea Party (1773) 162
Boston, Tea Party Express, Tax Day protest 59, 66
Bradley Foundation 44
Brookings Institution 44
Brown, Scott 91
Buck, Ken 91, 179
Buckley, William F. 99
Bush, George H.W. 59
Bush, George W. 26, 81, 82, 84

Cain, Herman 61, 179
Campbell, John 84
Capital Research Center 44
Carender, Keli, activism 73–4, 93
Cato Institute 102, 104
Cavuto, Neil 65
Christian Right
    free market ideology 102
    and the Tea Party 106–7
Citizens for a Sound Economy 88
Citizens United 76
    political advertising 44–5
civil rights movement 2, 15, 37, 61, 77, 78fn1
    non-violence 83
    tactics 83
Clarke, Edward Young 22
Cleaver, Emmanuel 84, 85
Clinton, Hillary 45
Club for Growth 86, 106
Coffee Party 79
collective action 17
    response to threats 18–19
collective identity
    definition 151
    nature of 152
    as process 151–2
    see also Tea Party movement, collective identity
Columbus Tea Party 105
conservative movements 18, 21–2
    definition 17
conspiracism
    and creeping socialism 112–13
    dissemination of 112
    and social movements 111–12
    and the Tea Party 8, 112–15
Coors family 43

corporate funding of
    conservative nonprofits 43–4
    grassroots campaigns 44
    political activism 45
    Tea Party movement 45
corporate philanthropy, Kristol on 43
Coulter, Anne 42
Crist, Charlie 89
curvilinear framework of opportunity, Tilly 80, 83
cycle of contention, and social movements 126

Davis, David Brion 111
Declaration of Independence 149, 163
Dicks, Norman 74

Ecuador, social movement partyism 58
Ellis, Tibi 108–9
emotion management
    and ICT 125–6, 127, 176
    in social movements 125–6
    Tallahassee Tea Party 131–3, 135, 138–9, 141–3, 176
ethnic conflict 18–19
Evans, Hiram Wesley 22

Facebook, Tea Party, use by 9, 126, 128, 129, 131, 132, 133, 134, 135, 138, 141, 143, 144, 154
Federalist Society 43
Federation for American Coal, Energy, and Security, support for Tea Party 49
Federation for American Immigration Reform 90
The Fiery Cross, newspaper 24
financial bailout (2008–2009) 79, 81
Flaherty, Peter 129
Founding Fathers 16, 24, 29, 107, 160, 162, 163, 167, 168
Fox News, support to
    Mitt Romney campaign 65
    Republican Party 65
    Tea Party movement 3, 6, 30, 36, 38, 41–2, 48, 60, 68, 175
Frank, Barney 84, 85
Frederick, Sherman 107

FreedomWorks 3, 6, 86, 105
    Koch brothers, association with 40, 64
    Tea Party movement, links 40, 103
    Tea Party Patriots, formation of 58
    see also Tea Party Patriots
Friedman, Milton 43

Gadsden Flag 4
Giffords, Gabrielle 153
Gingrich, Newt 116, 179
    To Save America 114
Goldberg, Robert Alan 111, 112
Goldman, Andrew 40
Good, Chris 40
Grabaskas, David 105
Graham, Lindsey 90
Greenspan, Alan 104

Hands off Texas group 59
Hannity, Sean 42, 48, 65, 85
health insurance industry, support for Tea Party 50
Heritage Foundation 44, 102
Hofstadter, Richard 100, 104
Huckabee, Mike 102

ICT (Internet Communication Technology)
    and emotion management 125–6, 127, 176
    and social movements 47, 86
    Tallahassee Tea Party 133, 135, 143, 144, 176
    and the Tea Party 9, 30, 150, 180
    and Tea Party Patriots 40
identity *see* collective identity
immigration issue, Tea Party 4, 8, 90, 107
The Imperial Night-Hawk, newspaper 23
internet *see* ICT
Istook, Ernie 87

Jefferson, Thomas 163
John Birch Society 3, 100, 111
John M. Olin Foundation 43

Kagen, Steve 60
Kazin, Michael 100, 109
Kibbe, Matt 59, 181
King, Martin Luther 83

Index

Koch brothers 86, 88, 100, 177
   FreedomWorks, association with 40, 64
Koch, David 104
Koch, Fred 100
Kristol, Irving 45
   on corporate philanthropy 43
Kroyman, Anna 35
Ku Klux Klan (1920s) 5, 110
   anti-Catholic 23
   and economic hardship 24
   expansion 22–3
   membership 23
   and power devaluation, of white middle-class 25
   Tea Party movement, comparison 24, 26, 28–9, 30, 31

Latin America
   "pink tide" 58
   social movement partyism 57–8, 67
LeBon, Gustave 15
Lepore, Jill 115
Lewis, John 84
Lilla, Mark 99
Limbaugh, Rush 42, 81

McCain, John 2, 81
McCarthyism 104, 116
Maddow, Rachel 65
Malkin, Michelle 42, 112–13, 129
Mayer, Jane 40, 86
Meckler, Mark 181
media, Tea Party support 30, 36, 38, 41–2
Miller, Dan 59
Miller, Joe 41, 87
Miller, Laura 100
Moveon.org group 93
Must Know News 154, 159

NAACP 79
National Association of Manufacturers 100
National Tea Party Federation 88
Nevada Patriots 50
New Deal 100, 101, 104, 116
New World Order 114
Nicaragua, social movement partyism 58

Obama administration
   health care reform (ObamaCare) 1, 2, 27, 79, 92, 104, 150
   passage of 181
   Tea Party opposition 77, 79, 89, 92, 104, 139, 140, 157, 181
Obama, Barack 59
   demonization of 113
   election victory 2, 26, 81, 179
   satirized 139, 140
ObamaCare *see* Obama administration, health care reform
Occupy Wall Street movement (2011) 176, 178
O'Donnell, Christine 41, 91, 102, 106, 179
O'Hara, John 129
Ohio Freedom Alliance 105
Our Country Deserves Better 41, 87
   Tea Party Express, formation of 58
   see also Tea Party Express

Palin, Sarah 41, 88, 106
Patriot Movement, and the Tea Party 111
Paul, Ron 80, 105, 107
Pelosi, Nancy 85, 139
Pledge of Allegiance 149, 162, 163, 165, 167
political opportunity theory 80–82
   African American activists 80
political parties
   resource mobilization theory 63–4
   resources 64
populism
   and middle-class status anxiety 100
   Tea Party movement 99–100, 115–16
Postel, Charles, *Populist Vision* 100
power, and exchange 20
power devaluation
   and interpretive processes 21
   and the Tea Party 26–31, 178
   white middle-class 25
power devaluation model 5, 17, 19–22, 114, 178
   dynamics **20**
   and threats, perceived 178
Presidential election (2008) 5
producerism, and the Tea Party 109–10
progressive movements 18
   definition 17

protest, nature of 15–16

racism
  color-blind 28–9
  Tea Party movement 8, 29, 82
Rand, Ayn, *Atlas Shrugged* 164
Reagan, Ronald 29, 84
Reid, Harry 139
religious right movement
  activism 49
  resources 49
  see also Christian Right
Republican Party
  electoral losses 61, 66
  links
    Fox News 65
    Tea Party Caucus 60–61, 136
    Tea Party Express 41, 58, 87
    Tea Party movement 6–7, 8, 55,
      56–7, 59, 60, 64–5, 66, 175
    Tea Party Patriots 58
  protest turn 3, 55, 57, 58
resource mobilization theory 46–51
  political parties 63–4
  Tea Party movement 64–6, 85–6
RINOs (Republicans in Name Only) 114
Robinson, Dale 88
Rogin, Michael 104
Romney, Mitt 109, 179
  support from Fox News 65
Rove, Karl 116
Russo, Sal 87
Ryan, Paul 49

Sanders, Bernie 91
Santelli, Rick, CNBC rant 1, 4, 35, 42, 81,
  113, 129
Santorum, Rick 179
Savage, Michael 42
Scalia, Antonin 44
Scott, Rick 136
Simmons, William Joseph 22
Skocpol, Theda 46, 61, 68
Skousen, W. Cleon 102
social movement
  activism 15
  society 7
  unionism 7, 55

social movement partyism 7, 55–6, 67
  Bolivia 58
  Ecuador 58
  Latin America 57–8, 67
  Nicaragua 58
  studies 56
  threats, perceived 58, 67
  USA 67
social movement society 76, 77, 93, 176
social movement theory
  resources in 36–8
  and the Tea Party 78–93, 176
social movements
  African Americans 83
  bottom-up, examples 38
  conservative 150–51
  and conspiracism 111–12
  and cycle of contention 126
  and democratic participation 77
  emotion management 125–6, 127
  and ICT 47, 86
  mobilization 2, 35–6
  part of political system 57
  and populist conservatism 75, 77
  and race 82
  threats, perceived 114
  three-layers 38–9, 46, 48
  top-down resource mobilization 46–51
    and agenda of corporate funders
      48
    cultural processes 47–8
    and grassroots supporters 48
    infrastructure development 47
    movement emergence and decline
      46–7
  theorizing of 46–51
  of white people 83, 84
  see also civil rights movement
Sons of Liberty 162
Soros, George 177
Specter, Arlen 81, 89
Steinhauser, Brendan 129
Stephenson, D.C. 22, 24
Student League for Industrial Democracy 3
student protests, left-wing bias 3
Students for a Democratic Society 3

Take Back America movement 66, 73, 74

Tallahassee Tea Party
    controversial issues, avoidance of 134–5
    criticism of 136–7
    differences of opinion 134
    electoral success 136
    emergence 129
    emotion management 131–3, 135, 138–9, 141–3, 176
    on Facebook 133, 134, 135, 138, 141, 143
    ICT use 133, 135, 143, 144, 176
    local groups 130–31
    Obama administration, criticism of 139, 140
    pride and patriotism 133–5, 144
    Republican Party, disillusionment with 137–8
    research project 8–9, 126, 128–44
        data and methods 128–9
        respondents, demographics 129, 130
    researchers, suspicion of 141
    unions, criticism of 141–3
TARP 2
Tea Party Caucus 104
    Republican Party, links 60–61, 136
Tea Party Express 1, 106
    Boston, Tax Day protest 59, 66
    expenditure 87
    formation, by "Our Country Deserves Better" group 58
    Republican Party, links 41, 58, 87
Tea Party movement
    activism
        example 156–62
        and narrative of American history 162–3
    African Americans, negative views on 26
    America, use of founding narratives 79–80
    Americans for Prosperity, links 66, 103
    "astroturf" organization, labeled as 3, 40, 41, 55, 78
    challenge of 1
    collective identity 3, 4, 9–10, 47–8, 150
    inclusion and exclusion criteria 168–70
    instability of 170
    management 4
    mapping 152, 165–7
    multidimensionality 9, 156–64
    overarching narrative 167–8
    "we the people" notion, use of 9, 10, 153, 156, 162, 165, 168, 180
    and conspiracism 8, 112–15
    Constitution, romanticizing of 163, 168, 175
    corporate funding 45
    countermovements 79
    cultural support 41–2
    decline 46–7
    democratic rhetoric 92–3
    and economic recession 5, 31
    electoral fortunes 42, 67, 91, 179
    elite supporters 6
    emergence 1, 2, 18, 36, 55
        reasons for 80–81, 101–3, 175
    entitlement, notion of 84–5
    event organization 42
    Facebook, use of 9, 126, 128, 129, 131, 132, 133, 134, 135, 138, 141, 143, 144, 154
    Florida see Tallahassee Tea Party
    Fox News, support from 3, 6, 30, 36, 38, 41–2, 48, 60, 68, 175
    framing, big government threat 103
    FreedomWorks, links 40, 103
    government spending, negative view of 26–7, 29
    and ICT 9, 30, 150, 180
    ideologies 8, 100, 180
    immigration issue 4, 8, 90, 107
    Ku Klux Klan (1920s), comparison 24, 26, 28–9, 30, 31
    media attention 30, 36, 38, 41–2, 47, 175
    membership 3–4, 16, 62, 180
        diversity 180
        map **62**
        prior activism 180
    mobilization, rapid 63–6
    motivations 150

name origin 4
nature of 4–5
Obamacare, opposition to 77, 79, 89, 92, 104, 139, 140, 157, 181
online infrastructure 9, 47
patriotic agenda 30
policy issues 89–91
political identity 3
political landscape, impact on 49, 177–8
populism 99–100, 115–16
and power devaluation 26–31, 178
racism 8, 29, 82
recruitment 180
Republican Party, links 6–7, 8, 55, 56–7, 59, 60, 64–5, 66, 175
research on
    data and methods 153–6
    further 176–81
resource mobilization theory 64–6, 85–6
resources 3, 6, 36, 39–42
    sources of 39–40, 67–8, 85–6, 177
and social movement theory 78–93, 176
social networking platforms, use of 154
    see also Facebook
supporters 42
    Christian Right 106–7
    coalitions 86–9
    conspiracists 8, 112–15
    demographic 103
    Federation for American Coal, Energy, and Security 49
    fiscal conservatives 103–5
    health insurance industry 50
    libertarians 105
    Patriot Movement 111
    producerism 109–11, 115
    white racialism 107–9
survival of 182
threats, perceived 2, 5, 7, 8, 26, 61, 63, 67, 74, 80, 82, 103, 112, 139, 177
as top-down movement 6, 39
and violence, threat of 83–4
    see also Tallahassee Tea Party
Tea Party Nation 41
    conference organization 87–8
Tea Party Patriots
    formation by FreedomWorks 58
    funding 3, 6
    as grassroots movement 40, 87
    and ICT 40
    internal dissent 181
    Nevada 50
    Republican Party, links 58
    website 35, 66
    White County group 35
    see also FreedomWorks
The Tea Party and Revolution 88
Texas, Tea Party rally (2009) 59, **60**
Thee-Brenan, Megan 101
Thomas Theorem 114
Tilly, Charles 61, 63, 80
    curvilinear framework of opportunity 83
Truth, Dr, *The New Democrat: A Parody in Celebration of the Tea Party Movement* 139–40
Tyler, Elizabeth 22

United States Constitution, Tea Party romanticizing of 163, 168, 175
USA, social movement partyism 67

van Susteren, Greta 65

Wall Street Journal 42
Washington Post 50
"we the people" notion, Tea Party use of 9, 10, 153, 156, 162, 165, 168, 180
Weyrich, Paul 49
white people, social movements 83, 84

Young Americans for Liberty 105

Zernike, Kate 101
    Boiling Mad: Inside Tea Party America 115